PEARSON   ALWAYS LEARNING

Going from Stress to Success
to Success

A Student Workbook for the Fundamentals of Speech Class

Seventh Edition

by Penny Joyner Waddell, Ed.D.

Excerpts taken from

Simon & Schuster Handbook for Writers, Ninth Edition
by Lynn Quitman Troyka and Douglas Hesse

DK Guide to Public Speaking
by Lisa A. Ford-Brown

Cover Art: Courtesy of Photodisc/Getty Images.

Excerpts taken from:

Simon & Schuster Handbook for Writers, Ninth Edition
by Lynn Quitman Troyka and Douglas Hesse
Copyright © 2009 by Pearson Education, Inc.
Published by Prentice Hall
Upper Saddle River, New Jersey 07458

DK Guide to Public Speaking
by Lisa A. Ford-Brown
Copyright © 2011 by Pearson Education, Inc.
Published by Allyn & Bacon
Boston, Massachusetts 02116

Copyright © 2013, 2012, 2011, 2010, 2009, 2007, 2006 by Pearson Learning Solutions
All rights reserved.

This copyright covers material written expressly for this volume by the editor/s as well as the compilation itself. It does not cover the individual selections herein that first appeared elsewhere. Permission to reprint these has been obtained by Pearson Learning Solutions for this edition only. Further reproduction by any means, electronic or mechanical, including photocopying and recording, or by any information storage or retrieval system, must be arranged with the individual copyright holders noted.

All trademarks, service marks, registered trademarks, and registered service marks are the property of their respective owners and are used herein for identification purposes only.

Pearson Learning Solutions, 501 Boylston Street, Suite 900, Boston, MA 02116
A Pearson Education Company
www.pearsoned.com

Printed in the United States of America

5 6 7 8 9 10 V0UD 19 1817 16 15

000200010271780898

EEB/VP

ISBN 10: 1-269-44796-3
ISBN 13: 978-1-269-44796-6

New to This Edition

The Revised 5th Edition of *Going from Stress to Success* has been designed to include important changes in structure, appearance, and content that make this text more user friendly for students and instructors.

Structure and Content:

- The structure of the textbook has changed to a coil bound text with perforated tear-out worksheet pages.
- The textbook contains instructional material, worksheet pages, and is bundled with **Tools for Success**, a course online access card.
  - **Instructional Material**
    - The Fundamentals of Speech
    - Organizing a Speech
    - Conducting Research
    - Delivering a Speech
    - Types of Speeches
  - **Worksheets**
    - Speech Evaluation Worksheets
    - Peer Evaluation Worksheets
    - Self-Evaluation Worksheets
    - Outline Evaluation Worksheets
    - Assignment Worksheets
  - **Tools for Success**
    - MyCommunicationLab
    - E-Book—*Going from Stress to Success*
    - Resources
      - Alternative Media Index
      - Video Quizzes
      - American Rhetoric Quizzes
      - 100+ Classic and Contemporary Speeches
      - National Communication Association
      - ABC News Top Videos
      - ABC News Top Stories
    - Composition Assistance
      - MyOutlineBuilder
      - Topic Selector
      - New York Times Topics Index
      - Pearson Online Writing Tutor
    - PowerPoint presentations
      - First Day of Class
      - Overcoming the Fear of Public Speaking

- Audience and Speaker Responsibilities
- Organizing a Speech
- Selecting a Topic
- Writing an Outline
- Conducting Research
- Creating Effective Visual Aids and Handouts
- Presentation Skills
- Dressing for a Speech
- Non-verbal and Verbal Communication Skills
- Public Speaking Confidence Center
  - Quick and Dirty Tips
- Research
  - MySearchLab
  - Avoiding Plagiarism
  - Plagiarism Check
  - MLA, APA, CMS Guidelines
  - Autociting Tool
  - Understanding a Research Assignment
  - Examples of Written and Verbal Citations
- MySpeechFeed
  - Recent Speeches in the News
  - Applicable Questions
- MediaShare
  - Upload Video for Instructor
  - Upload Video for Peer Review
- Multimedia Library
  - Audio and Video
  - Classic and Contemporary Speeches
  - Introduction Speeches
  - Informative Speeches
  - Persuasion Speeches
  - Special Occasion Speeches
  - Speech Preparation Tools
- Quizzes and Exams
  - American Rhetoric Video Quizzes
  - Chapter Quizzes
  - Comprehensive Exams
- Pearson 24/7 Tech Support

MyCommunicationLab

Contents

"There is no elevator to success.
You must take the stairs . . . one step at a time."

Anonymous

Whether you are a first year college student, a young professional in a growing corporation, or a parent attending a PTA meeting with your child, you will soon realize the value of feeling comfortable while speaking in public. At some point you will be required to stand before a group of people and speak. Understanding the fundamentals of speech will allow you to have a better command of the speech process and to feel more confident each time you have the opportunity to speak before others.

For the purpose of the course in which you are enrolled, we will begin at a base level of understanding, add information and instruction as the course progresses, and have opportunities to practice your new skills.

It is important to realize that in the communication process, public speaking is very different from conversational speaking. Public speaking is formal and planned communication. When preparing to speak in public, you will need to spend time organizing, writing, and rehearsing your speech. Public speaking usually involves research to support the topic and stories or illustrations to help make your point. Most of all, it must be organized in such a fashion that includes an introduction, body, and conclusion. You will also want to use Standard English grammar and vocabulary as you speak and omit casual, slang, or off-color language. Before we get into the details of crafting your speech, we will look at some of the aspects you will need to consider.

Overcoming the Fear of Public Speaking

"Know your limitations",

JAMES CALVIN JOYNER

So, you say that speaking in front of a group is not one of your favorite activities? You are in good company! When asked to list their top ten fears, most people will list public speaking before other fears such as spiders, snakes, heights, or death. Why do you think most of us get nervous when we are in a situation that requires us to stand and speak in front of others?

The fear of speaking in public is often referred to as stage fright. A majority of you will find that you tend to be anxious about speaking in public. You might feel as though you are exposed when standing in front of a group. You think everybody is looking at every detail and waiting to find fault with your speech. You are afraid of not doing a good job or not measuring up to the performance of others. Mark Twain said it best when he said, "There are two kinds of speakers, those that are nervous, and those that are liars!" (American University). There are any number of reasons why most people feel anxious in public speaking situations, but there is good news. Feeling anxious or nervous is quite often one of the tools you need in order to succeed.

When nervous, your body produces extra **adrenaline** to help you respond to a stressful situation. This causes your heart to beat faster; sometimes your hands may shake, your knees may feel weak, and you may perspire. All of these reactions are normal. Often it is the extra adrenaline that gives you the energy, animation, and enthusiasm to help you do a better job. Some people will even say they enjoy that rush of adrenaline because it makes them feel vitalized as they are making a presentation.

Now that we have established that you are absolutely normal, here are three basic things to remember that will help you overcome the fear of public speaking:

1. Nobody is perfect;

2. If you do not tell them, they probably will not know;

3. Your audience wants you to succeed.

Have you ever met a perfect person in your life? Have you ever heard a perfect speech without any mistakes? It might help you to know that in this world, there is no such thing as a perfect person or a perfect speech. Even the best speakers stumble over words, forget to make points, lose their place, forget

to pause at a crucial spot, or say things that are unplanned. Knowing that little fact from the beginning should help you to feel more at ease. Just remember **nobody is perfect,** and unless you are superhuman, at some point you will also fall into that category. Most of the time, your audience will not be aware of mistakes because they will be focusing on the message.

This brings us to the next point. Because the audience may not be aware of your mistakes, you are not obligated to bring it to their attention. **If you do not tell them, they probably will not know.** You have your speech outline on the lectern in front of you and your instructor will have an outline; however, your audience usually will not have one. Therefore, they probably will not notice a small mistake here or there. One of the biggest reasons speakers are concerned with making mistakes is that they view the speech making process as a performance rather than a process for communicating an idea. When speakers feel they are being judged by the audience, they are more nervous and more apt to make mistakes.

In the public speaking class **your audience wants you to succeed;** they will cheer for you and support you as you go through the learning process. If you make a mistake, no one is going to rush through the door with a shepherd's staff, hook you around the shoulders and drag you out into the hall. Just remember that after you have given your speech, your audience will also be taking turns standing in front of you. With this in mind, you can be assured that your audience will be looking for all of the ways you are succeeding and will not dissect every word you say to find fault in your speech.

Within the first couple of days in this speech class, your instructor may assign you to a **Speech Group.** The purpose of this group is to provide you with a team that will offer support and cheer for you as you go through the learning process. Unsure about your speech topic? Talk to your Speech Group. Need an audience to practice in front of before the actual speech? Talk to your Speech Group. Unsure if your outline is the correct form? Talk to your Speech Group. You will be amazed at the many areas where your Speech Group will help you

to do a better job. As the course progresses and you begin to make speeches, your Speech Group also becomes your **Tech Team.** At that time, their purpose will somewhat shift to include duties such as:

- Assisting with visual aids (PowerPoint, video, DVD, charts, easels, etc.);
- Assisting with handout distribution;
- Assisting with set up and break down;
- Acting as a light crew;
- Acting as a sound crew.

Although you may not realize it now, your Speech Group/Tech Team will provide the support and encouragement you need to help overcome the fear of public speaking. Throughout this workbook you will note references to your Speech Group or Tech Team, so get cozy with the terms. You will be hearing them often.

Now that we have established the basics, here are five additional points to help you overcome the fear of public speaking:

1. Show what you know;
2. Think positively;
3. Visualize your success;
4. Speak every time you get the opportunity;
5. Rehearse, Rehearse, Rehearse.

When choosing a speech topic, carefully consider choices that would include things you already know something about or things that interest you. It becomes so much easier to talk to a group when you are telling them about something that you have experienced. In other words, **show what you know!** Especially when it comes time for the demonstration speech, you will want to demonstrate something with which you feel comfortable. With any speech you will want to conduct research to add facts to support the topic. However, it is much more interesting to research and write about a topic that is familiar.

Have you ever wondered about folks who cán walk up to the lectern, make a presentation, and never break a sweat? Chances are they have developed confidence. The way to achieve confidence is through your thought process. **Think positively!** Most of you have heard the phrase, "Believe it, Achieve it!"

Remember the story of *The Little Engine That Could*? Speakers who think negatively about themselves are more apt to make mistakes and experience stage fright than speakers who think positively about themselves. Psychologists call it "self talk"; others call it the "power of positive thinking." In either case if you enter a situation telling yourself, "I can do this and I can do a great job," you will exude confidence and appear much more successful.

Prior to giving your speech, **visualize your success.** Imagine yourself walking confidently from your seat to the lectern, presenting a strong speech, and returning to your seat knowing that you have done your very best. Although this is an aspect of thinking positively, it provides you with a mental picture of your success and will help you create a realistic image in your mind. Make sure that you go through this process several times prior to presenting your speech. The more you visualize your success, the greater your chances are of presenting a successful speech.

Do you remember learning to drive a car? How many times did you have to practice backing out of a parking spot before you were confident with your driving skills? How many times did you have to practice parallel parking before you got it right? Another way to overcome the fear of public speaking is to **speak every time you get the opportunity.** You have decided to take a fundamental speech course. You have signed up for the class. Now you have started the course; therefore, you have taken the first crucial steps! Instruction received through this course will give you the tools, knowledge, and experience to be successful.

Once you have learned how to craft your speech, it will be important that you **rehearse, rehearse, rehearse!** You have heard the phrase, "Practice makes perfect," yet, in the beginning of this chapter you were told that "nobody is perfect." We can rewrite that phrase for the speech class to say, "Rehearsal helps you do your best." After all, it is your best that is the ultimate goal. The more you rehearse, the better you will do. Rehearsal helps you to get a more accurate idea of the length of your speech. If the speech is too short, you will know it and can add additional points, more information, or a story to illustrate your point. If the speech is too long, you will know it, and take measures to reduce the content so that you stay within your time limit. The most important thing about rehearsal is that it will reduce stage fright as you overcome the fear of public speaking and you will be successful in this class!

Personal Report of Public Speaking Anxiety Assessment

This instrument is composed of thirty four statements concerning feelings about communicating with other people. Please work quickly and record your first impression. Indicate the degree to which the statements apply to you by selecting:

1—Strongly agree
2—Agree
3—Undecided
4—Disagree
5—Strongly disagree

1	2	3	4	5	
				☒	1. While preparing for giving a speech, I feel tense and nervous.
				☒	2. I feel tense when I see the words "speech" and "public speaking" on a course outline.
			☒		3. My thoughts become confused and jumbled when I am giving a speech.
☒					4. Right after giving a speech I feel that I have had a pleasant experience.
		☒			5. I get anxious when I think about a speech coming up.
			☒		6. I have no fear of giving a speech.
				☒	7. Although I am nervous just before starting a speech, I soon settle down after starting and feel calm and comfortable.
		☒			8. I look forward to giving a speech.
				☒	9. When the instructor announces a speaking assignment in class, I can feel myself getting tense.
	☒				10. My hands tremble when I am giving a speech.
		☒			11. I feel relaxed while giving a speech.
				☒	12. I enjoy preparing for a speech.
		☒			13. I am in constant fear of forgetting what I prepared to say.
				☒	14. I get anxious if someone asks me something about my topic that I do not know.
☒					15. I face the prospect of giving a speech with confidence.
☒					16. I feel that I am in complete possession of myself while giving a speech.
☒					17. My mind is clear when giving a speech.
☒					18. I do not dread giving a speech.
		☒			19. I perspire just before starting a speech.
		☒			20. My heart beats very fast just as I start a speech.
	☒				21. I experience considerable anxiety while sitting in the room just before my speech starts.
				☒	22. Certain parts of my body feel very tense and rigid while giving a speech.
				☒	23. Realizing that only a little time remains in a speech makes me very tense and anxious.
☒					24. While giving a speech, I know I can control my feelings of tension and stress.

☐ ☐ ☑ ☐ ☐ 25. I breathe faster just before starting a speech.

☑ ☐ ☐ ☐ ☐ 26. I feel comfortable and relaxed in the hour or so just before giving a speech.

☐ ☐ ☐ ☐ ☑ 27. I do poorer on speeches because I am anxious.

☐ ☐ ☐ ☐ ☑ 28. I feel anxious when the teacher announces the dates of the speaking assignment.

☐ ☑ ☐ ☐ ☐ 29. When I make a mistake while giving a speech, I find it hard to concentrate on the parts that follow.

☐ ☐ ☐ ☐ ☑ 30. During an important speech, I experience a feeling of helplessness building up inside of me.

☐ ☐ ☐ ☐ ☑ 31. I have trouble falling asleep the night before a speech.

☐ ☐ ☑ ☐ ☐ 32. My heart beats very fast while I present a speech.

☐ ☑ ☐ ☐ ☐ 33. I feel anxious while waiting to give my speech.

☐ ☐ ☐ ☐ ☑ 34. While giving a speech, I get so nervous that I forget the facts that I really know.

The purpose of this assessment is to make you aware if you have anxiety when speaking in public. ADD numbers in the columns to show a total and then add the column totals together to get your score.

MY SCORE IS: ___110___

An Allyn & Bacon Product. Copyright 2007 Pearson Education, Inc.

Explanation of Personal Report of Public Speaking Anxiety (PRPSA) Assessment
- Scores between 34–84 indicate a low level of anxiety—very few public speaking situations would produce anxiety.
- Scores between 85–92 indicate a moderately low level of anxiety about public speaking.
- Scores between 93–110 indicate moderate anxiety in most public speaking situations.
- Scores between 111–119 indicate moderately high level of anxiety about public speaking.
- Scores between 120 –170 indicate a very high level of anxiety in most public speaking situations.

McCroskey, James C. and Richmond, Virginia P. (1998). *Communication: Apprehensive, Avoidance, and Effectiveness,* fifth edition. Boston: Allyn & Bacon. Print

Audience Analysis

The art of speaking is quickly becoming the science of speaking due to the diversity of audiences. Before you decide on a speech topic or write the first word of your speech, the first step should be to conduct an audience analysis.

- What do you know about your audience?
- What does your audience need to learn from you?
- Why will your audience be meeting?
- What motivates your audience?
- What concerns or objections might your audience have?
    - Will members of your audience have allergies or aversions to animals or food products that you might use?
    - Will members of your audience be offended by a topic that contains religious or political views?
- What do you know about the place where you will be speaking?

The answer to these questions will play an important role in the success of your speech. If you are not reaching your audience for a specific purpose, you could be wasting their time. Audiences come in various ages, beliefs, backgrounds and emotional states; therefore, flexibility and adaptability in communication are critical skills.

Also, you will need to consider the place where you will speak to the audience.

- Is it a large room?
- Is it a small room?
- Will your audience be able to hear you without a microphone?
- What do you need to do to ensure that your audience will be able to hear your speech?
- Are you comfortable with speaking into a microphone?
- Can you arrive early enough to practice with a microphone prior to the speech?
- What type chairs will your audience be using?
- Are the chairs comfortable or uncomfortable?
- Will your speech be conducive to the physical situation?

- Do you need a computer and projector in order to use a PowerPoint Presentation?
- If using posters, can the audience see them?
- If you are unable to provide the things you need in order to be successful, it becomes your responsibility to request such things from the group who invited you.

Understanding the place is just as important as **understanding your audience.** You might want to arrive early and walk around the room. Sit in the different seats to see what your audience will see. Thinking of things like this will help you get a better perspective so that you can accommodate your audience's needs. Listen to hear what your audience will hear:

- Are there noises that might be distracting to your audience?
- How are the acoustics?

- Does the projector make a buzzing sound?
- What happens when the air conditioning or heating system turns on?

Making the transition from your seat to the lectern is often a stressful situation; therefore, you will want to practice moving from where you will be seated to the place where you will be speaking. Take note of obstacles such as desks, chairs, or steps that might be in your way.

If possible, plan to arrive early and greet the audience as they arrive. Chatting with the audience will help you create a relationship with them before you are on stage. Just remember, it is easier to speak to a group of friends than to a group of strangers!

On the next page, you will find an "Audience Analysis Worksheet" which should help as you plan your speeches for this term.

Audience Analysis Worksheet

Note: Conduct an audience analysis prior to presenting a speech.

TYPE/PURPOSE OF SPEECH:_____

_____

What time of day will the speech be held? _____

How many people will be in the audience? _____

What percentage of the audience is female? _____

What percentage of the audience is male?_____

Is there a large gap in the gender of my audience members?_____

What is the average age of the audience? _____

Is there a large gap in the age of my audience members?_____

What is the educational status of my audience? _____

What is the cultural background of my audience? _____

_____

_____

Are there any restrictions that might limit my topic?_____

_____

_____

_____

What is the perceived disposition of the audience toward my topic?_____

_____

_____

_____

What is the perceived disposition of the audience toward me? _____

_____

_____

_____

_____

What does my audience expect from me? _____

_____

_____

_____

_____

What topic would be most suitable to my audience? _____

_____

What kind of information should I share with my audience? _____

_____

_____

_____

Collecting Information for an Audience Analysis

As you conduct an Audience Analysis, you will need to consider the demographics of your audience. Your instructor may have you conduct the Audience Analysis as a classroom activity, or you may be asked to e-mail your information to each classmate and compile the information on your own time. If you have to rely on e-mail, the following chart will help you to compile data needed to complete the Audience Analysis Worksheet.

AGE	17–25	25–35	36–45	Older than 45
GENDER	Male	Female		
EDUCATIONAL STATUS	High School Diploma	Associate's Degree	Bachelor's Degree	Graduate Degree
CULTURE/ETHNIC BACKGROUND				

Audience Responsibilities

You thought this was a speech class, and now you are finding out that you also have audience responsibilities. Overwhelmed? Don't be. In a fundamental speech class you will listen to your peers as they present the required speeches. In turn, they will be the audience for your speech.

Let's spend some time learning about the audience's responsibilities. It should go without saying that when a speaker is in front of a group, the audience's first responsibility is to **listen.** Audience members are not to ask questions of the speaker unless invited to do so. Audience members should also not comment aloud to anything the speaker says. In some cases, a speaker will ask the audience a question and will expect an answer. In that event, it is acceptable to answer the speaker, but it is advisable that the audience member raise a hand to be acknowledged before verbally answering the question.

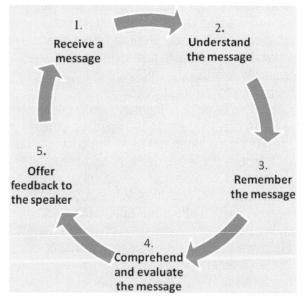

1. Receive a message
2. Understand the message
3. Remember the message
4. Comprehend and evaluate the message
5. Offer feedback to the speaker

This part of the communication process is not always as clear as it sounds in the definition. Due to the diversity of culture, language, age, religious background, and gender found in the average classroom, it is not surprising to understand why listening can be so difficult. Add to that the various experiences, lack of sleep, hunger, or whatever else might be on the audience member's mind and it is a wonder that we hear anything at all.

Listening Skills

Ask any good salesperson and she will tell you that if you want to increase sales, try listening. Ask a college professor and he will tell you that his best students are the ones who listen! Don't stop there! Ask a corporate executive and you will also learn that successful business people understand the art of listening. Empowerment comes from having good listening skills; however, it does not come naturally. Listening is a learned skill and it is an important skill to learn!

Listening is a different activity than hearing. Even if you are not trying, you may hear something. Hearing is a physical process which occurs as sound waves vibrate on our eardrums and impulses from the inner ear carry a sound to our brains to be perceived. Listening, on the other hand, is an activity instead of a process. For listening to occur, the listener must pay careful attention to the message and comprehend the message. Not only do we need to pay attention to verbal communication sent our way, but we also need to understand non-verbal communication. Reading a speaker's non-verbal language is just as important as physically hearing the message the speaker is attempting to communicate.

Often, we have poor listening skills because we fail to concentrate on the speaker's message. We might listen too hard, jump to conclusions, focus on speech delivery and personal appearances, or interrupt the listening process by thinking of other things. While most of these bad habits affect our ability to listen, we can learn to become more effective listeners.

Here are a few pointers to help you become a better listener:

1. **Try to see the speaker's point of view.** This is often referred to as **empathetic listening** as you try to understand the speaker's meaning and offer support for the speaker. The speech class will be composed of a diverse audience with varying points of view. It is important that you do not dismiss the speaker's presentation because you think or believe differently.

   Keep an open mind. Try to see the speaker's point of view and be objective as you listen. Often your personal feelings toward the speaker or the subject might alter what you actually think you hear.

   Avoid making a judgment until you have heard all the speaker has to say. Try not to be critical of the topic or the speaker.

2. **Resist Distractions.** Outside noises, unrelated thoughts, the speaker's distracting habits, and other forms of distractions can keep us from hearing the speaker's message. Silence your cell phone, close your laptop, and remove all distractions from your seating area. Make a conscious effort to focus all attention on the speaker. Realize that it is impossible to completely eliminate physical and mental distractions, in spite of our best attempts.

   The listener now begins to employ **critical listening** skills as he/she listens to the speaker's message, mentally reviews what the speaker says and thinks of ways to apply what has been said.

   One final word of advice, avoid concentrating on the speaker's appearance or on delivery skills, especially if they tend to be distracting.

3. **Focus on verbal and non-verbal messages.** When a speaker's verbal and non-verbal messages are in alignment, you will gain a better understanding of the actual message. Since so much of our communication is non-verbal, we tend to believe what we see more than what we hear. Ask yourself, "Are the speaker's non-verbal cues confirming what he or she is saying?" To understand more about verbal and non-verbal messages, please read Chapter Four.

4. **Take notes and create an outline.** As the speaker begins the presentation, make an effort to write down the main points, sub-points, and note evidence or research that support the points. This type of listening is known as **informative listening** because the listener is hoping to learn something from the speaker. Actively listening through note taking can help you to become a more effective listener because you are listening for specific details that you want to remember.

   Audiences have a responsibility to listen to a speaker. During the speech class, you will be listening to many speeches and completing peer-evaluations during each speaker's presentation. This activity will help you to become a better listener. Pay close attention to your classmate's speeches, listen for details, and make notes of areas where the speaker excels or needs improvement. As you conduct this activity, you will discover things that will help you to become a better speaker. You'll see behaviors and actions that you will want to model; in contrast, you will also see behaviors and actions that you want to avoid.

5. **Be an active listener.** Becoming an effective listener is a result of being an active listener. Enjoying the speaker and the content of the speech produces **appreciative listening!** With this in mind, audience members should send non-verbal messages to the speaker that we understand or appreciate what is being said. Lean forward in your seat toward the speaker, establish eye contact with the speaker, and nod your head or smile to let the speaker know that you are listening to the message.

As you posture your body to face the speaker, establish direct eye contact, and use non-verbal cues to let the speaker know you are listening, you are exhibiting active listening skills. Some experts say that simply exhibiting a listening posture helps us to become more effective listeners.

Want to find out more about listening skills? Visit **http://www.listen.org** online. This is an association of people concerned with the study and teaching of listening and are dedicated to learning more about the impact that listening has on all human activity.

Name: _____ Class: _____

What Kind of Listener Am I?

Self-Assessment Listening Inventory

Answer: YES – NO – SOMETIMES

Learning How to Listen

_____ Do I pay attention?

_____ Do noises interrupt my attention?

_____ Do I judge the speaker's ideas without letting my ideas get in the way?

_____ Do I find the speaker's personal habits distracting? (Throat clearing, playing with hair/note-cards/lectern, etc.)

Listening For Information

_____ Can I organize in my mind what I hear so that I can remember it?

_____ Can I think of questions to ask about ideas that I do not understand?

_____ Do I understand the meaning of unknown words from the rest of what the speaker says?

Listening Carefully

_____ Can I separate facts from explanations or from opinions?

_____ Can I tell the difference between important and unimportant details?

_____ Can I pick out unsupported points that a speaker makes?

_____ Can I accept points of view that are different from my own?

_____ Can I evaluate the speaker and what the speaker is saying?

Listening Creatively

_____ Do I identify specific words or phrases that impress me as I listen?

_____ Do I get caught up in the story or poem so that I believe the action is truly taking place?

_____ Can I put what I hear into my own words so that I can recount it to others?

_____ Can I listen to what the speaker is saying and try to feel what the speaker feels?

_____ Can I find hidden meanings: the meanings that are revealed by subtle verbal and non-verbal cues?

Given the situations and speaker variables, responses to these questions may not always be the same for each speech. However, this assessment should give you a good idea of your average listening skills.

If you said YES at least 16 times, you are a good listener.
If you said YES at least 14 times, you are an average listener.
If you said YES less than 12 times, you are a poor listener.

Peer Evaluations

The public speaking classroom is a perfect place to learn about listening skills and audience responsibilities. One responsibility will be for you to evaluate and provide a peer evaluation for each speaker. Some instructors may ask students to submit an evaluation in writing, while other instructors encourage oral evaluations.

Written Evaluations are conducted during the speaker's performance. A written form or rubric is suggested because it will contain specific details that should be addressed. Also, each speaker will be evaluated using the same rubric, making each evaluation fairer.

Oral Evaluations are usually conducted immediately following the speaker's performance so that classmates make observations while the speech is still fresh on their minds. This is especially important if there are several speeches scheduled in the same day. Instructors may choose to focus the oral evaluation on the presentation skills of the speaker or on the content of the speech.

Why do we ask you to evaluate your classmates?

The answer is simple. As you observe the speeches of your classmates, you will notice areas where your classmates' skills are strong or weak. Consequently, you will find yourself making a conscious effort to learn from your classmates' strengths. The same thing is true about your classmates' weaknesses! As you see someone fidgeting with their hair during a speech, wrapping a leg around the lectern, or flailing note-cards in the air as they speak, you will say to yourself, "I must be sure not to do that because it is distracting."

Peer evaluations also provide you with an opportunity to analyze each section of the speech. Students actively judge the attention step, listen for the speaker's credibility, discover the purpose/need of the speech, and listen for the thesis sentence which lists three main points to be covered. Then students will listen as the speaker develops the three main points. An evaluation will also be made of the summary and appeal to action, as you listen for strong concluding comments that will keep audience members thinking about the topic. Next, it is important to evaluate the visual aids and handouts. Finally, it is important to evaluate the speaker's language and the delivery aspects of the speech. Here is an example of a peer evaluation rubric that you may use:

Does the speaker accomplish the following?

SPEECH CONTENT	EXCELLENT	GOOD	AVERAGE	FAIR	POOR
Introduction:					
Attention Step					
Establish Need (Relevance)					
Establish Credibility					
Thesis (States Main Points)					
Transition to First Point					
Body:					
I. Main Point					
Transition to Second Point					
II. Main Point					
Transition to Third Point					
III. Main Point					
Transition to Conclusion					

Conclusion:				
Summary (Restate Main Points)				
Appeal to Action (BANG!)				
Presentation Skills				
Use of Research				
Used Scholarly Research				
Verbally Cited Research				
Number of Sources Used:_____				
Research Supported Topic				
Visual Aids and Handouts:				
Design				
Visibility				
Clarity				
Use				
Setting Up				
Handling and Timing of Aids				
Language:				
Vocabulary				
Correct Sentence Structure				
Correct Grammar Usage				
Delivery Techniques:				
Voice				
Volume				
Rate				
Vocal Quality				
Vocal Variance				
Enthusiasm for Topic				
Gestures				
Eye Contact				
Poise and Confidence				
Appearance				
Movement				
Entrance				
Exit				
Time of Speech:				

Identify three areas to improve for the next presentation:

1.

2.

3.

The end result is a win-win for everyone. Your fellow classmates will benefit by reading your peer evaluation comments and you will benefit by offering them. It may also surprise you to realize just how much you will look forward to reading the evaluations offered by your instructor and by your peers. It doesn't matter whether you are the audience member offering the evaluation or the speaker receiving an evaluation, participating in this classroom exercise is sure to make you a better public speaker and will strengthen your listening skills!

For more information, log into:

CHAPTER 2 CONTENTS—ORGANIZING A SPEECH

During this section you will learn how to determine a purpose for your speech, select and narrow a topic, create an outline, make useful notes, and choose visual aids and handouts to support your speech. A strategic plan in the organizational process will help you to achieve your goals. The following diagram will show you the order in which you should proceed:

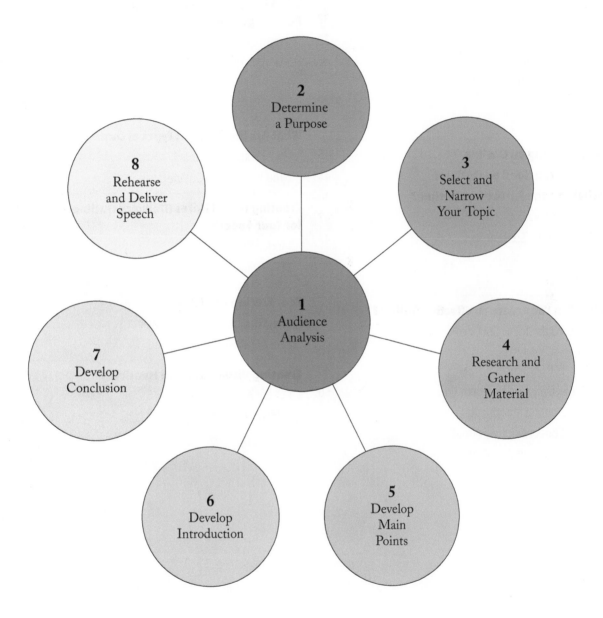

Goals and Strategies

Without a doubt you have heard the saying, "If you don't aim for something, you'll hit nothing every time." Goal setting is important with anything that you do. Setting goals and determining strategies of how to achieve your goals will be the tool that separates the successes from the failures. A quick look at your class syllabus will let you know when each speech is due. You'll also need to note when outlines are due because often they are due prior to your speech date. Goal setting will also help you to plan and prepare so that you have plenty of time to organize, research, and gather materials to present a successful speech.

Just a hint—you can not determine a purpose, choose a topic, research the topic, organize and outline your speech, create a visual aid, create a handout, and have adequate rehearsal in two or three days. These things take time, and your ability to set goals and scorecard your progress will help tremendously. How do you scorecard your progress? Develop a timeline that you plan to follow and as each part of the plan is accomplished, you will note the progress on the scorecard.

TIMELINE FOR A SPEECH PRESENTATION

WEEKLY PLAN	TASKS TO BE COMPLETED
Week #1:	Conduct Audience Analysis
	Determine the Purpose of the Speech
	Select and Narrow the Topic
	Develop Central Idea/Thesis of the Topic
Week #2:	Research and Gather Supporting Materials
	Develop Main Points and Sub-Points
	Develop the Introduction
	Develop the Conclusion
	Complete the Outline
Week #3:	Create a Visual Aid
	Create a Handout
	Make Useful Notes for the Presentation
Week #4:	Rehearse, Rehearse, Rehearse
	Deliver the speech

"Rome wasn't built in a day," and neither will your speech be constructed and presented the same day. As you studied the timeline for speech preparation, you might have been surprised to realize the persuasion speech will take several weeks to complete.

Once you have a goal, your next job is to determine strategies needed to accomplish the goal. The first strategy is a commitment to work hard. Ronald Reagan, past President of the United States, once said, "My philosophy of life is that if we make up our mind what we are going to make of our lives, then work hard toward that goal, we never lose—somehow we win out." We can also apply this philosophy to speech making.

So, get busy! Set your goals, determine your strategy, and work hard. You might just surprise yourself!

1

Determining the Purpose

Each time you plan to speak in public, you should have a clear sense of purpose or a goal. With the speeches required during this course, you will be given a direction in which to work. Every speech will have a general purpose and a specific purpose. The general purpose will fall into one of three categories: inform, entertain, and/or motivate. The specific purpose will define the general purpose and should always be written in a full sentence format. The following table should make this clearer:

TYPE OF SPEECH	GENERAL PURPOSE	SPECIFIC PURPOSE
Introduction	Inform	The purpose of an Introduction Speech will be to introduce yourself or someone else and inform the audience about the subject's past, present, and future.
Central Idea	Inform	The purpose of a Central Idea Speech will be to inform the audience of something you have learned in life.
Demonstration	Inform (Instruct)	The purpose of a Demonstration Speech will be to demonstrate (instruct) something of value to the audience.
Persuasion	Motivate	The purpose of a Persuasion Speech will be to persuade the audience to change their way of thinking about something and to motivate the audience to do something.
Special Occasion	Inform Entertain Motivate	The purpose of a Special Occasion Speech will change according to the category chosen (Ceremonial, Work Related, Political, or Social Event). The speaker must be sure to understand the occasion and the audience because this type of speech may inform, entertain, and/or motivate.
Group Presentation	Inform Entertain Motivate	The purpose of a Group Presentation will be to present a topic through a group effort. Each group member will work individually and collectively to make a presentation for the audience which may inform, entertain, and/or motivate.

While that may seem basic enough, it can often mislead you into thinking that stating a purpose is all you need to do in order to fulfill the assignment. Nothing could be farther from the truth. As you designate a purpose for each speech, you are actually creating a set of plans to achieve a particular goal. You are also creating a roadmap which will determine how you plan to have the audience respond to your speech. Just as a roadmap helps you to plan a trip and moves you successfully from one location to another, determining the purpose for your speech will provide the criterion that determines whether your speech will be successful. You may ask yourself, "What is your destination?" The road map shows where you start and where you finish. Do you want to take the back roads on your trip to avoid traffic? Do you want to take the interstate so that you can get to your destination quicker and with less confusion? Determining the purpose of your speech will do the same thing. It will show where your speech should start and where it should end. It's the place between starting and ending that will take careful consideration. Your main points will determine if you take the direct route or if you decide to take a more creative route.

This is where your audience analysis really comes in handy. Refer back to your notes as you are thinking of the purpose for your speech. Are you providing your audience with information? If so, you might want to stop and think about what they might already know regarding the topic. If they are completely unfamiliar with your topic, your purpose might be to provide them with information to expand their way of thinking. You will also want to think of your listener's perspectives about a subject. With the persuasive speech, your purpose should be to offer enough strong research and clear information that will motivate the audience.

Determining the purpose of your speech will offer you the opportunity to:

- Develop a strategic plan,
- Identify constraints,
- Identify opportunities,
- Achieve your goal.

2
Selecting a Topic

Most of you would probably agree that the hardest part of a public speaking assignment is choosing a topic! When asked to give a speech in a special situation, you may not have the luxury of choosing the topic. However, whenever you have complete freedom to select your topic, there are several factors to consider.

1. Will it interest the audience?
2. Will it be meaningful to the audience?
3. Is your topic worth the audience's time?
4. Is your topic appropriate for your audience?
5. Is it a topic that you know something about?
6. Is the topic important to you?
7. How much time are you allowed?
8. Are you willing to conduct research on this topic?
9. Do you have a clear purpose that can be developed?

In Chapter One, you learned that the primary concern of the speaker is the audience. With that as the center of your focus, determine your purpose prior to selecting a topic. Just a bit of advice for you—speakers tend to enjoy the speaking process so much more when they choose a subject that interests them or a subject in which they feel they have achieved credibility. Still can't decide on a topic? Here are a few strategies to help you get started.

1. Meet with your Speech Group and ask for ideas;
2. Look through books or magazines;
3. Listen to a news station or radio;
4. Surf the internet looking for suggestions; Google search "speech topics" to see what you can find;
5. Brainstorm with your family or friends.

Once you have chosen a topic, you will need to narrow the topic to fit your purpose and time restraints. If the topic has been chosen for you, this step can be eliminated. Effective speaking begins with effective planning.

By this point in your speech preparation, you have a better understanding of yourself, your audience, and your speech topic. Become selective, make careful choices, and begin to focus on content. Just doing this will help you communicate more clearly, concisely, and confidently. Concentrating your focus will better enable you to get your message across. And that's what matters!

TOPIC SUGGESTIONS FOR AN INFORMATIVE/CENTRAL IDEA SPEECH:

AIDS

Alcoholism/Drug Addiction

Artificial Insemination

Attention Deficit Disorder

Atomic Energy

Bargain Shopping

Become a Millionaire

Bigamy

Body Piercing

Carpooling Tips

Cloning

College Requirements

Coping With Online Courses

Euthanasia

Facebook Accounts

Feed Your Family for $100.00 per Week

Finding Balance

Gangs

Gardening as a Hobby

Global Warming

Going Green

Health Benefits of Naps

Healthcare Options

Home Schooling

How Much Television is TOO Much?

Importance of a College Education

Kindergarten for 3-Year Olds

Labor Unions

Laser Surgery

Learning Disabilities

Learning Foreign Languages

Meditation

Music Genres

Paranormal Activity

Planning Your Funeral

Prison Alternatives

Privacy Rights

Private Schools vs. Public Schools

Raising Healthy Children

Recycling

Reincarnation

School Bus Safety Procedures

Sororities and Fraternities

Smoking Policies

Student Financial Aid Policies

Television Viewing Habits

The Dangers of Driving Drunk

Traveling

Twittering

Vegetarianism

Volunteering

What's So Wicked about Wikis?

Working from Home

TOPIC SUGGESTIONS FOR A DEMONSTRATION SPEECH:

How to Apply Make-up

How to Arrange Flowers

How to Ask for a Date

How to Bake a Cake

How to Change a Diaper

How to Change a Tire

How to Clean a House

How to Clean Shoes

How to Create a Website

How to Dance

How to Decorate a Birthday Cake

How to Decorate for Christmas

How to Facebook

How to Fold a Flag

How to Hang Wallpaper

How to Juggle

How to Make Biscuits

How to Make Brownies

How to Make Egg Rolls

How to Make a Mojito

How to Make an Origami Swan

How to Make Play Dough

How to Make a Picture Frame

How to Manage Your Time

How to Organize Your Closet

How to Pack a Suitcase

How to Paint a Room

How to Plan a Party

How to Plant Tomatoes

How to Play Basketball

How to Play Cards

How to Play Dominoes

How to Set a Table

How to Shop Using Coupons

How to Study for an Exam

How to Tie a Necktie

How to Use Twitter

How to Use a Cell Phone

How to Wash a Window

How to Waltz

How to Wax Your Legs

How to Wrap a Gift

How to Write a Resume

How to Write a Speech

TOPIC SUGGESTIONS FOR A SPECIAL OCCASION SPEECH:

Accepting an Award

Announcements

Commemorative Presenting an Award

Dedication (Building, Religious)

Eulogy

Farewell

Graduation or Commencement

Inspirational

Installation (Private or Political Office)

Nomination (Office or Award)

Public Relations

Reports

Retirement

Roast

Toast

Tribute (Person or Group of People)

Welcome

TOPIC SUGGESTIONS FOR A PERSUASION SPEECH:

Abolish Abortion

Adopt a Grandparent

Adopt Children from the United States

Avoid Artificial Sweeteners

Abolish Gun Control

Abolish the Death Penalty

Abolish Welfare

Apply for Scholarships

Allow Gay Marriages

Ban Beauty Contests

Ban Dog Fighting

Ban Unsolicited Telephone Calls

Be a Consumer Advocate

Be a Mentor

Be a Patriot

Become a Vegetarian

Begin Sex Education in Pre-School
Buy Organic
Capital Punishment
Care for Your Elders
Celebrate Achievements
Curfews for Teenaged Drivers
Do Random Acts of Kindness
Do Not Drink and Drive
Do not Use Drugs
Do Not Smoke
Donate Blood
Donate Organs
Dress for Success
Drink Water
Eat Healthy
Eat Less Meat
Eliminate Pesticides in Food Production
Eliminate Racial Profiling
Enforce Animal Rights
Enforce Capital Punishment
Enforce Gun Control
Establish a Living Will
Exercise
Freedom of Speech
Get Involved
Get Out of Debt
Get More Sleep
GIVE
Go Back to School
Grow a Vegetable Garden
Invest in Your Future
Join a Club
Join a Community Theater
Learn How to Cook
Learn How to PLAY
Learn How to Ride a Horse
Learn How to Speak Spanish
Learn How to Quilt
Legalize Marijuana

Limit Senior Citizen Drivers
Lose Weight
Lower the Legal Drinking Age
Make a "Bucket List"
Make Handmade Cards
Mandatory Community Service
Organize Your Home
Prioritize Your Life
Practice Safe Sex
Plan for Your Retirement
Plan for Your Death
Practice Birth Control
Prayer in Schools
Quit Eating Fast Food
Quit Smoking
Raise the Driving Age for Teenagers
Raise the Minimum Wage
Require School Uniforms
Register to Vote
Ride a Motorcycle
Right to Bear Arms
Say "NO" to Drugs and Alcohol
Save Money
Search Your Family History
Support Breast Cancer Research
Support the Arts
Support United States Commerce
Take a Computer Course
Teach Your Children to Save
Think About Others
Train Your Dog
Travel to a Foreign Country
Visit Shut-Ins
Volunteer
Walk
Wear Bike Helmets
Wear a Seatbelt
Write Letters

TOPIC SUGGESTIONS FOR GROUP PRESENTATIONS:

Choose a Country – report on different aspects
    Culture
    Foods and Entertaining
    Government
    Sports
    Clothing Styles

Choose a College – report on different aspects
    History
    Courses Offered
    Sports
    Campus Life
    Costs Involved

Choose a Sport – report on different aspects
    Minor Leagues
    Major Leagues
    Mascots
    Fans
    Current Events
    Past History

Plan a Meal – include recipes
    Appetizers
    Soup
    Salad
    Main Course
    Desserts
    Beverages
    Decorations

Plan a Travel and Study Abroad Trip
    Who?
    When?
    Where?
    How?
    Other Considerations?

Make a Sales Presentation
    Product
    Demonstration
    Costs
    Benefits

Choose a Hobby – report on different aspects
    Time Involved
    Money Involved
    Benefits
    Getting Started
    Making Money with your Hobby

Speech Topic Proposal

Student: _____   **Class:** _____

Date: _____

Speech Category	Title and Purpose of Speech	Three Main Points
Introduction Speech	Title: Purpose:	1. Past 2. Present 3. Future
Central Idea/Informative Speech	Title: Purpose:	1. 2. 3.
Persuasion Speech (See Chapter Five for a detailed breakdown)	Title: Purpose:	1. Problem/Need 2. Solution/Satisfaction 3. Visualization of Results

Speech Category	Title and Purpose of Speech	Three Main Points
Special Occasion Speech	Title: Purpose:	1. 2. 3.
Demonstration Speech	Title: Purpose:	1. 2. 3.
Group Presentation Names of Group Members: 1. 2. 3. 4. 5.	Title: Purpose:	1. 2. 3.

Congratulations! You have conducted an audience analysis, determined the purpose (general and specific) for your speech and completed the hardest part of all as you selected and narrowed your topic. Now begins the fun part!

RESEARCH

Once you have made the decision about the topic for your upcoming speech, it is time to begin the research process and gather materials that are necessary for the success of your presentation. Although this is the fun part, this is also a very large and sometimes overwhelming job! That's why it is important to narrow your topic!

As you prepare to locate materials and select research that will not only support your topic, but add to your credibility as a speaker, it becomes necessary to learn more about the research process. Please take the time and effort to thoroughly study Chapter Three in this textbook. You'll learn about the methods of research, how to use interviews as a source of research, and how to use the internet and the library to find the sources you need. More importantly, you will learn about plagiarism and how to avoid it by correctly citing research in your written outline and drafts and verbally citing sources in the speech presentation.

Conducting research will also provide ideas about ways to organize your speech and will help you to make decisions regarding which main points should be developed. After you have made decisions about the research you plan to use and about the main points you want to cover, it is time to begin the writing process.

the audience analysis should be used to help in the planning process from choosing your topic to gathering supporting materials and developing visual aids.

Have you ever been in a class where the instructor enjoyed being center stage everyday and spent the entire class talking and talking without asking for a response from the class? It might have reminded you of a scene from the famous "Peanuts" cartoon in which the teacher droned on and on, "Mwa, mwa, mwa, mwa, mwa, mwa." BORING! In comparison, have you ever been in a class where the instructor conducted class in more of a discussion forum? You might have been asked questions that invoked thought or motivated you to think of something in a creative way. The difference between the two instructors is one who prefers a speaker-centered approach or one who prefers an audience-centered approach. In any public speaking situation, the emphasis should always be on the audience and not on the speaker.

As you write for your audience, do not think of them as a classroom full of students having to hear your speech because they need a grade. Instead, think of them as individuals and find out as much as you can about them so that you can offer a presentation that will be more appealing. Yes, you are crafting a speech for a speech class in order to get a grade; however, the most important thing to remember is that you will be addressing an audience. Your ability to grasp and retain the attention of your audience will make you a more successful speaker.

Have you ever heard someone say, "That speaker had us in the palm of his hands?" You can achieve this, too, when you write for your audience, giving them information they need to know, demonstrating how to do something, or persuading them to change their way of thinking.

3
Writing for Your Audience

Once you have completed an audience analysis, you will be in a better position to craft a speech that will benefit your audience. Depending on your audience, your writing style may vary. Information you have compiled from

4
Writing Style

Everybody has style. You show it in the way you dress, the type book bag you carry, and the car you drive. Did you know that you also show your style with the way you craft a speech and deliver it? That's right! Your

speech will also show style. That is how you get the attention of your audience, keep their attention, and leave them wanting more. Style. So, how is it achieved?

1. Get organized;
2. Get the audience's attention;
3. Get to the point;
4. Get the audience motivated.

The first step in creating style with your writing is to consider a plan to organize your ideas. Although you may want to begin with the introduction, move to the three main points of the body, and finally write the conclusion, there is a better way to construct a speech. Good writers will tell you to always start with the body and then write the introduction and conclusion after you've developed the main points. To **get organized** and decide how to order the body of your speech, you must realize that this is an important step in the speech making process and requires considerable thought.

5
Clustering and Webbing

During one of your introductory English classes, you probably learned to use **clustering and webbing** or mapping as a system of outlining to help organize ideas before drafting a formal outline. If you haven't used this type of brain storming technique before, you may want to take a few minutes and try it because it helps make your ideas visible in a drawing! Many speech students will agree that clustering and webbing helps them to see potential ideas that they may use when designing a speech. Like any brainstorming activity, you will use some of the ideas and others will be rejected. Let's get started!

First, begin with a blank sheet of paper. Near the top draw a circle and write your topic inside the circle. Next, begin to write any ideas that relate to the topic. As you brainstorm ideas, be sure to cluster or group ideas that seem to belong together. Continue with the activity until you think you have exhausted your ideas. Now, draw circles around each cluster or group. Count the number of groups and these become your main points. All supporting points become your sub-points. Just a note: this will not be a neat paper. You will have ideas written here and there, lines drawn through ideas that you rejected, and big circles highlighting your groups or clusters of ideas. For those of you who like things a little neater, here is a pre-made clustering and webbing diagram ready for you to use – simply insert your ideas.

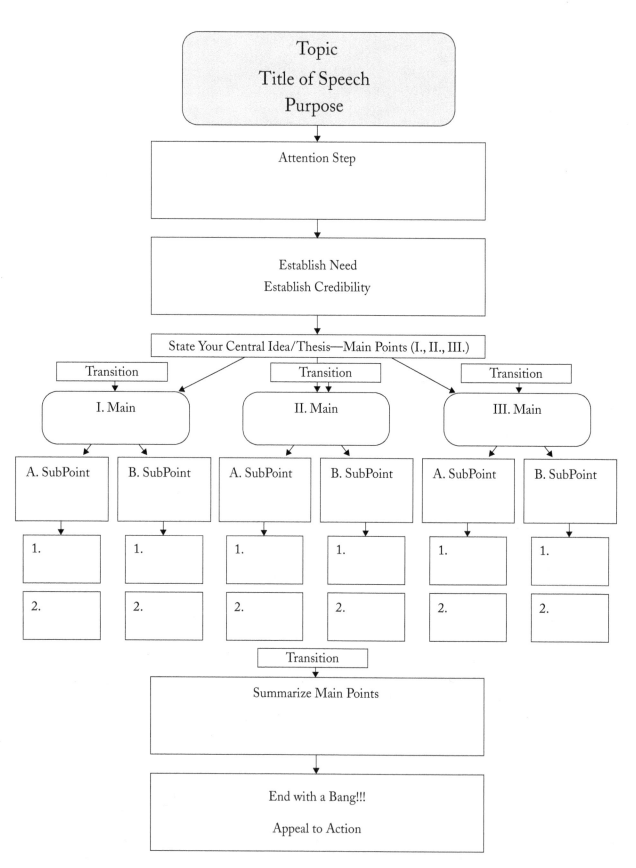

6
The Body of the Speech

Now that you have a better idea of your topic and the points you wish to develop, it is time to decide how you would like to present your main points. This can be done by using one of the following strategies:

STRATEGIES:	DEFINITION:
Chronological	With the Introduction Speech, you should order your speech in a **chronological** manner. Simply start with the beginning and move from the present to the future. Another way to use chronological ordering is in the demonstration speech as you demonstrate ordered steps that should be followed to accomplish a goal.
Logical	The **logical** strategy is used when the main points are ordered in a way that makes sense. Simply start with the most important point and then develop the next two points according to their level of importance to the topic. It is always a good idea to follow a logical order in presenting information. An example of this is a speech about walking for exercise. The first point may cover the health benefits of walking. The second point may describe how to begin a walking routine, and the third point may list the equipment needed to walk for exercise.
Spatial	**Spatial** strategies are used when the speaker chooses to discuss a topic dealing with space. The recruitment department of your college will use this strategy when taking a group of potential students on a guided tour of the college. The tour guide will begin at a place near the beginning of the tour and will then design the body of the tour around items of interest at the college.
Cause-Effect	Some writers choose to use a **cause-effect** strategy; whereas, others may choose to use a problem-solution, or a compare-contrast strategy. With the *cause-effect* strategy, the writer first states a situation and then uses points to establish the resulting effects. One example might be an informative speech in which the speaker is telling the audience about flu shots. The situation would be established and then the main points would detail the positive results from having a flu shot.
Problem-Solution	When using the **problem-solution** strategy, the speaker will detail a problem and then offer realistic solutions for solving the problem. As a third point, the speaker would list the benefits of solving the problem. This strategy is often used for persuasion speeches and is also known as Monroe's Motivated Sequence. Further instructions regarding the use of the problem-solution strategy is discussed in Chapter Five.
Compare-Contrast	The **compare-contrast** strategy works well in informative speeches where the speaker wants to compare how two things are similar and then offer a contrasting view of how the same two things are different. For example, you might compare how community colleges and four-year universities are similar and then you might offer contrasting views about how the two types of institutions are different.
Pros-Cons	The **pros-cons** strategy involves informing the audience of the positives and negatives about something and allowing the audience to make their own deductions. For example, the speaker might bring up the idea of using sugar instead of a sugar substitute. Once the topic was established, then the speaker would list the benefits of using sugar and the consequences of using a sugar substitute.

Regardless of the organizational strategy that you choose, it is important to arrange ideas by adding sub-points to support and clarify the main points.

7

The Introduction

The next step is to **get the audience's attention.** This crucial step provides the audience with their first impression of the speaker and the speaker's message; consequently, it should be written only after the body of the speech has been developed.

How do you get the audience's attention so that they want to hear more? The answer is the introduction step of the speech. During this step, you should get the audience's attention, explain the relevance of the topic, establish speaker credibility, and preview the three main points which will be presented.

During the first few seconds of your speech, the audience will decide if you know about your topic and if you are worthy of being heard. Speakers have to earn the right to be heard; therefore, your attention getting tactics should be strong. Some speakers choose to begin their speech with a story while others begin with startling statistics, a quote, a short poem or lyrics to a song, an alarming statement, thought provoking questions, or humor.

After presenting a strong introduction, the speaker's next goal is to **get to the point** by placing clear transitional sentences between each main point. Transitions are also known as connectors or links because they offer cues for the audience to follow. You'll read more about creating transitions later in this chapter as we discuss outlining techniques.

8

The Conclusion

"Success is not measured by what one brings, but rather by what one leaves."

UNKNOWN

The final step is to **get the audience motivated.** In your outline, it will be shown as the conclusion. During your speech, you will need to provide a verbal signal that you are moving toward the conclusion. Some speakers say, "In conclusion…" while others might say, "Let's review…". A strong conclusion leaves your audience with a lasting impression of the information you have shared. Providing a brief summary will allow the audience to review the main points that you have developed. The summary is followed by an appeal to action. Many speakers choose to end the speech using some of the same strategies they used to introduce the speech. One strategy is to refer back to the story used in the introduction and finish the unfinished story in the concluding appeal. In other words, keep the audience thinking about the message that you have delivered. The ultimate goal is to motivate your audience to action and end your speech with a BANG!

Constructing an Outline

Why Do You Need an Outline?

"Why do I need an outline?" is possibly the question most frequently asked by beginning speakers. One of the best ways to see the value of an outline is to think of it as a piece of architecture.

Visualize the tallest building in your town or on your campus. Think about how each nail, each beam, each panel, and each floor support relates to the next. What would happen if a beam were missing or in the wrong place? The result would be disastrous, right? What happens if a doorway is missing or too small and you can't get from one room to the other? (Sounds like a moment out of *Alice in Wonderland*, doesn't it?)

Doorways, stairwells, and halls allow us to move smoothly through a building by linking the rooms and floors together. Architects create a sound structure and use elements of design such as space, line, shape, texture, and color to design a safe, functional, and pleasing building. Without a plan, the building could be useless, unsightly, and likely to fall apart.

The same is true for a speech. Successful speeches contain distinctive features and components that are carefully structured for a particular function and pleasing effect. The process of outlining your speech will help you build that strong foundation and will make the process of creating a speech faster as well as easier.

Many students see outlining a speech as just busywork required by the instructor and do not see its value at first. Like most things worth creating, a speech is more than just the sum of its parts.

You must be selective in what materials you use, and you must build them in a way that will hold your speech together and allow your audience to move easily through your information. Your outline is the blueprint you use to make sure everything is properly supported, in the right place, and easy to maneuver.

Think about the last time you wrote a paper. You probably went through several drafts of the paper, crafting exactly what you wanted to write, making sure that readers could follow your essay and feel that they gained something from your paper. For most writers, that perfect paper does not happen on the first try.

Crafting a successful speech is a similar process. When you prepare a speech, you need to go through the stages of inventing; researching; drafting; editing; proofreading; and, when possible, peer reviewing before you give the speech. Creating outlines is the most effective way for you to achieve these important steps.

An outline helps you:

- Ensure that your main points relate to your central idea.
- Select the appropriate organizational pattern and keep it consistent.
- Make sure your subpoints are related and subordinate.
- Evenly distribute your support materials and investigate the quality of the material.
- Formulate links between parts of the speech.
- Design a speech your audience can follow and recall.
- Create a permanent record of your speech.

So, creating an outline is more than just busywork!

CONFIDENCE BOOSTER

Knowing your material is the best way to lower your anxiety, and the best way to learn it is to be exceedingly meticulous, comprehensive, and systematic when creating the outline of your speech.

Constructing an Outline was taken from *DK Guide to Public Speaking* by Lisa A. Ford-Brown.

What Are the Parts of an Outline?

Creating a visual image in your mind of a basic outline will help you understand its parts and help you create an outline. Here is the basic blueprint for most outlines.

1 **Introduction**
2 **Body of the Speech**
3 **Conclusion**
4 **Source Page**

INTRODUCTION

Link
I.   First main point
        A. First subpoint of I
            1. First subpoint of A
                a. First subpoint of 1
                b. Second subpoint of 1
            2. Second subpoint of A
        B. Second subpoint of I
Link
II.   Second main point
        A. First subpoint of II
        B. Second subpoint of II
            1. First subpoint of B
            2. Second subpoint of B
    Link
III.   Third main point
        A. First subpoint of III
        B. Second subpoint of III
    Link

CONCLUSION

SPEECH BODY

1
Introduction

The *introduction* opens the speech, grabs the audience's attention, and focuses it on the topic.

2
Body of the Speech

The **body** contains the central portion of the speech, including the main points, the multiple layers of subordinate points, and the links. It is, essentially, what you want to tell your audience about the topic.

Main points are the essential ideas you must cover or the main claims you wish to make, and they directly relate to your central idea. Most speeches will have two or three main points, but some speeches (usually process or persuasive) will have more—around five.

Subpoints (also called *subordinate points* or *supporting points*) offer information to support and relate back to the main point. You can have multiple layers of subpoints (e.g., your subpoints can have their own subpoints).

Links (also called *transitions*) act much like hyperlinks on your computer, which serve to make a logical jump between two places on your computer. Links in your speech will make logical connections between parts of your speech.

3
Conclusion

The **conclusion** ends your speech and takes one last moment to reinforce your main ideas as well as to "wow" your audience.

4
Source Page

Many instructors will require a page at the end of your preparation outline that indicates the sources you used in your speech. You will create this page just as you do for a formal research paper, often using the style manual for the *Modern Language Association (MLA)* or the *American Psychological Association (APA)*. Style manuals are guides for writing and documenting research. Your instructor may require you to purchase a style manual, or you may just use the one located in your library's reference section. Make sure you have the correct style manual and that it is the most current. Certain software packages (including Word) can help you adhere to a style, although you should always check the citations and page format for accuracy.

How Can You Create an Effective Outline?

1 **Record the Topic, Specific Purpose, and Central Idea**
2 **Use Full Sentences**
3 **Cover Only One Issue at a Time**
4 **Develop the Introduction and Conclusion**
5 **Use Correct Outline Format**
6 **Use Balanced Main Points**
7 **Employ Subordination**
8 **Plan Out Formal Links**
9 **Use Proper Citations**

In this section, you will encounter the nine qualities of an effective outline. It is important to note that not all of the qualities are necessary for different types of outlines. For example, you will not include full sentences in the outline you use for delivering your speech (the delivery outline). However, full sentences are almost always a requirement in the outline you create as you craft your speech (the preparation outline). If you are not sure what your assignment requires, ask your instructor.

A section later in this chapter will discuss the three types of outlines and their uses. However, for now, you should realize that correct preparation outline format is the basis of all types of outlines, and it is important that you begin early to use as many of the qualities as possible.

Let's look at each of the nine qualities as well as how two speakers, Jessamyn and Zamir, work to incorporate each into their outlines. Jessamyn is a big NFL football fan and wants to give her class a brief history of the game. Zamir owns a café in the City of Jackson and is concerned about an overabundance of pigeons. His café has an outdoor seating area, where pigeons have become a problem and a potential health hazard. His speech proposes that the city institute a plan to decrease the pigeon population.

1

Record the Topic, Specific Purpose, and Central Idea

You should include the topic, specific purpose, and central idea at the top of the outline as a title framing the speech. Doing so will help you keep these elements of your speech in the forefront of your mind as you create the rest of the outline.

Topic: ....

Specific Purpose: ....

Central Idea: ....

2

Use Full Sentences

You should write each outline component in full sentences. Writing in full sentences forces you to think in complete thoughts and will help you learn the speech as well as gauge its length. If you use only words or phrases in the preparation outline, you may struggle for the right words when giving the speech. Below, see how Jessamyn rewrote her working points as full sentences.

INCORRECT

I. The beginning of football
   A. Two different sports
      1. English soccer player 1823 and rugby
      2. Between 1880 and 1883, Yale's rugby players changed rules

CORRECT

I. The game of football has come a long way since its beginnings.
   A. Football is actually adapted from two different sports (Ominsky).
      1. While playing soccer in 1823, an English soccer player got frustrated and picked up the ball and started running with it, creating the sport of rugby.
      2. Between 1880 and 1883, as rugby grew in popularity, one of Yale's rugby players conceived a new set of rules for the game, very similar to today's football game.

3
Cover Only One Issue at a Time

Covering only one issue at a time in each outline component will help you keep your speech simple enough for delivery and will keep you from writing the speech as a manuscript. The best way to adhere to this quality is to write only one sentence per component in the body of the speech. For example, Zamir noticed that his first point looked more like a paragraph:

INCORRECT

> I. The City of Jackson needs to institute a plan to decrease the numbers of pigeons that infest it each year, breeding everywhere and roosting on buildings, because they spread diseases to humans and other animals and contaminate our waterways. The pigeons…

Avoid using words like **and**, **or**, **because**, or **but** to connect two independent issues in one sentence.

Zamir corrected this problem by breaking the paragraph down into points, each containing only one issue at a time.

CORRECT

> I. The City of Jackson needs to institute a plan to decrease the number of pigeons.
> A. Each year, thousands of pigeons flock to the city.
>   1. They breed everywhere.
>   2. They roost on many buildings.
> B. Pigeons spread disease.
>   1. They carry germs that affect humans.
>   2. They carry germs that affect animals.
>   3. They can contaminate our waterways.

4

Develop the Introduction and Conclusion

Most instructors suggest creating your introduction and conclusion after you create the body of the speech. For now, recognize that they are an integral part of the preparation outline. Beginning speakers tend to cut corners in the development of a speech by deciding to improvise the introduction and conclusion as they speak. This practice sets you up for serious problems at critical moments in the speech. Speech anxiety is often the highest at the beginning, making the practice of "thinking on your feet" frustrating and often impossible. Therefore, you may forget crucial parts of the introduction and conclusion. Polish and practice them as you do the rest of the speech. Below are Jessamyn's NFL speech introduction and conclusion. Notice the major parts in each one.

EXAMPLE OF INTRODUCTION

Attention material: A friend of mine used to say that she thought the game of football looked like a bunch of chickens running around with their heads cut off.

Relevance to audience: If you are anything like my friend, then you probably don't appreciate the fall and winter seasons the same as I do. My hope is that during the next few minutes you will develop an understanding and appreciation for the sport of National Football League (NFL) football.

Credibility material: As sister to a high school player, a daughter of a military football coach, and an unwavering fan of the game, I enjoy watching and playing the sport with my brothers.

Preview of speech: Today, I want to share a brief history of the game of football, the development of the NFL, and how the league is set up today.

EXAMPLE OF CONCLUSION

Summary statement: The NFL is a complex association, but once you have an understanding of football's history, the development of the NFL, and how the league is currently set up, it is much easier to comprehend.

Audience response statement: So now that you have a basic working knowledge of the NFL, the next time you are flipping through the channels on a Sunday afternoon, maybe, just maybe, you will turn on a football game and enjoy it like I do.

WOW statement: Join me for some FOOOOTBALL!

5
Use Correct Outline Format

The format of an outline should be very systematic, helping you to logically structure your speech and aiding you in your delivery. You should always use correct outline formatting in the body of the speech. The following guidelines will help you.

DISTINGUISHING MAIN POINTS

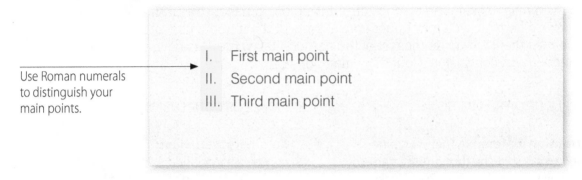

Use Roman numerals to distinguish your main points.

I. First main point
II. Second main point
III. Third main point

PATTERN OF SYMBOLS

Use a consistent pattern of symbols (e.g., uppercase letters, numbers, and lowercase letters).

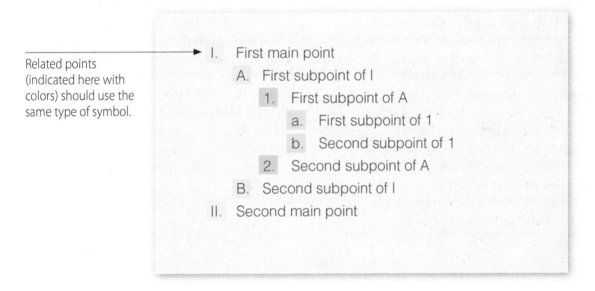

Related points (indicated here with colors) should use the same type of symbol.

I. First main point
  A. First subpoint of I
    1. First subpoint of A
      a. First subpoint of 1
      b. Second subpoint of 1
    2. Second subpoint of A
  B. Second subpoint of I
II. Second main point

SUBPOINTS

Each subpoint must have at least two subdivisions if it has any. Think of it like cutting up an apple. If you cut up an apple, you have at least two pieces. You may end up with more pieces, but you cannot divide something without a result of at least two.

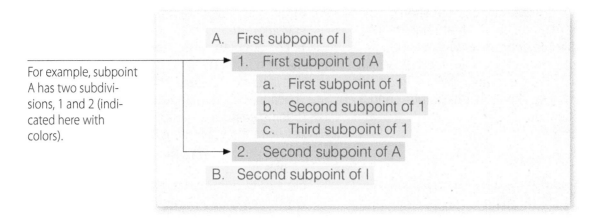

For example, subpoint A has two subdivisions, 1 and 2 (indicated here with colors).

ALIGNMENT OF POINTS IN YOUR OUTLINE

Your main points should line up closest to the left margin of the page, and each subsequent subdivision should be indented further to the right.

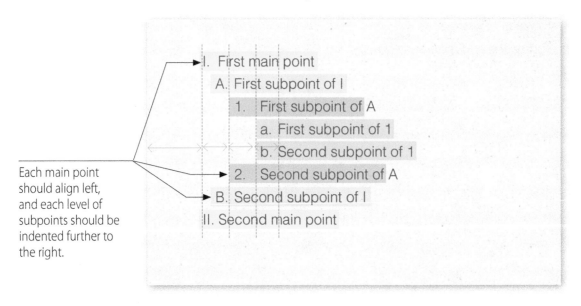

Each main point should align left, and each level of subpoints should be indented further to the right.

6

Use Balanced Main Points

Your main points should be equal in importance to each other. They will directly relate to the overall topic but should not overtly relate to each other. Each main point should coordinate with the others. For example, Jessamyn created these three relatively balanced main points. Point 1 is a bit shorter in duration, but points 2 and 3 are almost equal:

Specific purpose: To inform my audience about the National Football League (NFL).

I. A brief history of the game of football explains the evolution of the NFL.

II. The NFL has come a long way since its beginnings.

III. Today, the NFL has a unique organizational setup.

Notice that each point is unique and relates back to the specific purpose.

7

Employ Subordination

The components of your outline following each main point should be properly subordinate to the point above them. In other words, any statement that comes under a point must *not* be equal to or of greater importance than the point directly above it. An easy test for this is to read the main point, mentally insert "because" or "for," and then read the subpoint. If doing so makes a logical connection between the main point and the subpoint, the subpoint is subordinate.

Let's return to Zamir's speech on pigeon control to demonstrate how this works. On the next page, see how Zamir works through the first main point to check for subordination. He uses the *"because* or *for"* test to make sure he has followed the principle of subordination.

I. The City of Jackson needs to institute a plan to decrease the number of pigeons.

    A. Each year, thousands of pigeons flock to the city.

        1. They breed everywhere.

        2. They roost on many buildings.

    B. Pigeons spread disease.

        1. They carry germs that affect humans.

        2. They carry germs that affect animals.

        3. They can contaminate our waterways.

First, Zamir tested the connections between the main point and its subpoints A and B:

↓ Main point I

The City of Jackson needs to institute a plan to decrease the number of pigeons **because** each year, thousands of pigeons flock to the city.

↑ Subpoint A

↓ Main point I

The City of Jackson needs to institute a plan to decrease the number of pigeons **because** pigeons spread disease.

↑ Subpoint B

Then, he tested the connections between a subpoint, such as B, and its subpoints (1, 2, and 3):

↓ Subpoint B   ↓ B's subpoint 1

Pigeons spread disease **because** they carry germs that affect humans.

↓ Subpoint B   ↓ B's subpoint 2

Pigeons spread disease **because** they carry germs that affect animals.

↓ Subpoint B   ↓ B's subpoint 3

Pigeons spread disease **because** they can contaminate our waterways.

8
Plan Out Formal Links

You should include links between major components of the speech. An effective speaker will lead the audience almost effortlessly from one point to another, and formal links will make this seem smooth, not jolting. Jessamyn used this link between her first main point about the history of the NFL and her second main point about the NFL's current structure:

> Now that we understand the formation of the National Football League, let's look at the structure of the NFL today.

Jessamyn placed the link on her preparation outline here:

II. The NFL has come a long way since its beginnings.
   A. Football is actually adaptations made to two different sports (Ominsky).
      1. While playing soccer in 1823, an English soccer player got frustrated and picked up the ball and started running with it, creating the sport of rugby.
      2. Between 1880 and 1883, as rugby grew in popularity, one of Yale's rugby players conceived a new set of rules for the game, very similar to today's game.

   (Link: Now that we understand the formation of the National Football League, let's look at the structure of the NFL today.)

III. Today, the NFL has a unique organizational setup.

➔ See "What Can You Use to Link Your Speech Parts Together?" on page 58 for how to write effective links.

9
Use Proper Citations

You should include in-text citations within the outline itself and a page with sources listed according to an acceptable style manual.

In the speech outline, you can do your in-text citations one of two ways, depending on what your instructor requires or what works best for you. Your first option is to follow your style manual. In this example, Jessamyn followed the MLA style of using *parenthetical citations*, or placing the citation information in parentheses at the end of a sentence:

> II. The NFL has come a long way since its beginnings.
>   A. Football is actually adaptations made to two different sports (Ominsky).

Alternatively, Jessamyn could incorporate the citation into the outline text to help her remember to give it during the speech. This method is especially useful for beginning speakers.

For example:

> II. The NFL has come a long way since its beginnings.
>   A.   According to Dave Ominsky and P.J. Harari, in *Football Made Simple: A Spectator's Guide*, football is actually adaptations made to two different sports.

Before you decide how to cite your sources within the outline text, make sure you first check your instructor's requirements for the speech. Your instructor may stipulate how you create in-text citations.

PRACTICING ETHICS

Using proper citations in your outline will help you remember to cite your sources orally, preventing you from plagiarizing portions of your speech.

What Can You Use to Link Your Speech Parts Together?

1 **Transitions**
2 **Signposts**
3 **Internal Previews**
4 **Internal Reviews**

On page 45, you learned that links are one of the important parts of your speech's body. Links (also called transitions and connectives) make logical connections between the parts of your speech.

Think of a computer hyperlink—usually a word, symbol, image, or other element in a document or on a Web site that links, when you click on it, to another section in the same document/site or to a completely new document/site. Just as a hyperlink serves to make a jump between two related places, a speech link creates a bridge between two sections of your speech.

Many instructors require your speech links to be part of your preparation outline. Transitions, signposts, internal previews, and internal reviews are four types of links you can use.

1
Transitions

Transitions are words or phrases signaling movement from one point to another as well as how the points relate to each other. Transitions fall into the following categories.

TYPE OF TRANSITION	EXAMPLES
Time transitions are words and phrases that demonstrate a passing of time.	Let's move on to… Now that we have… We are now ready… In the future… Meanwhile… Later… Next…
Viewpoint transitions demonstrate a change in your view of a situation.	On the other hand… However… Conversely… Although… But…
Connective transitions simply unite related thoughts.	Also… Another… In addition… Moreover… Not only… but also…
Concluding transitions signal the end of a section within the speech or the ending of the entire speech.	Therefore… Thus… As a result… Finally… In conclusion… To summarize…

2
Signposts

Signposts are words or phrases that signal to the audience where they are with regards to related thoughts and/or what is important to remember. Some of the most common signposts are:

- First… Second… Third…
- Argument #1… Argument #2… Argument #3…
- My first reason… My second reason…
- Above all, remember…
- Keep in mind…
- The most important aspects are…

For example:

> The first step in preparing a strawberry patch is to locate a well-drained, sunny location.

After presenting the details of how to select a great place for the strawberry patch, you would use the same type of signpost to signal the remaining steps as you progress through the speech, offering details for each.

> The second step is to prepare the soil in the patch prior to planting.…

> The third step is to select the best type of strawberry plants for your location and usage.…

> The fourth step is to place the plants in the ground properly.…

> The fifth step is to care for the plants to produce the best fruit possible.…

3
Internal Previews

As links, **internal previews** are like mini introductions and look like detailed signposts. These statements tell the audience what will be covered next in the speech. Here are a few examples:

> Let's look at how the NFL consists of 32 teams, two conferences, and four divisions.

> To prepare the tomatoes for drying, you need to select the best fruits, wash them, and thinly slice them. Let's look at the preparation process in greater detail.

> There are many reasons why we need universal health care. However, I would like to focus on how a universal system would decrease the numbers of uninsured citizens, improve the access to proper care for those already insured, and help regulate the cost of care.

An internal preview is a great way to link your introduction and the body of your speech. It can act as the preview of your full speech, as in the last example above.

TIP: Signposts

Be careful to avoid conflicting or repeating signposts. For example, if your speech is on baking a cake, you might correctly say, "The first step is to gather ingredients." But you should then avoid signposts that make your subpoints sound similar, such as "The first ingredient is flour. The second is eggs." By the time you get to your second main point of "The second step is to mix," your listeners will be confused.

4
Internal Reviews

Internal reviews (also known as *internal summaries*) are like mini conclusions. They summarize what you have just covered in the previous section of your speech. Here are a few internal review examples:

> It is our responsibility to offer health care to every U.S. citizen, to improve access, and to lower care costs that force a need for a universal system.

> Knowledge, persistence, and charisma are what make a great salesperson.

> To review, you need a well-drained and sunny location, loamy soil, and certain nutrients to create the best strawberry patch.

> The steps for preserving tomatoes by drying are selecting tomatoes that dry well, preparing them for the drying process, using the proper drying process for the equipment you have, and storing the tomatoes in a dry, cool place.

Often you will combine internal previews and internal reviews with a transition, as these examples do.

> Now that you have selected the right location for the strawberry patch, prepared the soil, and purchased the correct plants for your climate, it is time to plant the strawberries properly.

> Now that we have discussed the evolution of football and the establishment of the NFL, we can move on to considering ....

TIPS: Effective Links

- Creating your links ahead of time and placing them in the correct spots will help you remember to use them, and you won't struggle for words during the delivery of the speech. You should write out the links completely on the preparation outline. You might also use an abbreviated version of your links in your delivery outline so that you remember to include them.

- You can use nonverbal cues to add emphasis to your links. Pausing, gesturing, changing locations or facial expressions, and increasing or decreasing your pitch or rate are some ways to help signal that a link is occurring.

What Are the Different Types of Outlines?

1 **The Working Outline**
2 **The Preparation Outline**

1
The Working Outline

Working outlines are usually handwritten attempts to organize your thoughts as you progress through the early stages of creating a speech—especially as you do research. These outlines will change often and will be a combination of complete thoughts, words, and phrases. Think of them as a way to record your thoughts, narrow in on your main points, and play around with organizational strategies. Your working outline is mostly for your eyes only. You should attempt to use correct outline form, but this is still a very free-flowing stage. For example, Steven is giving a classroom speech about fair trade chocolate. His topic, specific purpose, central idea, and working outline are shown on the next page.

Steven remembered how important it is to formulate and record his topic, specific purpose, and central idea as he created his working outline. Doing so helps him remain focused during his research. He plans to refer back to his specific purpose and central idea often so that he does not stray from his goal.

Topic: Fair Trade Chocolate

Specific Purpose: To inform my audience about fair trade chocolate.

Central Idea: Fair trade chocolate is more than just expensive chocolate; it is responsible chocolate.

Like many beginning students, Steven found it helpful to create his potential main points as questions during this stage of the speech process. This can help Steven stay focused as he conducts research that answers each of the questions. Later, he will change his main points into declarative sentences.

I.   What is fair trade chocolate?

II. Why is chocolate an issue?
  A.   process of harvesting and where
  B.   chocolate is harvested by slaves

III. Where can you purchase fair trade chocolate locally?
  A.   stores
  B.   online
  C.   what's not fair trade

2

The Preparation Outline

Preparation outlines (also known as *formal* or *full-sentence outlines*) will be much longer and more detailed than working outlines. Designing a preparation outline allows you the opportunity to give the necessary time, effort, and thought to creating a successful speech.

The entire outline will adhere to correct outline form. The introduction, body, and conclusion will be clearly marked and connected with detailed links. The outline will end with a complete and correct source page, listing all the sources cited in the speech. You should follow your instructor's requirements for how to present the outline, but in most cases, it will be:

- Typed
- Double spaced
- Formatted in a specific and consistent way
- Handed in prior to or on the day you give your speech

The basic format of a preparation outline should look similar to the template at right. This template is the standard pattern you can use to create most speech outlines.

Student name	Class
Date	Instructor name

Topic
General purpose
Specific purpose
Central idea

INTRODUCTION
    Attention-getter
    Credibility material
    Relevance to audience
    Preview of speech

(Link from introduction to first main point)

BODY
    I. First main point
        A. Subpoint
        B. Subpoint
            1. Subpoint of B
            2. Subpoint of B
            3. Subpoint of B

(Link between first and second main points)

    II. Second main point
        A. Subpoint
        B. Subpoint
            1. Subpoint of B
            2. Subpoint of B
        C. Subpoint

(Link between second and third main points)

    III. Third main point
        A. Subpoint
            1. Subpoint of A
              a. Subpoint of 1
              b. Subpoint of 1
            2. Subpoint of A
        B. Subpoint
        C. Subpoint

(Link to conclusion)

CONCLUSION
    Summary statement
    Audience response statement
    WOW statement

        Works Cited (or References)

Steven's preparation outline looked like this.

Steven Barker   COMM 110
October 22, 2010   Dr. Smith

Topic: The facts surrounding fair trade chocolate are astounding.
General purpose: To inform
Specific purpose: To inform my audience about fair trade chocolate.
Central idea: Today, I want to share what fair trade chocolate is, why chocolate is an issue, and where you can purchase fair trade chocolate.

INTRODUCTION
Attention-getter: Raise your hand if you have had any chocolate today. Raise your hand if you have had any chocolate in the last week. How about the last month? Or the last year?
Relevance to audience: For those of you who raised your hands and even those of you who didn't, what you are about to hear will surely make you think twice before the next time you eat a chocolate candy bar.
Credibility material: As a member of the Christian Social Justice Committee, I have become concerned about fair trade chocolate.
Preview of speech: Fair trade chocolate is becoming a global concern in our culture today. To understand its impact, we have to answer the following three questions. What is fair trade chocolate? Why is chocolate an issue? Where can one buy fair trade chocolate?

(**Link:** First, what is fair trade chocolate?)

BODY
I.   Fair trade, according to FairTradeFederation.org, is an economic partnership based on dialogue, transparency, and respect.
     A. Fair trade essentially is a combination of several ideals.
        1. It is set in place to provide safe work environments for industries.
        2. It allows for adequate levels of pay for all employees in industry.
        3. It prevents the practice of slavery in all associated industries.
        4. It ensures the rights of children.
     B. Fair trade chocolate is chocolate that is harvested and prepared by individuals who receive fair wages for the work that they do.

(**Link:** Second, why is chocolate such an issue?)

II. Chocolate harvested by slaves is such a big issue because of the limited product alternatives for consumption in the United States.

    A. It is estimated that there are more than 27 million modern-day slaves throughout the world (Batstone).

    B. The manner in which the chocolate-harvesting slaves are procured as well as how they are treated is horrendous.

        1. According to the 2001 documentary *Slavery*, these slaves are sometimes bought from parents for as little as $30.

        2. They are also taken from street corners in neighboring countries after being promised food and wealth.

    C. Ghana Africa grows cocoa for export.

        1. It is the world's largest exporter of cocoa beans.

        2. It is also the largest among the slave industry.

    D. The United States is the world's largest importer of cocoa beans.

(**Link:** Finally, where can one buy free trade chocolate?)

III. There are several places to purchase free trade chocolate.

    A. The Internet is the best place to purchase chocolate.

        1. Sweetearth.com deals specifically with fair trade.

        2. So does Divine Chocolate at divinechocolateusa.com.

    B. The Mustard Seed, which is located in downtown Columbia, is a fair trade only store that sells Divine Chocolate.

    C. Kaldi's Coffee also sells fair trade chocolate. Their store is located in downtown Columbia right next to the Mustard Seed.

    D. Some common chocolates are not fair trade.

        1. Hershey, Nestle, Mars, and Lindt chocolates make up more than 75 percent of the chocolate that most stores carry.

        2. These brands of chocolate are not slave free.

As you can see, free trade chocolate is available locally and via the Internet.)

CONCLUSION

Summary statement: Fair trade chocolate has become a big issue throughout the world today. Now you know what fair trade chocolate is, why chocolate has become an issue, and where you can purchase fair trade chocolate.

Audience response statement: You can now make an informed choice to eat responsible chocolate, or not.

WOW statement: I will leave you today with a gift. This is a sample of Divine Chocolate. This is what chocolate should taste like, because no little kid was forced to make it for you. This chocolate is slave free and guilt free. It is Divine!

Works Cited

"About Fair Trade." *FairTradeFederation.org*. Fair Trade Federation, 2007. Web. 19 Oct. 2009.

Batstone, David. *Not for Sale: The Return of the Global Slave Trade—and How We Can Fight It*. New York: Harper, 2007. Print.

Slavery. Dir. Kate Blewett and Brian Woods. Narr. Kate Blewett and Brian Woods. British Broadcasting Channel, 2001. Film.

Name: _____   Class: _____

Instructor's Name: _____   Date: _____

Speech Brainstorming Worksheet

Use the Speech Brainstorming Worksheet to help gather your thoughts prior to typing an outline. This worksheet can be used for any type of speech that you will ever need to present (Introduction, Central Idea, Demonstration, Persuasion, Special Occasion, or Group Presentation). Additional copies of this worksheet are in your Tools for Success/MyCommunicationLab online portal!

Speech Category: Write the type of speech (Introduction, Informative, Demonstration, Persuasion, Special Occasion, or Group Presentation)

_____

Speech Title: Give your speech a clever title.

_____

General Purpose: Write the general purpose (Is the purpose of the speech to Inform? Instruct? Entertain? Motivate?).

_____

Specific Purpose: Write the specific purpose in full sentence format (What do you plan to accomplish by presenting this speech?).

_____

_____

_____

Introduction:

Attention Step: Write all you plan to say in full sentence format. (How will you get the audience's attention?)

_____

_____

_____

_____

_____

Establish Need/Relevance: Establish why this topic should interest the listener (full sentence).

_____

_____

_____

Establish Speaker Credibility: Establish why *you* are qualified to speak about this topic (full sentence).

Forensics

Thesis (Preview) Statement: Clearly state the three main points you plan to cover (full sentences).

1. What is a fingerprint
2. Why we use fingerprints
3. How to correctly fingerprint

(Transition: Transition from the Introduction Step to the First Main Point. Write the transition in full sentence format.)

Body: *Be sure to parenthetically cite research used.*
I. First Main Point A fingerprint
   A. First Sub-Point _____
     1. First Sub-Sub-Point (Note: Not all points will have Sub-Sub Points).

     2. Second Sub-Sub-Point _____
   B. Second Sub-Point _____
     1. First Sub-Sub-Point _____
     2. Second Sub-Sub-Point _____

(Transition: Transition from the First Main Point to the Second Main Point. Write the transition in full sentence format.)

II. Second Main Point _____
   A. First Sub-Point _____
     1. First Sub-Sub-Point (Note: Not all points will have Sub-Sub Points).

     2. Second Sub-Sub-Point _____
   B. Second Sub-Point _____
     1. First Sub-Sub-Point _____
     2. Second Sub-Sub-Point _____

(Transition: Transition from the Second Main Point to the Third Main Point. Write the transition in full sentence format.)

III. Second Main Point _____
   A. First Sub-Point _____
      1. First Sub-Sub-Point (Note: Not all points will have Sub-Sub Points).

         _____

      2. Second Sub-Sub-Point _____
   B. Second Sub-Point _____
      1. First Sub-Sub-Point _____
      2. Second Sub-Sub-Point _____

(Transition: Transition from the Second Main Point to the Third Main Point. Write the transition in full sentence format.)

_____

_____

_____

Conclusion:

Summary: Write in full sentence format. Summarize **ALL** main points.

1. _____

2. _____

3. _____

Appeal to Action: End with a **BANG**! Leave your audience thinking about your speech!

_____

_____

Speech Outline Checklist

Before each speech, follow this checklist to make sure your outline is in order.

The Outline:
- ☐ Typed
- ☐ Uses correct outline format
- ☐ Includes header (student's name, class ID, professor's name, date)
- ☐ Includes headings (shown in bold letters on the example outline)
- ☐ Includes a Speech Category
- ☐ Includes a Title
- ☐ Includes a General Purpose and a Specific Purpose

Introduction:
- ☐ Written in a full sentence format
- ☐ Includes an Attention Step
- ☐ Establishes Need/Relevance
- ☐ Establishes Speaker Credibility
- ☐ Clearly stated Thesis/Preview Statement

Body:
- ☐ Uses Roman Numerals (I., II., III.), capitalized letters for Sub-Points (A., B., C.), and numbers for Sub-Sub-Points (1., 2., 3.)
- ☐ Develops three main points using key words or phrases
- ☐ Used transition sentences

Conclusion:
- ☐ Written in a full sentence outline format
- ☐ Summarizes all main points
- ☐ Uses an appropriate final appeal

Presentation Aids (*Note: Visual Aids are not required for ALL speeches*):
- ☐ Includes a separate Visual Aid Explanation Page
- ☐ PowerPoint Slides follow outline and are effectively designed
- ☐ Handout is usable, effectively designed, and one for each audience member

Research:
- ☐ Follows MLA Guidelines
- ☐ Required number of sources are included
- ☐ Uses reliable research
- ☐ Uses various types of research (magazines, journals, books, interviews)
- ☐ Uses timely research (less than five years old)
- ☐ Includes parenthetical citations within the document
- ☐ Includes a Works Cited page

Creating Useful Notes (Delivery Outline) for Your Speech

1 Index Cards
2 File Folders

Believe it or not, you are well on your way to a successful speech. Next you will need to prepare a **delivery outline** which will become useful notes to carry you through the speech. Your notes should not be the same typed outline page that you give to your instructor. This actually needs to be constructed in a different way so that you can use it as a tool to keep yourself organized and calm as you speak. The following are some suggestions for you, but just remember that you should choose the strategy that works best for you.

1
Index Cards

Index Cards are often used by public speakers. They will write out the full introduction and conclusion and bullet point the main points. There is a great deal of speculation about what size card to use and what color to use. It has been said that blue index cards are a good choice because the color blue calms the speaker. Others believe they can read their writing better on a white card. One word of warning—if you choose to use index cards, you should use only **one** card and write on only **one** side of the card. All too often speakers, nervous to be speaking in front of a group, will drop their card/cards and the more cards you use, the more you will have to pick up. In other words—keep it simple!

2
File Folders

File Folders happen to be my tool of choice. They just look neater. The speaker walks to the lectern holding a plain black file folder (looking professional), gets to the lectern, opens the file folder, and places it on the surface (still looks professional). During the course of the speech, the speaker usually will not pick up a file folder; whereas, if the speaker is using an index card, he may be tempted to pick up the card and hold it the entire speech (not professional at all!). The speaker who uses the file folder can glance down occasionally, find their notes, and then look back up to their audience (still professional). Here are some things that you should do:

1. Choose a solid color file folder—Black or navy blue is best.
2. Type the introduction, main points, and conclusion.
3. Cut the sections apart.
4. On the top left side, tape or glue the introduction.
5. On the middle left side, place the list of the three main points (I., II., III.).
6. On the top right side, place the list of all main points and sub points.
7. On the bottom right side, place the conclusion.
8. Color code sections for easier recognition.
9. Notes should always be **a large, bold font** so they are easy to read. Write out your introduction and conclusion. Everything else should be well organized key words that are used to jog your memory. Don't read your notes to the audience; use them as a tool to keep you on track.

Here is an Index Card example for you to follow:

Introduction:
    Attention Step:
    Establish Need:
    Establish Credibility:
    State Central Idea/Thesis:
Transition/Link
    I. First Main Point
        A. Sub Point
        B. Sub Point
Transition/Link
    II. Second Main Point
        A. Sub Point
        B. Sub Point
Transition/Link
    III. Third Main Point
        A. Sub Point
        B. Sub Point
Transition/Link
Conclusion summarizes three main points and ends with a BANG!

Here is a File Folder example for you to follow:

Introduction:
Attention Step:
Establish Need:
Establish Credibility:
State Central Idea/Thesis:

List Three Main Points
    I. Main Point
        Transition/Link
    II. Main Point
        Transition/Link
    III. Main Point
        Transition/Link

I. First Main Point
    A. Sub Point
    B. Sub Point
II. Second Main Point
    A. Sub Point
    B. Sub Point
III. Third Main Point
    A. Sub Point
    B. Sub Point

S P E E C H

Conclusion summarizes three main points and ends with a BANG!

"We were born to succeed, not to fail."

HENRY DAVID THOREAU

Peer Editing Guidelines

1 Responsibilities of the Reader
2 Responsibilities of the Writer

Some instructors will require students to produce a written speech in addition to an outline. This assignment should be drafted using the outline as a guide and will usually involve three drafts: first, second, and final. As a class activity, you may be asked to peer-edit another classmate's written first draft. If this is the case, it is a good idea to understand the peer editing process. Speech writing will utilize your skills regarding grammar, punctuation, spelling, word usage, and the writing process. There are five stages involved:

1. Pre-writing

2. Drafting

3. Revising

4. Editing and proofreading

5. Publication

During the speech prewriting process, you will conduct an audience analysis, consider the purpose, decide upon a topic, research and gather information, brainstorm with your speech group, and organize your speech. As you begin to put your thoughts on paper, the drafting stage will allow you the opportunity to focus on the content you plan to share. This stage is often called **free-writing,** because you will need to write freely without worrying about the mechanics which will be expected in your final draft. The third stage, revising, allows you to take a closer look at the content before sharing the draft with your peer editor.

The editing and proofreading stage is where **peer editing** enters the picture. Working with a peer editing group will offer you a chance to write for an audience other than your instructor. Knowing your group will be peer editing your written speech draft will encourage you to think ahead about how you can explain your topic more clearly for the audience. In the beginning, you will feel a bit self-conscious realizing others in your group will be reading and critiquing your work. A critique is much different than when someone criticizes your work. A critique is positive and constructive. You should remember that all drafts which precede the final draft are works in progress. Anxious feelings will soon change as you realize that peer editing can also be a confidence builder as your peers offer positive feedback as well as constructive criticism. Peer-editing provides the opportunity to discuss the topic and receive helpful suggestions. Enter this stage with an open mind and invite your peers to correct anything they find which will improve your speech. Encourage your peer editors to actively search for areas which need correction such as grammar, spelling, punctuation, and word usage; however, they should also review the quality of research and inclusion of research documentation throughout the written speech.

After the peer editing process has been completed, you may choose to incorporate the suggested corrections in the next draft. Caution should be used at this stage because not every suggestion made by your peers will be correct. You will need to consider suggestions and check your grammar books to make sure suggestions are valid. If you deem the suggestions valid, then you should make the corrections. The final stage is often called the publication stage. It is at this point that you submit the final written speech to your instructor for a grade.

Now that you have a clear understanding of the writing process, you should realize the reader and the writer both have responsibilities in the peer editing process.

1
Responsibilities of the Reader

- **Take your time.** Before you begin to peer edit someone's work, make sure that you realize this is a time intensive process. You will want to devote an adequate amount of time to each of your peers as you edit their written persuasion speech, remembering that they are also taking the time to peer edit your written speech.

- **Read the written speech twice.** The first time you read the speech, you will need to become familiar with the topic, make notes, or mark places which seem unclear or vague. The second time you read the speech, you will try to understand what the reader is trying to accomplish, and you may begin to make suggestions. If you have a hard time understanding the reader's thoughts after two readings, you should let the writer know.

- **Ask questions.** As you read the written speech and begin the peer editing process, you should feel confident to ask for clarification about anything that seems vague or incorrect.

- **Assume the role of the instructor.** Begin to notice obvious errors which might include grammar, spelling, punctuation, and word usage; however, don't just concentrate on the mechanics. You should focus on content, organization, format, and MLA documentation. Pay careful attention to the overall structure of the written speech. If there are a few areas which need help, bring this to the attention of the writer. You will also need to ask, "Did the writer meet the objectives of the assignment?"

- **Don't correct the errors.** As a peer editor, it is not your job to correct the errors that you see. Instead, you should bring them to the writer's attention so that the writer can make the corrections.

- **Offer positive feedback.** It is always good to offer positive praise when praise is due, but make sure your comments are honest.

- **Be constructive.** When peer editing, you will need to keep comments constructive. Making all positive comments such as, "You are doing great," or "I liked your attention step," will not actually help your writer to improve his or her work. Instead, make sure you give them constructive ideas which will help them to become a better writer. Focus on how your classmate can change the written speech in order to gain improvement.

- **Be specific** in both praise and criticism.

2
Responsibilities of the Writer

- **Be prepared.** On the day assigned for peer editing, it is the writer's responsibility to have a completed draft of the written speech including a Works Cited page.

- **Explain the purpose.** As you present your written speech to your peers, explain the purpose of your speech as well as any other information which will help with the editing process.

- **Keep an open mind.** The feedback you receive today could help you to achieve a higher grade on your written speech. Do not get your feelings hurt if someone makes suggestions with which you do not agree. Listen to your peers. You have the option of whether you make the change or not, but you still must listen to suggestions. If you feel bruised by the suggestions made, remind yourself that suggestions are about your writing, not about you. Realize the benefit available to you by having someone else review your work before you have to submit it to an instructor.

- **Ask questions.** If someone makes a suggestion that you do not understand, you may ask questions regarding the suggestion.

- **Make a decision.** Following the peer editing process, you have the choice of whether you will make the corrections suggested by your peer editor or ignore the suggestions. Choose carefully because the final draft is the draft which will be submitted to your instructor.

Creating Visual Aids and Handouts

1 **Visual Aids**
2 **Handouts**

Now that you have completed the hard part, it's time to work on the fun part. Whether or not you have had classes in graphic design, you will be able to create a professional visual aid and handout, but it takes a bit of effort.

First, you need to understand why visual aids and handouts are necessary for a speech presentation. Instructional designers maintain that using visual aids and handouts clarifies the topic, generates interest, and promotes retention of the material. In fact, the more senses involved during your presentation, the longer your audience will remember the message that you have delivered.

Communication experts tell us that we remember only about 10% of everything we hear; however, if we hear and see something, our retention rate may increase up to 50%. Add touch or activity to the presentation and our retention rate may rise as much as 85%. As a result of visual aids, audiences are more likely to retain the primary essence of the presentation. Still, a handout is needed to help the audience members recover the final 15%. I'm sure that you will agree visual aids and handouts are crucial to a successful presentation. Without them, your audience will forget your message in about the same time that it takes for you to exit the stage.

There are three design principles to help in the visual aid and handout planning process: figure/ground, hierarchy, and gestalt. Each of these principles may be used separately or in conjunction with one another, in order to create or manage visuals for clearer understanding and retention.

Figure/Ground designs allow the audience to choose which information is most important. The visual aid designer may use larger font, bolder font, brighter colors, and/or spacing to bring important information into the forefront. Through this method, the most important information is thrust, visually, in front of the audience. As the audience sees the larger, bolder information, they perceive that particular information as being important and worthy of consideration. Here is one example of figure/ground:

> Figure/ground
> brings
>
> # I M P O R T A N T
>
> information
> to the front

Do you see how the word, **IMPORTANT,** jumps out from the slide? Simply using a bolder, larger font and adding a space between each letter, we are able to incorporate the figure/ground principle.

The same principle can be achieved by moving less important information to the background. As a result, the audience sees the smaller, less obtrusive fonts and perceives that particular information as less important.

> **Figure/Ground**
> can also move
> less important
> information
> to the
> background

Hierarchy is an organizational tool which utilizes bar graphs, line graphs, pie charts, and maps to draw the audience's attention. Outlines, directional arrows, and lists are another way of using the hierarchy principle. Tables and diagrams can also be positioned to show the most important information and the least important information. This principle is based upon the way that our mind organizes and groups things of importance together. Additionally, it incorporates the way that we note things of great importance and things of less importance.

In a PowerPoint presentation, we often see the hierarchy principle used as designers create headings and bullet points to list items of importance first. Here are some examples of hierarchy:

> **Three Visual Aid Design Principles:**
> - **Hierarchy**
> - Figure/Ground
> - Gestalt

The next example is a pyramid design which shows the hierarchy principle noting the largest section as the most important and the smallest section as the least important.

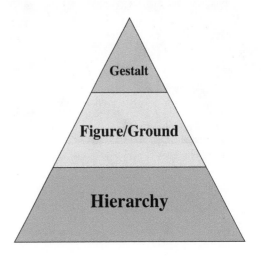

Organizational schemas are another example of the hierarchy principle.

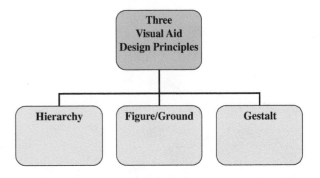

Notice the line graph below which helps move the eye from one bar of information to the next. Designers are able to show the audience in one quick graphic exactly where they want the audience to focus.

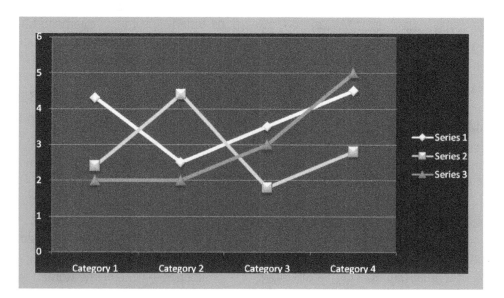

Tables are another version of the hierarchy principle. Note how the designer is able to incorporate information through a table which gets right to the point of the speech topic – the number of females and males enrolled in each Public Speaking course.

100 STUDENTS ENROLLED	GENDER 61 F=FEMALE 39 M= MALE	
25	18F	7M
25	12F	13M
25	15F	10M
25	16F	9M

The **gestalt** principle usually incorporates figure/ground and hierarchy, and is based upon the "big picture". In fact, gestalt is a German word which means the whole is greater than the sum of many parts. This principle incorporates the use of words and visuals to produce one primary thought. When using a PowerPoint presentation, a gestalt design could sport a heading and a picture that illustrates the point. Notice the question marks along with the picture that mirrors the heading?

Here is a great example of gestalt. One picture tells you everything you should remember about visual aid and handout design:

- Did you notice the arrow and the added spaces in "Keep it *Going*"?

- Take a look at the different type of font used in "Keep it Interesting".

- How about the simple, boring font in "Keep it Simple"?

- Notice the gray and smaller font in "Keep it in the Background".

- How about the larger and bolder font in "Keep it **L A R G E**"?

- Of course, you wouldn't want to pass up the main block which is located at the top and lets you know the entire slide is about "Visual Aid Tips".

What does this mean? If you ever see a visual aid and it seems to have elements of figure/ground and hierarchy, then you can bet you are looking at a great example of gestalt! Now that you understand a little about the three design principles in creating effective visual aids and handouts, you will want to consider what visual aid best suits your purpose and which type of handout would be most useful for your audience.

1
Visual Aids

You have several options: PowerPoint presentations, video clips, music, overhead transparencies, flip charts, posters, your own body, other classmates, and objects that visually support your topic. Here are some things to consider:

1. Keep It Simple Sweetie! (KISS)

- Limit each visual to one main idea.

- Don't clutter up posters or slides with too many things.

- Use very little text.

- Bullet format key words instead of complete sentences.

- Limit your text to no more than six lines.

- Use the same font throughout your speech—Times New Roman is preferred.

- Use the same color throughout your speech.

- Use graphics such as charts, graphs, or pictures.

- Use no more than one slide for every one minute of speech time.

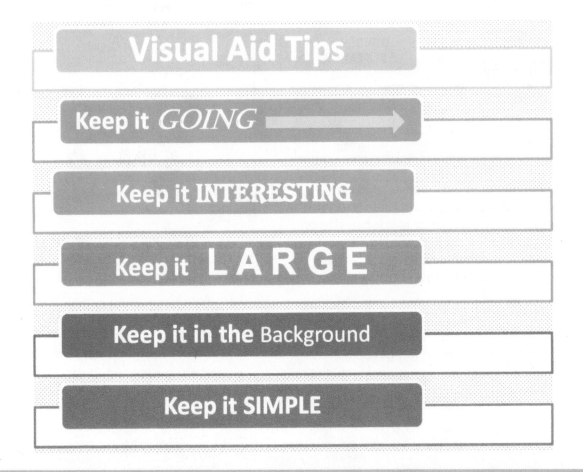

- If using a video/DVD clip, limit the scene to show only what is necessary. A good rule is to have no more than 30 seconds of video or music for a 5-minute speech or 45 seconds for a 10-minute speech. Speeches that last 30 minutes or more may incorporate a longer video or music clip.
- Cue video/DVD clip to desired scene.
- Check audio level and contrast.
- Dim audience lights, but do not turn them off.
- Explain the purpose of the video/DVD clip before playing it.
- Show interest in the video/DVD clip and watch it enthusiastically.
- Summarize the main point of the clip after you have shown it.

2. Keep It Large.

- Make sure that everyone in your audience can see it, including the guy who sits in the very back row—and especially your instructor, who is usually in the back of the room during speech day!
- Use at least a 24-point font if working with PowerPoint.

3. Keep It Interesting.

- Don't turn your speech into a dull slide show!
- Make sure that your visual aids support the message.
- Try to use more than one type of visual aid, especially for longer speeches.
- You don't have to have a different visual for each point—but only show the visual that pertains to the point you are making. If you change to another point and you don't have a visual for that point, show a blank slide—or remove the visual that is displayed.
- NEVER write on a dry-erase board for your visual aid unless you are an artist and you choose that as a medium to illustrate a point—and then make sure your markers are working properly. You will also want to test different colors to see which ones are more easily seen from a distance.
- When using a table display:
  - Cover the table with a table cloth;

- Position the table so that items are visible;
- Make sure items on the table can be seen—use boxes, cubes, or stands to elevate items, if necessary;
- Pick up items as you discuss them and show them to the audience;
- Rehearse your speech using the table display.

4. Keep Your Visuals in the Background.

- Talk to your audience, not to your visuals.
- Use your Speech Support Group as a Tech Team and have them manipulate the visuals for you. If you have several posters, enlist them to help you set up and take down. If you are using a PowerPoint presentation, give them a script and have them operate the computer while you speak.
- Direct your listeners' attention to the visual aids, but make sure that you are using good eye contact with your audience at all times.

5. Keep It Going.

- In life, things happen! Computers crash; CDs, or jump-drives malfunction; posters fall down. Be prepared for anything. Remember Murphy's Law? Always back up PowerPoint presentations on two or three different mediums so that if one doesn't work, you will have a backup. If the computer in your classroom is Internet capable, you can always e-mail a copy to yourself and retrieve it from your e-mail. Since the visual aid grade is a big portion of your overall grade, you will not want to make a presentation without one! So, be prepared!
- Always have an alternative plan in case your first plan isn't working. Just remember, that if for some reason your visuals fail during the course of your speech, "the show must go on," and you must continue.
- Be comfortable with the equipment that you are going to use.
- Rehearse with your visuals so that you are comfortable with them.
- Pack all of your speech supplies prior to speech day so that you will be ready to go!

2
Handouts

Many of the same rules for visual aids apply to handouts, so you will want to review the "Keep It Simple Sweetie" section as you consider your design.

1. Design an appealing handout.
2. Use quality paper, usually heavy card stock.
   - Use color paper for visual variety.
   - Use color fonts and pictures to create interest.
3. Use a brochure or book format when applicable.
4. Use diagrams, charts, pictures, or graphs to illustrate a point.
5. Design should support your spoken message, but not restate what you have already said during your speech.
6. Have enough handouts for each member of your audience.
7. Use technical writing skills as you design the handout:
   - Use bullet format with key words;
   - Keep headings simple and to the point;
   - Use simple borders to encase headings;
   - Use concrete words instead of abstract words;
   - Limit the handout to one theme;
   - Use one type of font;
   - Use color;
   - Include phone numbers, Web sites, addresses, etc., for additional information.
8. Laminate handouts when needed to protect the content.
9. Tell the audience about your handout during the speech and provide instructions/ directions for using the handout.

When using handouts, you will need to consider the following distribution suggestions:

1. **Avoid giving your handouts to the audience during the middle of the speech.** This is disruptive during a short speech and your audience will quit listening to you while they take their handout and begin looking at it.
2. **Give your handout at the beginning of your speech if** it will be used as a note taking aid, a fill-in-the-blank format, or if it will be used as a visual during the speech.
3. **Give your handout to the audience following the speech if** it is offering additional information for your audience to read later.
4. **Enlist your Speech Support Group/ Tech Team** to help with the distribution of handouts. The speaker must never distribute handouts, personally. Having your Tech Team distribute handouts will make your presentation appear more professional and will help ease some of your "stress" because you won't worry about forgetting to give them to your audience.

For more information, log into:

MyCommunicationLab

In this chapter, you will learn how to investigate a speech topic so that you will be confident in your understanding of the subject and will be able to speak intelligently about it. The process for finding materials to support your speech is called **research.**

As you are preparing speeches for the fundamental speech class, you will find that the first place to begin research will be from your own common knowledge or personal experience with the subject. This is especially true as you present the Speech of Introduction and the Central Idea Speech. Often you might include information that has been gleaned from a direct observation. These might include examples, illustrations, short stories, descriptions or explanations, opinions, or case studies in which you have directly observed a phenomenon that will support your topic. While this is a good starting point, students must remember that the audience will want to hear evidence, other than your own contributions, in order to form an opinion regarding their acceptance or rejection of your point of view. This will be especially useful during your persuasive speech.

After you have included information that you already know or have experienced, it is important to search for further documentation to support your topic. These are usually presented in the form of documents and quantitative support such as statistics or figures.

One mistake students often make when researching a topic is to use the first four or five items they find. For example, when asked to include five resources, students will use the first five resources they find on the internet or in the library regardless of the quality of the source or its apparent connection to the subject. The ultimate goal is to find five quality sources that support your argument or topic in such a way that leaves little doubt for the audience.

When research choices are made haphazardly, the results can be disastrous. Weak research can undermine the speaker's credibility, affect audience attention and reaction, and create confusion. Therefore, you should enter the research arena with these goals in mind:

- Find relevant, credible research that will support your topic,
- Find evidence that supports your view of the topic,
- Find research that will expand your knowledge of the subject,
- Find research that will clarify your topic for the audience,
- Find research that is current,
- Find research that is scholarly.

CHAPTER 3 CONTENTS—CONDUCTING RESEARCH

Research Criteria

The first questions you might ask yourself are:

- Where do I start?
- Where do I go to find good research material?
- How will I know it is good?
- What kind of research do I need?
- What supporting materials should I use?

Just the thought of conducting research for a speech can be overwhelming. By the time you have reached this stage, you should have reduced your topic so that you will stay within the time frame allotted. This very fact will help you to reduce the amount of research that is necessary. Taking a quick look at your outline will enable you to make decisions regarding the type of research you might need to support your topic. For example, if your topic involves bicycle safety for small children, you will want to include information and statistics that will get the audience's attention. First, you might ask yourself the following research based questions:

- Are you conducting research for support?
- Are you conducting research to supplement the knowledge you already have?
- Do you need statistics to get the audience's attention?
- Do you need a great quote, story, or anecdote to use in the conclusion?
- How timely does the research need to be?

Understanding this information will let you know where to start in the researching process.

It goes without saying that you will need to visit your college or community library to begin the process. If you are unsure about navigating in such a sterile, quiet, daunting environment, just ask for help! Librarians and their assistants are usually happy to help you understand the indexing system to reveal the material involved in your search. The library will provide you with numerous selections of newspapers, magazines, books, video, and audio sources. Before visiting the library, you will want to find out the library's operation hours and then make sure that you do the following:

- Take along all of the materials or supplies (note cards or paper, pencils or pens, travel drives, computer disks, and correct change for the photocopy machine) that you might need. Thinking ahead will make your library experience more positive.
- Take your outline so that you can reference areas that need research support.
- Develop a Works Cited page from potential sources, writing down all sources of interest.
- Check out books that might be relevant to your research.
- Photocopy newspaper articles or magazine articles that might be relevant to your research.

Of course, you will want to surf the Web to see the options available. Be sure to read the section in this chapter regarding "Using the Internet." Often you will find Internet material that has a hard-copy version. In this event, the source is still considered to be an Internet source. Many of the magazines and newspapers offer daily web entries that correspond to their hard-copy versions. As you choose Internet sources, please be sure to write down the complete online reference which should contain the title of the project, the database, the name of the author or the editor, the title of the article, date of publication, the URL (Universal Resource Locator) address enclosed in angle brackets (< >), and date you retrieved the article. This information will be necessary if you use the source.

After you have gathered several sources, you will want to begin reading and evaluating the sources. You will not have time to read every book, magazine, or newspaper article cover to cover. The first thing you will need to do is to note the copyright date of your source. Typically, most instructors will not want you to use anything that is over five years old unless it has historical significance. Internet, magazine, and newspaper sources should not be over three years old. After making sure the source is timely, you will want to identify certain elements within the source that happen to be most pertinent for your speech. When looking through the books you have chosen, you should begin with the Table of Contents and note which chapters might be of use.

Should you decide to include personal interviews, you will need to carefully evaluate the person/persons being interviewed. The interviewee should be recognized as an authority on the topic, and you will need to quote the exact words of the source. Care must be taken to determine if the source is biased or unbiased toward your topic. The interview must also be documented as a source in your research.

Be particularly cautious when using statistical research to support your topic. Your sources should be reputable, authoritative, and unbiased. Government and independent survey organizations usually provide more reputable statistics than private agencies. When using statistics, you will need to quote the primary source of information so that you will know the information has been cited accurately. You will also gain speaker credibility and audience attention when you use sources that are unbiased and do not tend to report according to their personal agenda.

Most researchers find it helpful to create a speech material file. This can be as simple as a file folder in which you add things that might be helpful as you plan your upcoming speeches. Some students designate a section in their speech class notebook in which to include ideas, quotations, clippings from newspapers, brainstorming sheets, anecdotes or stories that might be used. **Thinking ahead, planning as you go, and gathering materials ahead of time will make your job easier when you begin putting all of the pieces together for a speech.**

Methods of Research

This chapter will focus on the evaluation of materials to be used as you research a speech topic. **Evaluation** is a process of gathering information and making decisions regarding the worth or quality of information.

Most of you might think of evaluations in terms of testing in a classroom to determine how well you know the material. Evaluating research happens in much the same way. The final result will be to determine if a piece of research is useful to support your speech topic.

Why should we evaluate research material? Truthfully, there is so much information available and not all of it is valid. It might sound good as you read it, but do you know that it is factual? Is the book, magazine, or web site legitimate? Are the facts real or made up num-

bers from a bogus source? Evaluation is not as simple as it might sound. Some sources may sound legitimate on the surface but are not reputable. Often conducting an evaluation will reveal weaknesses or strengths of the source. You will need to ask yourself the following questions:

1. Who authored this piece of research?
2. What are their credentials?
3. Why would my audience respect this piece of research?
4. Is the content clear?
5. Is the content helpful?
6. Is the content informative?
7. Is the content accurate?
8. Is the content unbiased?
9. Is the source up to date?
10. Does the content support my topic?

The best advice is to use newspaper articles from larger newspapers (*The Wall Street Journal, The Business Chronicle, etc.*), magazine articles from reputable magazines (*Time, Newsweek, US News and World Report, etc.*), professional journals (*ERIC Digest, Phi Delta Kappan, Research and Improvement Reports and Studies, etc.*), books published by reputable publishers, reputable Internet sites (*Galileo*), and interviews from professionals. If you are ever unsure about a source, ask your instructor to help with the evaluation.

When asked to conduct a research project, you will want to use varied sources. For example, you might include one newspaper article, one magazine article, one book, a personal interview and an Internet site. Varying your sources and qualifying your sources will make you a more credible speaker and will gain the attention of your audience.

Using Interviews as a Source of Research

1 Suggestions for E-mail and Telephone Interviews

Interviews are defined by the asking and answering of questions. We hear interviews as they are conducted on radio news shows, we observe interviews on television or online, and we are interviewed by friends and business associates. Interviews are very different from social communication because they are goal oriented. Using an interview as a source of research, involves gathering information which may be used to discover meanings or uncover facts.

An interview with a professional person, who understands your topic, is an excellent source of research. Your instructor may require that you conduct a personal face-to-face interview and use this as research for one of your upcoming speeches. Telephone and e-mail interviews are also acceptable; however, students will not achieve the full benefit of conducting an interview unless it is a face-to-face interview. Before you conduct your first formal interview, it is important to understand something about the interview process. The following section will be divided into three areas of importance: before the interview, during the interview, and after the interview:

BEFORE THE INTERVIEW:

1. Decide who you would like to interview;
2. Prepare 3-5 interview questions;
3. Contact the interviewee;
4. Request an appointment;
5. Secure an audio recorder;
6. Arrive ten minutes early, dressed for the interview;
7. Have pencil/paper, recorder, questions;
8. Announce yourself to the receptionist;
9. Wait until announced;
10. Breathe.

After you have chosen a topic, you will have a clearer idea of the type of information needed to support your speech. A professional will provide you with credible information and a personal viewpoint which might not be achieved through any other method of research.

As you consider who you might interview, ask yourself the following questions:

- "What do I need to know?"
- "Who would have information to support my topic?"
- "Would this professional talk to me for thirty minutes?"
- "Will this professional share information with me?"

Only three to five questions are needed for a personal opinion interview. It is advisable to craft open-ended questions instead of question which yield a *yes* or *no* answer. An open-ended question is a broad question which allows the interviewee an opportunity

to expound upon an answer. A closed-ended question limits answer options and will severely stunt the interview process.

Some interviewees will request a list of questions prior to the interview. It is for this reason that you are asked to craft the interview questions prior to making the appointment with the interviewee. Here are some things to consider when preparing questions for the interview:

- Know something about your interviewee and his/her company;
- Show excitement and energy regarding your upcoming speech topic;
- Have pre-determined objectives for the interview.

To request an interview, write a formal letter or make a brief phone call. It is important that you introduce yourself and indicate the nature of the request. An example of an interview request letter/e-mail/telephone script is found at the end of this section.

Audio or video recording the interview will provide you with a valuable tool, especially as you begin the transcription process. Many students have audio recording devices available on their cell phones or MP3 players. If you do not have a recorder, borrow one. Remember to test the recorder prior to the interview, making sure that you completely understand how to start and stop the recorder. You will also want to check to make sure the batteries are fresh and will stay charged for a 30-minute interview.

Of course, you will want to arrive early, prepared, and dressed for the interview. It is always a good idea to visit the location prior to your interview. This allows you the opportunity of confirming directions and understanding the amount of time it takes to drive to the location.

Knowing how people in the office dress, will help you to know how to dress for the interview. While piercings and high fashion may be the *thing* in college, corporate America might not appreciate your fashion trends. Neatness and appropriate attire will help you to make a positive impression with the interviewee. A word of warning: keep clothing and hairstyles simple, and stay away from colognes and fragrances.

Conducting research about the interviewee and his/her company will help you to get a good idea about the content of your questions. Being prepared for the interview will reduce anxiety about the interview.

Announce yourself to the receptionist and be prepared to wait in a waiting area until the interviewee comes to meet you. As you wait, practice your "Stress to Success Breathing Exercises" (found in Chapter 4) to calm your nerves and to prepare yourself for the meeting.

DURING THE INTERVIEW:

1. Behave professionally;
2. Shake the interviewee's hand;
3. Wait until the interviewee invites you to sit;
4. Ask permission to audio record the interview;
5. Ask your questions, one at a time;
6. Wait patiently for the answers;
7. If necessary, clarify the questions;
8. After questions have been answered, stand up, extend your hand, and thank the interviewee for his/her time;
9. Ask for a business card to attach to your transcript;
10. Thank the receptionist for her assistance.

As you begin the interview, shake the interviewee's hand and establish eye contact during the greeting. Be seated and ask permission to record the interview. Place your recorder in plain sight of the interviewee. Turn on the recorder and say, "Thank you, Mr./Ms./Dr., for allowing me the opportunity to interview you today regarding (your topic). Explain that you will be using this interview to support your speech which will be presented at (place) on (date).

Some interviewee's will decline permission to audio or video tape the interview. If this is the case, do NOT record the interview; instead, be prepared to write the interviewee's answer to each question. It may be necessary to abbreviate words in order to write everything the interviewee says. If you are unsure of your writings, read the answer back to the interviewee and confirm your understanding of the material.

Begin with your most important question. Ask each question and allow the interviewee time to provide the answer. Resist the impulse to make comments while the interviewee is speaking. You will also avoid asking

questions which you have not planned to ask. Keep the interview short so that you do not infringe on the interviewee's time.

During the interview, you will need to use correct grammar, enunciate clearly, establish and maintain eye contact, and use positive non-verbal language. It is advisable to use your interviewee's name at least three times during the interview: once for the beginning question, once during the interview, and again for the closing question.

After you have completed the interview, thank the interviewee for taking the time to provide valuable information to support your speech. A friendly handshake before you exit the office is a professional gesture of appreciation. Be sure to ask for a business card as you leave. This will help you to get the correct mailing information for the follow-up thank-you note.

Don't forget the receptionist! You'll also need to thank her/him for assisting with the interview.

AFTER THE INTERVIEW:

1. Write a thank-you note;
2. Write a transcript of the interview;
3. Attach a business card to the transcript;
4. Include the research in your outline and speech

The interview is over, but your job has just begun. Within twenty four hours of the interview, you should have a thank-you note in the mail expressing appreciation for the interviewee's time and interest in your speech, and inviting the interviewee to attend your speech. Thank-you notes may be hard-copy typed, handwritten, or e-mailed. It is more professional to type the note and to mail it; however, it is also appropriate to send an e-mail. Regardless of the method, the interviewee will enjoy hearing from you. An example of the thank-you note will be found at the end of this section.

Your next job is to transcribe the interview. Include your personal information, the interviewee's contact information, and the interviewee's credentials prior to listing the questions and answers. An example of an interview transcript will be found at the end of this section.

Although you may be tempted to correct the interviewee's grammar or word choice as you type the transcript, you must resist the urge! Type the questions and answers exactly as they are presented. During your speech, you may paraphrase the quote to correct grammar or word choice and make it appropriate for your audience; however, it is not ethical to change the meaning of the quote.

Finally, decide how you will use the information to support your speech. Refer back to the speech outline and determine which main points could be strengthened by information from your interview. Don't forget to document the research in the outline and add the source to your Works Cited page.

Suggestions for E-mail and Telephone Interviews

While e-mail and telephone interviews may save you time and anxiety, your best interviews will be conducted face-to-face. In the event you are not able to conduct a personal interview, remember these advantages and disadvantages of e-mail and telephone interviews:

ADVANTAGES:

1. E-mail and telephone interviews can be a time saver;
2. E-mail questions are efficient and provide a written record;
3. E-mail questions allow the interviewee time to think of a response;
4. E-mail and telephone interviews are useful for people in other states, countries, time zones.

DISADVANTAGES:

1. Can not be sure *who* is replying to your e-mail or telephone questions;
2. E-mail restricts your ability to clarify or question the response;
3. E-mail and telephone questions must be specific;
4. Interviewer might not hear all that is said in a telephone interview;
5. E-mail and telephone interviews can not reveal non-verbal cues;
6. E-mails may be forwarded to strangers.

EXAMPLE: Information Request Letter

Letterhead Which Includes:

Your Name
Your Address
Your City, State, Zip Code
Your Phone Number
Your E-mail

Date

Name
Title
Organization
Address
City, State, Zip Code

Dear Mr./Ms./Dr. Last Name:

I am currently an undergraduate student at (Name of College/University), majoring in (Your Major), and enrolled in a Public Speaking course. On (Date of Speech), I will be presenting a speech about (Topic).

As a recognized expert in this field, I wanted to ask if you had information which could be presented to my classmates as a handout. There are (Number of Students) and one professor in the class. Your help in providing my classmates with relevant information regarding (Topic) would be most appreciated.

I would be happy to pay for any shipping and handling costs which may apply.

Sincerely,

(*Your Signature*)

Your Name

EXAMPLE: Interview Request Letter

(For e-mail or mail, but could also be used as a script for a telephone request)

Letterhead Which Includes:

Your Name
Your Address
Your City, State, Zip Code
Your Phone Number
Your E-mail

Date

Name
Title
Organization
Address
City, State, Zip Code

Dear Mr./Ms./Dr. Last Name:

I am currently an undergraduate student at (Name of College/University), majoring in (Your Major), and enrolled in a Public Speaking course. On (Date of Speech), I will be presenting a speech about (Topic). As a recognized expert in this field, I would like to conduct an informational interview with you in order to learn more about this topic.

The interview should last about thirty minutes and will consist of three to five questions regarding (Topic). I will contact you by telephone on (Date) to see if we can schedule a meeting. Thank you for considering my request.

Sincerely,

(*Your Signature*)

Your Name

EXAMPLE: Thank-You/Follow-up Letter

Letterhead Which Includes:

Your Name
Your Address
Your City, State, Zip Code
Your Phone Number
Your E-mail

Date

Name
Title
Organization
Address
City, State, Zip Code

Dear Mr./Ms./Dr. Last Name:

Thank you for taking the time out of your busy schedule to talk with me about (Topic). I appreciate your time and consideration in preparing me for this speech at (Name of College/University). The information that you supplied will be used to support and strengthen my speech topic.

Please let me know if you would be available to attend the speech presentation on (Date) at (Time). The speech will be held at (Location). It would be an honor to have you join me, my classmates, and my professor (Name/Title of Professor) for this speech.

Thank you again for your time.

Sincerely,

(*Your Signature*)

Your Name

EXAMPLE: Interview Transcription

Interviewer:
Your Name
Your Address
Your City, State, Zip Code
Your Phone Number
Your E-mail

Interviewee:
Interviewee's Name
Interviewee's Title
Interviewee's Organization
Interviewee's Address
Interviewee's City, State, Zip Code
Interviewee's Phone Number:

Interviewee's Credentials: Detailed description of the professional's credentials and why you chose this professional to interview as a source of research for your topic.

Interview Date: _____

Question #1: _____

Interviewee's Response: _____

Question #2: _____

Interviewee's Response:: _____

Question #3: _____

Interviewee's Response: _____

NOTE: *Please include a copy of the interviewee's business card and the Thank-you note that you sent to the interviewee following the interview.*

Using the Internet

No doubt, many of you began using the Internet when you were in elementary school. It is probably hard for most students to remember when they had to go to the library and check out an encyclopedia in order to complete a project. Now you are able to point and click your way to mountains of information using a personal computer in the comfort of your home.

If you do not own a computer, your college will have computer labs that are set up with Internet capability for your use. Please check with your instructor to find out the hours of operation and be sure to ask about printer capabilities as you will want to print information retrieved from the Internet for use with projects. Some computer labs limit the numbers of pages you can print during each session. Again, it is important to check with your school to discover the limitations that might be imposed.

The **Internet** is a worldwide system of interconnected information and communication networks. Also referred to as the World Wide Web, WWW, or "the Web," it has become the dominant method of delivering and receiving information. When using the Internet, you will need to have access to the following:

- A computer (desktop or laptop),
- An Internet modem,
- Communications software,
- An Internet connection,
- An Internet provider.

Before you decide to jump into cyberspace you will first need to have a clear idea of the search you plan to conduct. Choosing specific descriptive keywords will save you time and aggravation. You can find web sites by using various search engines search. Each site will display a topic box in which you may type in your topic in the form of keywords. For example, if your persuasion speech is titled "Do Not Drink and Drive," you will want to type in keywords such as: drunken driving statistics, do not drink and drive, or the harms of drinking and driving. Just a brief warning, when typing in "drunk drivers" you will get over 1,990,000 sites.

In order to avoid wading through a million Web sites, you will want to conduct a **Boolean search.** This type of search is

more specific and allows you to narrow the number of Web sites at your disposal. Obviously this will save you a great amount of time, but will also narrow the search to items that are more specific to your topic.

Let's go back to your speech title. One way to narrow the information is to check on statistics that would involve drivers between the ages of 16 and 18. In this event, you will not just use the keywords, "drunk drivers," instead you will type in "drunk drivers + ages 16–18." Rewording the search eliminates about 200,000 sites. The more detailed you are in your search, the better chance you have of finding sites that will support your topic. Let's try this again, and this time we will type in "drunk drivers + ages 16–18 + girls." Now the results have reduced to just over 100,000 sites. Still another way to reduce the amount of information you receive would be to type in "drunk drivers + ages 16–18 + girls + Georgia," and your sites reduce again to just over 50,000 sites. One more addition will make your research more timely and still reduce the number of sites by typing in "drunk drivers + ages 16–18 + girls + Georgia + year 2010." At this point, you will have a search that is manageable and will provide information for the specified year.

Now you can understand why it is important to exercise clear judgments over the sites you plan to use. Even with a more detailed search, there are thousands of sites giving you information. Your first instinct will be to select the first sources that appear in the search; however, they might not be the best sources for your topic and may not meet the guidelines established by your instructor. Discretion is important.

 For those who are new to Internet use, try a quick tutorial at http://learnthenet .com/. This instructional site will walk you through the steps in English, Spanish, or French! It offers free mini courses and interactive labs that will help you get started. There are many other tutorials available on the WWW. Try to conduct a search for "internet tutorials" and see what you find. After you find the tutorial, scroll down the page until you find information you would like to learn. Click on the selected exercises and begin the journey.

Plagiarism

"No one can cheat you out of ultimate success but yourself."

RALPH WALDO EMERSON

We cannot complete a research discussion without offering a warning about **plagiarism.** This occurs when the writer uses someone else's ideas and claims them as his own. Students often find it tempting to copy, cut and paste, or duplicate work they find during the research process. Some students might ask a friend to write a paper or a speech for them, and other students will blatantly use another student's work substituting their own name and school information in the header. This is plagiarism.

The best way to avoid plagiarism is to make sure you are doing your own work and not using the work of someone else. You might remember a lesson your parents taught you as a child when they said, "Cheaters only cheat themselves." The more research you conduct and the more you work on a project, the more you will learn from the process.

It is also important to understand that many colleges and universities are now using software programs which will check your written work against all sources that have been published or submitted. If you have used information that is not your own work and if you have not cited the source of the information, you may rest assured that you will be charged with plagiarism.

Once you enter the corporate world, plagiarism can violate your reputation and your career. In order to teach students that plagiarism is a serious offense, many colleges and universities impose strict policies. Please check with your school to understand the penalties that are administered to students who plagiarize. Penalties range from failing the assignment to academic probation or expulsion from the institution. This is a serious matter.

Just to be safe, it is always a good idea to use direct quotations, place the quotes in quotation marks, and parenthetically cite the source in the outline and in written drafts. If you choose to **paraphrase** a quote, it is still important to parenthetically cite the source following your paraphrased information. There are some things which

cannot be paraphrased. For example, you cannot paraphrase dates, numbers, names, or places. Research containing hard information that cannot be paraphrased should be offered as a direct quote and parenthetically cited. In addition to in-text citations, a Works Cited Page should follow the written document and should contain complete citations for each source used.

Equally important, speakers should verbally give credit for ideas or phrases used during a presentation, and provide visual documentation of sources used for graphics displayed in visual aids and handouts. This is a good time to use the other lesson that your parents taught you when they said, "Better safe than sorry!"

How do you know when you should use MLA, APA, CSE, or CMS?

Students taking a fundamental public speaking course have usually had to complete a prerequisite English course prior to enrolling in speech. During the English course, you used MLA, APA, CSE, or CMS documentation guidelines to cite sources of research used in your written work. While it is always a good idea to ask your instructors which style of documentation they prefer, there are regulations which govern the type of documentation that should be used for various disciplines. To make this a little clearer for you, let's take a look at the different types of documenting.

MLA	Disciplines that cover language and literature should be documented using the **Modern Language Association (MLA)** guidelines. This textbook provides instructions for MLA citations of research used in the written speech and in the verbal speech presentation because Public Speaking falls into the category of languages and literature for which MLA citations were developed.
APA	Disciplines that deal with psychology, sociology, social work, criminology, education, business, and economics should be documented using the **American Psychological Association (APA)** guidelines.
CSE	The **Council of Science Editors (CSE)** guidelines are used when citing sources in the natural and applied sciences. Primarily, this includes subjects such as biology, chemistry, physics, astronomy, oceanography, material sciences, earth science, and atmospheric science.
CMS	The **Chicago Manual of Style (CMS)** guidelines are used when citing research that deal with the history of the arts and humanities. It is also interesting to note that publishers usually require the writers to use CMS when documenting research within their writings.

Verbally Citing Research

It is just as important to verbally cite sources during a presentation as it is to include parenthetical citations in a written draft. If you do not verbally cite sources during a presentation, you will be guilty of verbal plagiarism. Since verbal citations are not always covered in English textbooks, it important that time is spent here to learn the craft of verbally citing research.

Here are some things you need to know about verbally citing research: Why should I verbally cite a source? What needs to be cited? When do I verbally cite a source? How do I incorporate a verbal citation in my speech? How are different types of sources cited? Before you begin to get overwhelmed, take a deep breath and allow me to address these questions one at a time.

WHY SHOULD I VERBALLY CITE A SOURCE?

There is no question about it. Adding scholarly research to your speech presentation will substantiate the information you are providing for the audience. Supporting facts are much more powerful than simply using your own personal knowledge of a subject. As you add credible research, your own personal credibility will be strengthened, resulting in your listeners' willingness to believe what you are saying and to act upon your message. As you verbally cite the sources you have used, your audience will realize you have taken time to research the topic and they will also have more confidence in your ability as a speaker.

The other, much more obvious answer to the question, involves plagiarism. If you do not verbally cite sources that you use in the speech presentation then you will be guilty of verbal plagiarism. Not only does this affect your personal credibility, but also your goals of providing ethical communication for the audience.

WHAT NEEDS TO BE CITED?

Speakers should cite all sources of research used during the speech, just as a writer would cite all research used in a written draft. This means that you will verbally cite paraphrased or direct quotations, opinions or ideas of others, quantitative information, and any visual

materials (graphs, tables, charts, pictures, etc.) that do not belong to the speaker or are not considered to be public domain.

Speakers usually find that paraphrasing material in a speech is less complicated than providing direct quotes. For one thing, the speaker does not have to worry about incorrectly quoting the source. Another reason involves the speaker's presentation notes. When paraphrasing, the speaker only needs to include a couple of key words instead of a complete and lengthy quote. Suggestions for verbally citing research should be followed regardless of whether the information is paraphrased or directly quoted.

WHAT DOES NOT NEED TO BE CITED?

It is not necessary to cite your own original ideas or to cite sources which repeat commonly held ideas. For example, it is commonly understood that exercise along with proper nutrition is important to our good health. Since this type of sentence is common to most cultures, it is not necessary to include a source of research which states this commonly held idea. On the other hand, if your research takes this information and includes statistical evidence regarding this idea, you would need to cite the source where you found the statistics.

WHEN DO I VERBALLY CITE A SOURCE?

As with written citations, speakers should lead into all research with a verbal citation. In order to avoid redundancy, speakers should give a full verbal citation the first time the research is used in a speech and then refer to the author or the publication during subsequent mentions of the research.

Audiences like to know what the speaker is planning to share. It is for this reason that speakers should begin the citation by previewing the evidence. Usually, a transition sentence is a great time to move the audience toward the research that you will be providing.

After you preview the evidence and share the paraphrased or direct quote for your audience, it will be important to explain the evidence. After your verbal citation, you will not want to directly move to the next point.

Instead, take the time to interpret or justify the importance of the information you have just shared. It is your responsibility as a speaker to explain this information for the audience before moving to the next point.

HOW DO I INCORPORATE A VERBAL CITATION IN MY SPEECH?

Here is the big question that you want answered. Citing the research is where you insert the verbal citation into the content of your speech. There is a correct way of doing this that makes the transition from your words to the research smooth and seamless. Verbal citations should always begin by stating the name of the source, or in some cases, the organization. The purpose of this is to establish credibility for the source before introducing the information. If the audience perceives the source as credible, they will be more inclined to want to hear the information that you present. Whenever it is possible, your verbal citation should also include the publication date to let the audience know that your information is current.

When citing quantitative research/statistics, you will want to lead into the research using correct wording for the quote. If using a direct quote, you should precede the quote by saying, "and I quote", offer the quote, and then say "end quote". It is important to do this because audience members will not realize where your words end and the quote begins – unless you tell them. If you are paraphrasing the research, it is not necessary to follow this protocol.

Use a **signal verb** to provide the audience with a cue that you are about to interject research material. In the same way that you lead into a quote in your written work, you

will want to verbally lead into the quote for your speech presentation. It is also important to vary the verbs that you use and to use the words carefully so that they fit into the scope of your own language patterns. A list of signaling verbs that may be used is found below:

SIGNAL VERBS

Acknowledges	Describes	Interprets	Reveals
Advises	Disagrees	Lists	Says
Agrees	Explains	Maintains	Shows
Asserts	Emphasizes	Observes	Speculates
Believes	Expresses	Offers	States
Claims	Figures	Opposes	Suggests
Concedes	Finds	Regards	Tells
Considers	Generalizes	Replies	Thinks
Criticizes	Holds	Remarks	Wants
Denies	Implies	Reports	Wishes
Disputes	Insists	Responds	Wonders

Here are a few examples of Works Cited, written, and verbal citations:

BOOK BY ONE AUTHOR - MLA

Works Cited Page:	Waddell, Penny Joyner. *Going from Stress to Success.* 5th ed. New York: Pearson Publishers. 2011. Print.
Written Citation:	According to Waddell's book, *Going from Stress to Success,* "Listening is a learned skill and it is an important skill to learn" (15).
Verbal Citation: (direct quote)	According to Waddell's book published in 2011 and titled, *Going from Stress to Success,* - and I quote, "Listening is a learned skill and it is an important skill to learn" - end quote.

BOOK WITH TWO AUTHORS – MLA

Works Cited Page:	Wysocki, Ann Frances and Dennis A. Lynch. *The DK Handbook.* New York: Pearson Longman. 2009. Print.
Written Citation:	When drafting a paper, authors Wysocki and Lynch in *The DK Handbook* suggest that you "put your writing aside for at least several hours to get some distance from it, and then reread it" (218).
Verbal Citation: (paraphrased)	In their book, *TheDK Handbook,* published in 2009, Wysocki and Lynch provided details for drafting a paper and suggested that writers put their papers aside before rereading it to check the content.

BOOK WITH AN EDITOR - MLA

Works Cited Page:	Purdy, John L., and James Ruppert, eds. *Nothing but the Truth: an Anthology of Native American Literature.* UpperSaddleRiver: Prentice, 2001. Print.
Written Citation:	John Purdy and James Ruppert, who edited *Nothing but the Truth: an Anthology of Native American Literature,* provide insight and introspect into being Native American in today's society by sharing "The Softhearted Sioux" (406).
Verbal Citation: (paraphrased)	In their book, *Nothing but the Truth* from 2001, editors Purdy and Ruppert provide insight and introspect into being Native American in today's society. My favorite selection they shared was "The Softhearted Sioux", which is a delightful work of fiction.

SACRED TEXT - MLA

Works Cited Page:	*The Holy Bible: Authorized King James Version.* Grand Rapids, Michigan: Zondervan, 1971. Print.
Written Citation:	Although I am not an expert at being patient, *The Holy Bible* contains a passage that helps me to realize "to every *thing* there is a season, and a time to every purpose under the heaven" (Ecc. 3:1.762).
Verbal Citation:	Although I am not an expert at being patient, I recently read a passage in *The Holy Bible*, "Ecclesiastes", Chapter 3, Verse 1, which helps me to realize – and I quote, "to every *thing* there is a season, and a time to every purpose under the heaven" – end quote.

MONTHLY PERIODICAL ARTICLE WITHOUT AN AUTHOR – MLA

Works Cited Page:	"The Price is Wrong." *Economist.* 2 Aug. 2003: 58-59. Print.
Written Citation:	The *Economist* Newspaper reported that "mergers are more common when shares are overvalued" ("The Price is Wrong" 58-59).
Verbal Citation: (direct quote)	In a 2003 article from the *Economist* - and I quote, "mergers are more common when shares are overvalued" - end quote.

ARTICLE IN A DAILY NEWSPAPER – MLA

Works Cited Page:	Green, Penelope. "The Slow Life Picks Up Speed." *New York Times* 31 Jan. 2008, natl. ed.: D1+. Print.
Written Citation:	In speaking about the Slow Food movement, Penelope Green's *New York Times* article defines the movement as a mentality "which essentially challenges one to use local ingredients harvested and put together in a socially and environmentally responsible way" (D1).
Verbal Citation: (direct quote)	Green explains in a 2008 *New York Times* article that the Slow Food movement - and I quote, "essentially challenges one to use local ingredients harvested and put together in a socially and environmentally responsible way" - end quote.

PROFESSIONAL ONLINE HOME PAGE – MLA

Works Cited Page:	*National Communication Association*. Web. 22 March 2011.
Written Citation:	The National Communication Association (NCA) conducted research regarding group dynamics and recently reported that "Working in groups can be difficult, since members may have different priorities, opinions, and working styles".
Verbal Citation: (paraphrased)	In 2011, The National Communication Association, who is the country's largest communication organization, reported that group work can be a challenge due to the varied members who make up a group.

INTERVIEW – MLA

Works Cited Page:	Porter, Katie. Personal Interview. 21 December 2010.
Written Citation:	During an interview last week with Katie Porter, a real estate property manager from Atlanta, Georgia, I learned that the biggest part of a property manager's job is to "oversee the maintenance of the property" (3).
Verbal Citation: (direct quote)	During an interview conducted on December 21st of 2010 with an Atlanta, Georgia property manager, Ms. Porter pointed out that the biggest part of her job is to – and I quote, "oversee the maintenance of the property" – end quote.

To summarize, a verbal citation should begin with a preview transition statement, use signal verbs to alert the audience that research is going to be offered, include basic information (author, date, title) to establish credibility for the source, indicate if the research is quoted verbatim, and justify why the research was introduced. As you can see, conducting research for a speech is just one piece of the puzzle. The rest of the picture comes in view when we clearly offer evidence of the research in a way that is interesting and informative for the audience.

MLA Documentation

The 7th edition of the *MLA Handbook for Writers of Research Papers*, published in 2009 by the Modern Language Association, is the most current issue detailing MLA guidelines and should be followed when documenting research. Writers who wish to document research using MLA guidelines are encouraged to use this edition or to conduct a web search of online writing labs that use this edition. Updates and more information regarding MLA documentation can be found at http://www.mla.org.

Documenting research using MLA guidelines is much more than simply citing sources. First, you should make sure that your written work follows the MLA format as shown below:

MLA FORMAT

Margins should be 1 inch deep on top, sides, and bottom

Last name and page number in the upper right corner of each page

Header on the first page, left corner should include four lines:
(1) author's full name
(2) professor's name
(3) course ID
(4) day, date, year;

Title centered on page one and follows header

Times New Roman – 12 point font

Headings bolded

Double-spaced

MLA IN-TEXT PARENTHETICAL DOCUMENTATION

Placing the source information in parenthesis within written documents constitutes **parenthetical documentation.** Anytime research is used, the following information must be provided within the sentence, either in the opening statements before the research is presented or at the end of the sentence.

1. Author's name, if available

2. Title of the work

3. Page number

If you lead into the quote with the author's name, it is only necessary to include the page number at the end of the sentence. If an author's name is not available, lead into the quote with the title of the work and then include the page number at the end of the sentence.

Quotes that are longer than four typed lines should be included in the written document with **block indented** margins that are one inch or ten spaces from the left margin. Quotation marks are not used for block indented quotes and the parenthetical documentation will come after the end punctuation mark.

When using a source that has more than three authors, the writer could name all of the authors or use the first author's name, only. If only the first author's name is used, then the name should be followed with **et al.,** which is Latin for "and others".

MLA WORKS CITED

The Works Cited list will follow the document that includes research. Here are things to consider:

- *Works Cited* should be centered
- Only include research used within the written document
- Follow MLA Format
- Alphabetize all entries by the author's last name. If no author is named, alphabetize by the title's first word. If the title begins with A, An, or The, please alphabetize by the title's second word and move the A, An, or The to the end of the title. Example: "The Real Story about Organic Vegetables" should be listed on the Works Cited page and filed by the second word – "Real Story about Organic Vegetables, The".

MINI GUIDE TO THE MLA WORKS CITED LIST	
Book Online or Print	**Name of Author;**
	Title of Book (Italicize Books);
	Subtitle of Book, if Available;
	Place of Publication;
	Publisher;
	Date of Publication;
	Medium of Publication (Web or Print).
	Examples:
One Author	Last Name, First Name. *Title of Book: Subtitle of Book*. Place of Publication: Publisher: Year Published. Medium of Publication.
Two Authors	Last Name, First Name, and First Name Last Name. *Title of Book: Subtitle of Book*. Place of Publication: Publisher: Year Published. Medium of Publication.
Three Authors	Last Name, First Name, First Name Last Name, and First Name Last Name. *Title of Book: Subtitle of Book*. Place of Publication: Publisher: Year Published. Medium of Publication.
Four or More Authors	Last Name, First Name (of first author listed), *et al. Title of Book: Subtitle of Book*. Place of Publication: Publisher: Year Published. Medium of Publication.
Corporate Author	Name of Corporation. *Title of Book: Subtitle of Book*. Place of Publication: Publisher: Year Published. Medium of Publication.
Government Author	Government Name. Department of Gov't. *Title of Book: Subtitle of Book*. Place of Publication: Publisher: Year Published. Medium of Publication.
Editor	Editor's Last Name, First Name, ed. *Title of Book: Subtitle of Book*. Place of Publication: Publisher: Year Published. Medium of Publication.

Periodical	Name of Author;
(Journal, Magazine, or Newspaper)	**Title of the work (use quotation marks for articles or titles that are a part of a larger work;**
Publications – Online or Print	**Journal Title and Volume Numbers;**
	Date of Publication (Year);
	Page numbers; if no pages – n.pag.
	Medium of Publication (Web or Print);
	Date of Retrieval for Online Publications (Day Month Year).
	Examples:
Online	Last Name, First Name. "Title of Article." *Periodical Name*. Volume Number. Issue. (Published Year): Page #s. Web. Retrieval Day Month Year.
Print	Last Name, First Name. "Title of Article." *Periodical Name*. Volume Number. Issue. (Published Year): Page #s. Print.

Interview	Full Name of Interviewee;
	Type of Interview (Personal, Telephone, E-mail);
	Date of Interview (day, month, year);
	Examples:
Personal	Last Name, First Name. Personal Interview. Day Month Year.
Telephone	Last Name, First Name. Telephone Interview. Day Month Year.
E-mail	Last Name, First Name. E-mail Interview. Day Month Year.

Online Sources	Name of Author;
	Title of the Work (Italicize books, and use quotation marks for articles) or titles that are a part of a larger work;
	Title of the Web site (in italics) if different form the title;
	Version or Edition of the Website;
	Date of Publication (Day, Month, Year);
	Sponsoring Organization (if provided);
	Medium of Publication (Web);
	Date of Retrieval (Day, Month, Year);
	<URL Address>.
	Examples:
Webpages	Last Name, First name. "Title of Work". Website. Publication Day Month Year. Sponsoring Organization. Web. Retrieval Day Month Year. <URL Address>.
Personal Website	Last Name, First Name. "Name of Website". Home Page. Copyright Year. Web. Retrieval Day Month Year. <URL Address>.
Professional Website	Organizational Name. "Name of Website". Home Page. Copyright Year. Web. Retrieval Day Month Year. <URL Address>.
Online Database	Last Name, First Name. "Title of Article" Periodical. Volume. Issue. (Date): Pages. Name of Database. Subscription Service. Library. Web. Retrieval Day Month Year. <URL Address>.
Blog	Last Name, First Name. "Title of Blog Entry". Weblog Entry. Name of Weblog. Sponsoring Organization (if any). Date Posted. Web. Retrieval day Month Year. <URL Address>.

Other Sources	**Note: Requirements vary according to the type of source.**
	Author's Name,
	Title of Work
	Date
	Medium of Publication
	Examples:
Film	*Title of Work.* Director or Distributor. Year. Film.
Musical Recording	Last Name, First Name. *Title of Work.* Performer. Conductor. Work Performed. Year Issued. CD.
Art	Last Name, First Name. *Title of Work.* Art Description (ex. Oil on Canvas). Location.
Photograph	Last Name, First Name. *Title of Work.* Photograph Description (ex. Gelatin Silver Print). Location. Date.
Musical Composition	Last name, First Name. *Title of Work.* Musical Composition Description (ex. Symphony). Print.
Television/Radio	*"Title of Program".* Writer/s. Performer/s. Producer/s. Network. Station, Location. Date of Broadcast. Medium (Television or Radio).
Pamphlet	Organization. Published Location: Publisher, Year. Print.
PowerPoint	Last Name, First Name. *"Title of Presentation".* Location. Day Month Year. PowerPoint.

36

MLA Documentation

Following are two directories that point you to guidance you'll find in this chapter. The first lists examples of MLA in-text parenthetical citations. The second lists examples of MLA Works Cited entries.

Taken from Chapter 36 in *Simon & Schuster Handbook for Writers*, Ninth Edition, by Lynne Q. Troyka and Doug Hesse.

MLA

36a What is MLA style?

A DOCUMENTATION STYLE is a standard format that writers follow to tell readers what SOURCES they used in conducting their research and how to find those sources. Different disciplines follow different documentation styles. The one most frequently used in the humanities (Chapter 40) is from the Modern Language Association (MLA).

MLA style requires you to document your sources in two connected, equally important ways.

1. Within the text of the paper, use parenthetical documentation, as described in section 36b. Section 36c shows twenty models of in-text parenthetical documentation, each for a different type of source.

2. At the end of the paper, provide a WORKS CITED list of the sources you used in your paper. Title this list "Works Cited." It should include only the sources you've actually used in your research paper, not any

---

Important MLA Style Changes

As part of our continuing efforts to ensure that this book provides the most current information on documentation styles, the guidelines and examples in this chapter have been adapted from the Third Edition of *The MLA Style Manual and Guide to Scholarly Publishing* (2008). According to the MLA's Web site, this edition of the *MLA Style Manual* provides documentation style guidelines that will be used in MLA publications beginning in 2009. Thus, the guidelines in the sixth edition of the *MLA Handbook for Writers of Research Papers* should only be followed until the seventh edition is released in spring 2009. If you need more information regarding MLA style updates, check http://www.mla.org.

Although MLA citations should include the minimum amount of information necessary to allow readers to locate the original source, there are several new requirements for entries in works cited lists:

- Include the **medium of publication** for each entry, such as "Print" or "Web."
- Include the URL *only* when the reader probably could not locate the source without it.
- Include both an issue and volume number for scholarly journals.
- Use italics for titles instead of underlining for all works cited entries.

See Quick Reference 36.1 on page 600 for more guidance on these requirements.

---

you've consulted but haven't used. Section 36d gives instructions for composing a Works Cited list, followed by ninety-six models, each based on different kinds of sources (book, article, Web site, and so on) that you might use.

For an example of a research paper that uses MLA-style parenthetical documentation and a Works Cited list, see section 36e.2. As you read the research paper, notice how the two requirements for crediting sources work together so that readers can learn the precise origin of QUOTATIONS, PARAPHRASES, and SUMMARIES.

36b   What is MLA in-text parenthetical documentation?

MLA-style **parenthetical documentation** places SOURCE information in parentheses within the sentences of your research papers. Also called an *in-text citation,* this information is given each time that you quote, summarize, or paraphrase source materials. It signals materials used from outside sources and enables readers to find the originals.

If you include an author's name (or, if none, a shortened title of the work) in the sentence to introduce the source material, you include in parentheses only the page number where you found the material:

> According to Brent Staples, IQ tests give scientists little insight into intelligence (293). [Author name cited in text; page number cited in parentheses.]

For readability and good writing technique, try to introduce names of authors (or titles of sources) in your own sentences. If you don't include this information in your sentence, you need to insert it before the page number, in parentheses. There is no punctuation between the author's name and the page number:

> IQ tests give scientists little insight into intelligence (Staples 293).
> [Author name and page number cited in parentheses.]

When possible, position a parenthetical reference at the end of the quote, summary, or paraphrase it refers to—preferably at the end of a sentence, unless that would place it too far from the source's material. When you place the parenthetical reference at the end of a sentence, insert it before the sentence-ending period.

If you're citing a quotation enclosed in quotation marks, place the parenthetical information after the closing quotation mark but before sentence-ending punctuation.

> Coleman summarizes research that shows that "the number, rate, and direction of time-zone changes are the critical factors in determining the

MLA

extent and degree of jet lag symptoms" (67). [Author name cited in text; page number cited in parentheses.]

The one exception to this rule concerns quotations that you set off in BLOCK STYLE, meaning one inch from the left margin. (MLA style requires that quotations longer than four typed lines be handled this way.) For block quotations, put the parenthetical reference after the period.

> Bruce Sterling worries that people are pursuing less conventional medical treatments, and not always for good reasons:
>> Medical tourism is already in full swing. Thailand is the golden shore for wealthy, sickly Asians and Australians. Fashionable Europeans head to South Africa for embarrassing plastic surgery. Crowds of scrip-waving Americans buy prescription drugs in Canada and Mexico. (92)

36c What are MLA guidelines for parenthetical documentation?

This section shows examples of how to handle parenthetical documentation in the text of your papers. The directory at the beginning of this chapter corresponds to the numbered examples in the following pages. Most of these examples show the author's name or the title included in the parenthetical citation, but remember that it's usually more effective to include that information in your sentences in the paper itself.

1. Paraphrased or Summarized Source—MLA

According to Brent Staples, IQ tests give scientists little insight into intelligence (293). [Author name cited in text; page number cited in parentheses.]

In "The IQ Cult," the journalist Brent Staples states that IQ tests give scientists little insight into intelligence (293). [Title of source, author name, and author credentials cited in text; page number cited in parentheses.]

IQ tests give scientists little insight into intelligence (Staples 293). [Author name and page number cited in parentheses.]

2. Source of a Short Quotation—MLA

Given that "thoughts, emotions, imagination and predispositions occur concurrently . . . [and] interact with other brain processes" (Caine and Caine 66), it is easy to understand why "whatever [intelligence] might be, paper and pencil tests aren't the tenth of it" (Staples 293).

Coles asks, "What binds together a Mormon banker in Utah with his brother, or other coreligionists in Illinois or Massachusetts?" (2).

3. Source of a Long Quotation—MLA

A long quotation in MLA style consists of more than four typed lines. It's set off block style, indented one inch or ten spaces from the left margin. Never put quotation marks around a set-off quotation because the indentation and block style communicate that the material is quoted. At the end of an indented quotation, place the parenthetical reference after the end punctuation mark.

> Gray and Viens explain how, by tapping into a student's highly developed spatial-mechanical intelligence, one teacher can bolster a student's poor writing skills:
>
> > The teacher asked that during "journal time" Jacob create a tool dictionary to be used as a resource in the mechanical learning center. After several entries in which he drew and described tools and other materials, Jacob confidently moved on to writing about other things of import to him, such as his brothers and a recent birthday party. Rather than shy away from all things linguistic--he previously had refused any task requiring a pencil--Jacob became invested in journal writing. (23-24)

4. One Author—MLA

Give an author's name as it appears on the source: for a book, on the title page; for an article, directly below the title or at the end of the article.

> One test asks four-year-olds to choose between one marshmallow now or two marshmallows later (Gibbs 60).

Many nonprint sources also name an author; for CDs or DVDs, for example, check the printed sleeve or cover. For an online source, look at the beginning or end of the file for a link to the author, or at the site's home page. (For more information about citing electronic sources, see items 18 through 20.)

5. Two or Three Authors—MLA

Give the names in the same order as in the source. Spell out *and*. For three authors, use commas to separate the authors' names.

> As children get older, they begin to express several different kinds of intelligence (Todd and Taylor 23).

> Another measure of emotional intelligence is the success of inter- and intrapersonal relationships (Voigt, Dees, and Prigoff 14).

MLA

6. More Than Three Authors—MLA

If your source has more than three authors, you can name them all or use the first author's name only, followed by *et al.,* either in a parenthetical reference or in your sentence. In MLA citations, do not underline or italicize *et al.*

> Emotional security varies, depending on the circumstances of the social interaction (Carter et al. 158).

🔘 **Alerts:** (1) The abbreviation *et al.* stands for "and others." The Latin term *et* means "and" and requires no period. The term *al* is an abbreviation of *alii,* so it requires a period. (2) When an author's name followed by *et al.* is a subject, use a plural verb.

> Carter et al. have found that emotional security varies, depending on the circumstances of the social interaction (158). ●

7. More Than One Source by an Author—MLA

When you use two or more sources by an author, include the relevant title in each citation. In parenthetical citations, use a shortened version of the title. For example, in a paper using two of Howard Gardner's works, *Frames of Mind: The Theory of Multiple Intelligences* and "Reflections on Multiple Intelligences: Myths and Messages," use *Frames* and "Reflections." Shorten the titles as much as possible, keeping them unambiguous to readers and starting them with the word by which you alphabetize each work in your Works Cited list. Separate the author's name and the title with a comma, but do not use punctuation between the title and the page number. When you incorporate the title into your own sentences, you can omit a subtitle, but never shorten the main title.

> Although it seems straightforward to think of multiple intelligences as multiple approaches to learning (Gardner, *Frames* 60-61), an intelligence is not a learning style (Gardner, "Reflections" 202-03).

8. Two or More Authors with the Same Last Name—MLA

Use each author's first initial and full last name in each parenthetical citation. This is the only instance in MLA style where you use an initial in a parenthetical reference. If both authors have the same first initial, use the full name in all instances.

> According to Anne Cates, psychologists can predict how empathetic an adult will be from his or her behavior at age two (41), but other researchers disagree (T. Cates 171).

9. Work with a Group or Corporate Author—MLA

When a corporation or other group is named as the author of a source you want to cite, use the corporate name just as you would an individual's name.

In a five-year study, the Boston Women's Health Collective reported that these tests are usually unreliable (11).

A five-year study shows that these tests are usually unreliable (Boston Women's Health Collective 11).

10. Work Listed by Title—MLA

If no author is named, use the title in citations. In your own sentences, use the full main title and omit a subtitle, if any. For parenthetical citations, shorten the title as much as possible (making sure that the shortened version refers unambiguously to the correct source), and always make the first word the one by which you alphabetize it. "Are You a Day or Night Person?" is the full title of the article in the following citation.

The "morning lark" and "night owl" connotations are typically used to categorize the human extremes ("Are You" 11).

11. Multivolume Work—MLA

When you cite more than one volume of a multivolume work, include the relevant volume number in each citation. Give the volume number first, followed by a colon and one space, and then the page number(s).

By 1900, the Amazon forest dwellers had been exposed to these viruses (Rand 3: 202).

Rand believes that forest dwellers in Borneo escaped illness from retroviruses until the 1960s (4: 518-19).

12. Material from a Novel, Play, Poem, or Short Story—MLA

Literary works frequently appear in different editions. When you cite material from literary works, providing the part, chapter, act, scene, canto, stanza, or line numbers usually helps readers locate what you are referring to more than page numbers alone. Unless your instructor tells you not to, use Arabic numerals for these references, even if the literary work uses Roman numerals. For novels that use them, give part and/or chapter numbers after page numbers. Use a semicolon after the page number but a comma to separate a part from a chapter.

Flannery O'Connor describes one character in *The Violent Bear It Away* as "divided in two—a violent and a rational self" (139; pt. 2, ch. 6).

For plays that use them, give act, scene, and line numbers. Use periods between these numbers. For short stories, use page numbers.

Among the most quoted of Shakespeare's lines is Hamlet's soliloquy beginning "To be, or not to be: that is the question" (3.1.56).

The old man in John Collier's short story "The Chaser" says about his potions, "I don't deal in laxatives and teething mixtures . . ." (79).

For poems and plays that use them, give canto, stanza, and line numbers. Use periods between these numbers.

In "To Autumn," Keats's most melancholy image occurs in the lines "Then in a wailful choir the small gnats mourn / Among the river swallows" (3.27-28).

13. Bible or Sacred Text—MLA

Give the title of the edition you're using, the book (in the case of the Bible), and the chapter and verse. Spell out the names of books in sentences, but use abbreviations in parenthetical references.

He would certainly benefit from the advice in Ephesians to "get rid of all bitterness, rage, and anger" (*New International Version Bible*, 4.31).

He would certainly benefit from the advice to "get rid of all bitterness, rage, and anger" (*New International Version Bible*, Eph. 4.31).

14. Work in an Anthology or Other Collection—MLA

You may want to cite a work you have read in a book that contains many works by various authors and that was compiled or edited by someone other than the person you're citing. Your in-text citation should include the author of the selection you're citing and the page number. For example, suppose you want to cite the poem "Several Things" by Martha Collins, in a literature text edited by Pamela Annas and Robert Rosen. Use Collins's name and the title of her work in the sentence and the line numbers (see item 12) in a parenthetical citation.

In "Several Things," Martha Collins enumerates what could take place in the lines of her poem: "Plums could appear, on a pewter plate / A dead red hare, hung by one foot. / A vase of flowers. Three shallots" (2-4).

15. Indirect Source—MLA

When you want to quote words that you found quoted in someone else's work, put the name of the person whose words you're quoting into your own sentence. Give the work where you found the quotation either in your sentence or in a parenthetical citation beginning with *qtd. in*.

Martin Scorsese acknowledges the link between himself and his films: "I realize that all my life, I've been an outsider. I splatter bits of myself all over the screen" (qtd. in Giannetti and Eyman 397).

Giannetti and Eyman quote Martin Scorsese as acknowledging the link between himself and his films: "I realize that all my life, I've been an outsider. I splatter bits of myself all over the screen" (397).

16. Two or More Sources in One Reference—MLA

If more than one source has contributed to an idea, opinion, or fact in your paper, cite them all. Suppose, as in the following example, that three sources all make the same point. An efficient way to credit all is to include them in a single parenthetical citation, with a semicolon separating each block of information.

> Once researchers agreed that multiple intelligences existed, their next step was to try to measure or define them (West 17; Arturi 477; Gibbs 68).

17. Entire Work—MLA

References to an entire work usually fit best into your own sentences.

> In *Convergence Culture,* Henry Jenkins explores how new digital media create a culture of active participation rather than of passive reception.

18. Electronic Source with Page Numbers—MLA

The principles that govern in-text parenthetical citations of electronic sources are exactly the same as the ones that apply to books, articles, or other sources. When an electronically accessed source identifies its author, use the author's name for parenthetical references. If no author is named, use the title of the source. When an electronic source has page numbers, use them exactly as you would the page numbers of a print source.

> Learning happens best when teachers truly care about their students' complete well-being (Anderson 7).

19. Electronic Source with Paragraph Numbers—MLA

When an electronic source has numbered paragraphs (instead of page numbers), use them for parenthetical references, with two differences: (1) Use a comma followed by one space after the name (or title); and (2) use the abbreviation *par.* for a reference to one paragraph or *pars.* for a reference to more than one paragraph, followed by the number(s) of the paragraph(s) you are citing. Note that the practice of numbering paragraphs is rare.

> Artists seem to be haunted by the fear that psychoanalysis might destroy creativity while it reconstructs personality (Francis, pars. 22-25).

20. Electronic Source Without Page or Paragraph Numbers—MLA

Many online or digital sources don't number pages or paragraphs. Simply refer to those works in their entirety. Here are two examples referring to "What Is Artificial Intelligence?" by John McCarthy; this Web site does not use page numbers or paragraph numbers. Include the name of the author in your sentence; it is also helpful to include the title.

According to McCarthy, the science of artificial intelligence includes efforts beyond trying to simulate human intelligence.

In "What Is Artificial Intelligence?" John McCarthy notes that the science of artificial intelligence includes efforts beyond trying to simulate human intelligence.

36d What are MLA guidelines for a Works Cited list?

In MLA-STYLE DOCUMENTATION, the Works Cited list gives complete bibliographic information for each SOURCE used in your paper. Include only the sources from which you quote, paraphrase, or summarize. Never include sources that you consulted but don't refer to in the paper. Quick Reference 36.1 gives general information about the Works Cited list. The rest of this chapter gives models of many specific kinds of Works Cited entries.

Quick Reference 36.1 ▪ ▪ ▪ ▪ ▪ ▪ ▪

Guidelines for an MLA-style Works Cited list

TITLE
Use "Works Cited" (without quotation marks) as the title.

PLACEMENT OF LIST
Start a new page numbered sequentially with the rest of the paper, following the Notes pages, if any.

CONTENT AND FORMAT
Include all sources quoted from, paraphrased, or summarized in your paper. Start each entry on a new line and at the regular left margin. If the entry uses more than one line, indent the second and all following lines one-half inch (or five spaces) from the left margin. Double-space all lines.

SPACING AFTER PUNCTUATION
When typewriters were common, it improved readability to leave two spaces after punctuation at the end of a sentence. Computers have made this practice no longer necessary. The *MLA Handbook* uses one space, as does this book. Either style is acceptable. However, you should use two spaces if that's the style your instructor prefers. Always put only one space after a comma or a colon.

ARRANGEMENT OF ENTRIES
Alphabetize by author's last name. If no author is named, alphabetize by the title's first significant word (ignore *A, An,* or *The*).

continued >>

Quick Reference 36.1 (continued)

AUTHORS' NAMES

Use first names and middle names or middle initials, if any, as given in the source. Don't reduce to initials any name that is given in full. For one author or the first-named author in multiauthor works, give the last name first. Use the word *and* with two or more authors. List multiple authors in the order given in the source. Use a comma between the first author's last and first names and after each complete author name except the last. After the last author's name, use a period: **Fein, Ethel Andrea, Bert Griggs, and Delaware Rogash.**

Include *Jr., Sr., II,* or *III* but no other titles and degrees before or after a name. For example, an entry for a work by Edward Meep III, MD, and Sir Richard Bolton would start like this: **Meep, Edward, III, and Richard Bolton.**

CAPITALIZATION OF TITLES

Capitalize all major words and the first and last words of all titles and subtitles. Don't capitalize ARTICLES (*a, an, the*), PREPOSITIONS, COORDINATING CONJUNCTIONS (*and, but, for, nor, or, so, yet*), or *to* in INFINITIVES in the middle of a title.

SPECIAL TREATMENT OF TITLES

Use quotation marks around titles of shorter works (poems, short stories, essays, articles). Italicize titles of longer works (books, periodicals, plays).

When a book title includes the title of another work that is usually italicized (as with a novel, play, or long poem), the preferred MLA style is not to italicize the incorporated title: *Decoding* Jane Eyre. For an alternative that MLA accepts, see item 20 in 36d.1.

If the incorporated title is usually enclosed in quotation marks (such as a short story or short poem), keep the quotation marks and italicize the complete title of the book: *Theme and Form in "I Shall Laugh Purely": A Brief Study.*

Drop *A, An,* or *The* as the first word of a periodical title.

PLACE OF PUBLICATION

If several cities are listed for the place of publication, give only the first. MLA doesn't require US state names no matter how obscure or confusing the city names might be. For an unfamiliar city outside the United States, include an abbreviated name of the country or Canadian province.

PUBLISHER

Use shortened names as long as they are clear: *Random* for *Random House.* For companies named for more than one person, name only the first: *Prentice* for *Prentice Hall.* For university presses, use the capital letters *U* and *P* (without periods): **Oxford UP; U of Chicago P**

continued >>

MLA

Quick Reference 36.1 (continued)

PUBLICATION MONTH ABBREVIATIONS

Abbreviate all publication months except *May, June,* and *July.* Use the first three letters followed by a period (*Dec., Feb.*) except for September (*Sept.*).

PAGE RANGES

Give the page range—the starting page number and the ending page number, connected by a hyphen—of any paginated electronic source and any paginated print source that is part of a longer work (for example, a chapter in a book, an article in a journal). A range indicates that the cited work is on those pages and all pages in between. If that isn't the case, use the style shown next for discontinuous pages. In either case, use numerals only, without the word *page* or *pages* or the abbreviation *p.* or *pp.*

Use the full second number through *99.* Above that, use only the last two digits for the second number unless to do so would be unclear: 113-14 is clear, but 567-602 requires full numbers.

DISCONTINUOUS PAGES

A source has discontinuous pages when the source is interrupted by material that's not part of the source (for example, an article beginning on page 32 but continued on page 54). Use the starting page number followed by a plus sign (+): 32+.

MEDIUM OF PUBLICATION

Include the MEDIUM OF PUBLICATION for each Works Cited entry. For example, every entry for a print source must include "Print" at the end, followed by a period (if required, certain supplementary bibliographic information like translation information, name of a book series, or the total number of volumes in a set should follow the medium of publication). Every source from the World Wide Web must include "Web" at the end, followed by a period and the date of access. The medium of publication also needs to be included for broadcast sources ("Television", "Radio"), sound recordings ("CD", "LP", "Audiocassette"), as well as films, DVDs, videocassettes, live performances, musical scores and works of visual arts, and so on. (See examples 34–96.)

ISSUE AND VOLUME NUMBERS FOR SCHOLARLY JOURNALS

Include both an issue and volume number for each Works Cited entry for scholarly journals. This applies both to journals that are continuously paginated and those that are not.

WORKS CITED INFORMATION REQUIRED FOR ONLINE SOURCES

The following publication information should be listed for all online sources:

1. Name of the author, director, narrator, performer, editor, compiler, or producer of the work. If no author is given, begin the entry with the title of the work.

continued >>

Quick Reference 36.1   (continued)

2. Title of the work. Italicize the title, unless it is part of a larger work. Titles that are part of a larger work should be enclosed in quotation marks.

3. Title of the overall Web site (in italics) if this is distinct from the title of the work.

4. Version or edition of the site.

5. Publisher or sponsor of the site. If this information is not available, use n.p. (for no publisher).

6. Date of publication (day, month, and year, if available). If no date is given, use n.d.

7. Medium of publication. For all online sources, the medium of publication is "Web."

8. Date of access (day, month, and year).

URLs IN ELECTRONIC SOURCES

Entries for online citations should include the URL only when the reader probably could not locate the source without it.

If the entry requires a URL, enclose it in angle brackets <like this>. Put the URL before the access date and end it with a period. If your computer automatically creates a hyperlink when you type a URL (the text changes color, the URL is underlined, or both) format the URL to look the same as the rest of the entry by changing the font color to black, removing the underline, and making any other changes. In some applications, like Microsoft Word, you can use the command "remove hyperlink," which you can find on the "Insert" menu or by right-clicking on the hyperlink.

If a URL must be divided between two lines, only break the URL after a slash and do not use a hyphen.

36d.1   Following MLA guidelines for specific sources in a Works Cited list

The Works Cited directory above corresponds to the numbered entries in this section. Not every possible documentation model is shown in this chapter. You may find that you have to combine features of models to document a particular source. You'll also find more information in the *MLA Handbook for Writers of Research Papers*. Figure 36.1 provides another tool to help you find the Works Cited model you need: a decision-making flowchart.

BOOKS

Citations for books have three main parts: author, title, and publication information (place of publication, publisher, and date of publication). Figure 36.2 (p. 605) illustrates where to find this information and the proper citation format.

MLA

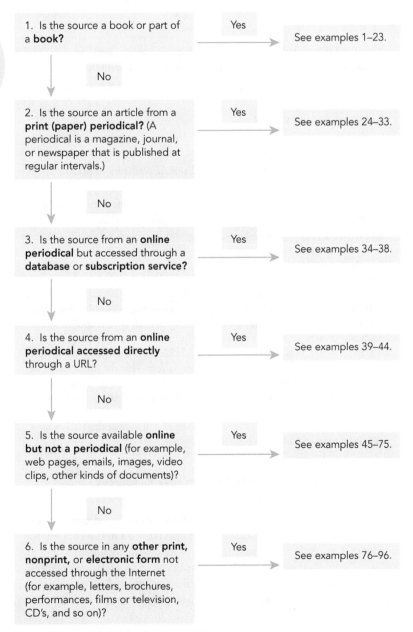

1. Is the source a book or part of a **book?**

Yes → See examples 1–23.

No ↓

2. Is the source an article from a **print (paper) periodical?** (A periodical is a magazine, journal, or newspaper that is published at regular intervals.)

Yes → See examples 24–33.

No ↓

3. Is the source from an **online periodical** but accessed through a **database** or **subscription service?**

Yes → See examples 34–38.

No ↓

4. Is the source from an **online periodical accessed directly** through a URL?

Yes → See examples 39–44.

No ↓

5. Is the source available **online but not a periodical** (for example, web pages, emails, images, video clips, other kinds of documents)?

Yes → See examples 45–75.

No ↓

6. Is the source in any **other print, nonprint,** or **electronic form** not accessed through the Internet (for example, letters, brochures, performances, films or television, CD's, and so on)?

Yes → See examples 76–96.

Figure 36.1 MLA Works Cited visual directory

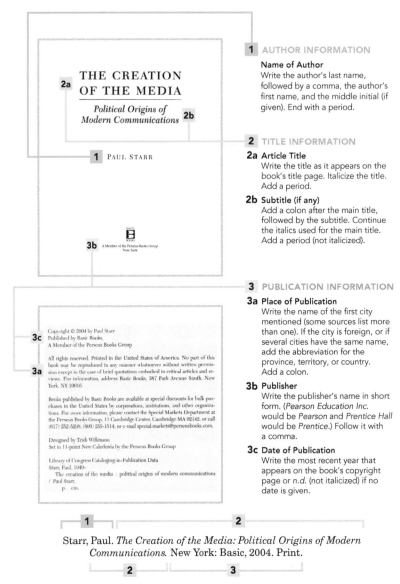

1 AUTHOR INFORMATION

Name of Author
Write the author's last name, followed by a comma, the author's first name, and the middle initial (if given). End with a period.

2 TITLE INFORMATION

2a Article Title
Write the title as it appears on the book's title page. Italicize the title. Add a period.

2b Subtitle (if any)
Add a colon after the main title, followed by the subtitle. Continue the italics used for the main title. Add a period (not italicized).

3 PUBLICATION INFORMATION

3a Place of Publication
Write the name of the first city mentioned (some sources list more than one). If the city is foreign, or if several cities have the same name, add the abbreviation for the province, territory, or country. Add a colon.

3b Publisher
Write the publisher's name in short form. (*Pearson Education Inc.* would be *Pearson* and *Prentice Hall* would be *Prentice*.) Follow it with a comma.

3c Date of Publication
Write the most recent year that appears on the book's copyright page or *n.d.* (not italicized) if no date is given.

Starr, Paul. *The Creation of the Media: Political Origins of Modern Communications.* New York: Basic, 2004. Print.

Figure 36.2 Locating and citing source information in a book

MLA

1. Book by One Author—MLA

Bradway, Becky. *Pink Houses and Family Taverns*. Bloomington: Indiana UP, 2002. Print.

2. Book by Two or Three Authors—MLA

Edin, Kathryn, and Maria Kefalas. *Promises I Can Keep: Why Poor Women Put Motherhood before Marriage*. Berkeley: U of California P, 2005. Print.

Lynam, John K., Cyrus G. Ndiritu, and Adiel N. Mbabu. *Transformation of Agricultural Research Systems in Africa: Lessons from Andreiya*. East Lansing: Michigan State UP, 2004. Print.

3. Book by More Than Three Authors—MLA

Give only the first author's name, followed by a comma and the phrase *et al.* (abbreviated from the Latin *et alii,* meaning "and others"), or list all names in full and in the order in which they appear on the title page.

Saul, Wendy, et al. *Beyond the Science Fair: Creating a Kids' Inquiry Conference*. Portsmouth: Heinemann, 2005. Print.

4. Two or More Works by the Same Author(s)—MLA

Give author name(s) in the first entry only. In the second and subsequent entries, use three hyphens and a period to stand for exactly the same name(s). If the person served as editor or translator, put a comma and the appropriate abbreviation (*ed.* or *trans.*) following the three hyphens. Arrange the works in alphabetical (not chronological) order according to book title, ignoring labels such as *ed.* or *trans.*

Jenkins, Henry. *Convergence Culture: Where Old and New Media Collide*. New York: New York UP, 2006. Print.

---. *Fans, Bloggers, and Gamers: Exploring Participatory Culture*. New York: New York UP, 2006. Print.

5. Book by Group or Corporate Author—MLA

Cite the full name of the corporate author first, omitting the first articles *A, An,* or *The*. When a corporate author is also the publisher, use a shortened form of the corporate name in the publication information.

American Psychological Association. *Publication Manual of the American Psychological Association*. 5th ed. Washington: APA, 2001. Print.

Boston Women's Health Collective. *Our Bodies, Ourselves for the New Century*. New York: Simon, 1998. Print.

6. Book with No Author Named—MLA

If there is no author's name on the title page, begin the citation with the title. Alphabetize the entry according to the first significant word of the title ignoring *A, An* or *The*.

The Chicago Manual of Style. 15th ed. Chicago: U of Chicago P, 2003. Print.

7. Book with an Author and an Editor—MLA

If your paper refers to the work of the book's author, put the author's name first; if your paper refers to the work of the editor, put the editor's name first.

Brontë, Emily. *Wuthering Heights*. Ed. Richard J. Dunn. New York: Norton, 2002. Print.

Dunn, Richard J., ed. *Wuthering Heights*. By Emily Brontë. New York: Norton, 2002. Print.

8. Translation—MLA

Kundera, Milan. *The Unbearable Lightness of Being*. Trans. Michael Henry Heim. New York: Harper, 1999. Print.

9. Work in Several Volumes or Parts—MLA

If you're citing only one volume, put the volume number before the publication information. If you wish, you can give the total number of volumes at the end of the entry. MLA recommends using Arabic numerals, even if the source uses Roman numerals (*Vol. 6* rather than *Vol. VI*).

Chrisley, Ronald, ed. *Artificial Intelligence: Critical Concepts*. Vol. 1. London: Routledge, 2000. Print. 4 vols.

10. Anthology or Edited Book—MLA

In the following example, *ed.* stands for "editor," so use *eds.* when more than one editor is named; also see items 9, 11, and 12.

Purdy, John L., and James Ruppert, eds. *Nothing but the Truth: An Anthology of Native American Literature*. Upper Saddle River: Prentice, 2001. Print.

11. One Selection from an Anthology or an Edited Book—MLA

Give the author and title of the selection first and then the full title of the anthology. Information about the editor starts with *Ed.* (for "Edited by"), so don't use *Eds.* when there is more than one editor. Give the name(s) of the editor(s) in normal order rather than reversing first and last names. Give the page range at the end.

Trujillo, Laura. "Balancing Act." *Border-Line Personalities: A New Generation of Latinas Dish on Sex, Sass, and Cultural Shifting*. Ed. Robyn Moreno and Michelle Herrera Mulligan. New York: Harper, 2004. 61-72. Print.

12. More Than One Selection from the Same Anthology or Edited Book—MLA

If you cite more than one selection from the same anthology, you can list the anthology as a separate entry with all the publication information. Also, list each selection from the anthology by author and title of the selection, but give only the name(s) of the editor(s) of the anthology and the page number(s) for each selection. List selections separately in alphabetical order by author's last name.

Bond, Ruskin. "The Night Train at Deoli." Chaudhuri 415-18.

Chaudhuri, Amit, ed. *The Vintage Book of Modern Indian Literature*. New York: Vintage, 2004. Print.

Vijayan, O.V. "The Rocks." Chaudhuri 291-96.

13. Signed Article in a Reference Book—MLA

A "signed article" means that the author of the article is identified. If the articles in the book are alphabetically arranged, you don't need to give volume and page numbers.

Burnbam, John C. "Freud, Sigmund." *The Encyclopedia of Psychiatry, Psychology, and Psychoanalysis*. Ed. Benjamin B. Wolman. New York: Holt, 1996. Print.

14. Unsigned Article in a Reference Book—MLA

Begin with the title of the article. If you're citing a widely used reference work, don't give full publication information. Instead, give only the edition and year of publication.

"Ireland." *The New Encyclopaedia Britannica: Macropaedia*. 15th ed. 2002. Print.

15. Second or Later Edition—MLA

If a book isn't a first edition, the edition number appears on the title page. Place the abbreviated information (*2nd ed., 3rd ed.,* etc.) between the title and the publication information. Give only the latest copyright date for the edition you're using.

Gibaldi, Joseph. *MLA Handbook for Writers of Research Papers*. 6th ed. New York: MLA, 2003. Print.

16. Introduction, Preface, Foreword, or Afterword—MLA

Give first the name of the writer of the part you're citing and then the name of the cited part, capitalized but not underlined or in quotation marks. After the book title, write *By* or *Ed.* and the full name(s) of the book's author(s) or editor(s), if different from the writer of the cited material. If the writer of the cited material is the same as the book author, include only the last name after

By. Following the publication information, give inclusive page numbers for the cited part, using Roman or Arabic numerals as the source does.

Hesse, Doug. Foreword. *The End of Composition Studies.* By David W. Smit. Carbondale: Southern Illinois UP, 2004. ix-xiii. Print.

When the introduction, preface, foreword, or afterword has a title (as in the next example), include it in the citation before the section name.

Fox-Genovese, Elizabeth. "Mothers and Daughters: The Ties That Bind." Foreword. *Southern Mothers.* Ed. Nagueyalti Warren and Sally Wolff. Baton Rouge: Louisiana State UP, 1999. iv-xviii. Print.

17. Unpublished Dissertation or Essay—MLA

State the author's name first, then the title in quotation marks (not italicized), then a descriptive label (such as *Diss.* or *Unpublished essay*), followed by the degree-granting institution (for dissertations), and, finally, the date. Treat published dissertations as books.

Stuart, Gina Anne. "Exploring the Harry Potter Book Series: A Study of Adolescent Reading Motivation." Diss. Utah State U, 2006. Print.

18. Reprint of an Older Book—MLA

Republishing information can be found on the copyright page. Give the date of the original version before the publication information for the version you're citing.

O'Brien, Flann. *At Swim-Two-Birds.* 1939. Normal: Dalkey Archive, 1998. Print.

19. Book in a Series—MLA

Goldman, Dorothy J. *Women Writers and World War I.* New York: Macmillan, 1995. Print. Lit. and Soc. Ser.

Mukherjee, Meenakshi. *Jane Austen.* New York: St. Martin's, 1991. Print. Women Writers Ser.

20. Book with a Title Within a Title—MLA

The MLA recognizes two distinct styles for handling normally independent titles when they appear within an italicized title. (Use whichever style your instructor prefers.) When using the MLA's preferred style, do not italicize the embedded title or set it within quotation marks.

Lumiansky, Robert M., and Herschel Baker, eds. *Critical Approaches to Six Major English Works:* Beowulf *Through* Paradise Lost. Philadelphia: U of Pennsylvania P, 1968. Print.

However, because MLA also accepts a second style for handling such embedded titles, you can set the normally independent titles within quotation marks and italicize them.

Lumiansky, Robert M., and Herschel Baker, eds. *Critical Approaches to Six Major English Works: "Beowulf" Through "Paradise Lost."* Philadelphia: U of Pennsylvania P, 1968. Print.

21. Bible or Sacred Text—MLA

Bhagavad-Gita. Trans. Juan Mascaro. Rev. ed. New York: Penguin, 2003. Print.

The Holy Bible: New International Version. New York: Harper, 1983. Print.

The Qur'an. Trans. Abdullah Yusuf Ali. 13th ed. Elmhurst: Tahrike Tarsile Qur'an, 1999. Print.

22. Government Publication—MLA

For government publications that name no author, start with the name of the government or government body. Then name the government agency. *GPO* is a standard abbreviation for *Government Printing Office,* the publisher of most US government publications.

United States. Cong. House. Committee on Resources. *Coastal Heritage Trail Route in New Jersey.* 106th Cong., 1st sess. H. Rept. 16. Washington: GPO, 1999. Print.

---. ---. Senate. Select Committee on Intelligence. *Report on the U.S. Intelligence Community's Prewar Intelligence Assessment of Iraq.* 108th Cong., 1st sess. Washington: GPO, 2004. Print.

23. Published Proceedings of a Conference—MLA

Rocha, Luis Mateus, et al., eds. *Artificial Life X: Proceedings of the Tenth International Conference on the Simulation and Synthesis of Living Systems.* Bloomington, IN. 3-7 June 2006. Cambridge: MIT P, 2006. Print.

PERIODICAL PUBLICATIONS—PRINT VERSIONS

Citations for periodical articles contain three major parts: author information, title information, and publication information. Figure 36.3 shows a citation for an article in a scholarly journal (see item 27).

24. Signed Article in a Weekly or Biweekly Periodical—MLA

Brink, Susan. "Eat This Now!" *US News and World Report* 28 Mar. 2005: 56-58. Print.

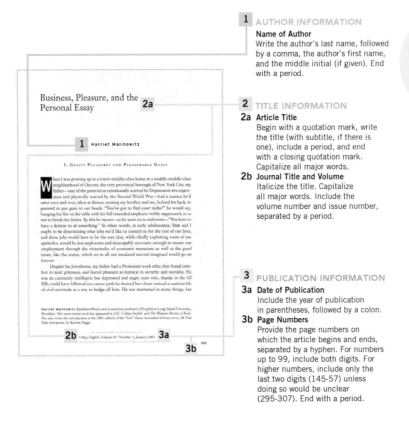

1 AUTHOR INFORMATION

Name of Author
Write the author's last name, followed by a comma, the author's first name, and the middle initial (if given). End with a period.

2 TITLE INFORMATION

2a Article Title
Begin with a quotation mark, write the title (with subtitle, if there is one), include a period, and end with a closing quotation mark. Capitalize all major words.

2b Journal Title and Volume
Italicize the title. Capitalize all major words. Include the volume number and issue number, separated by a period.

3 PUBLICATION INFORMATION

3a Date of Publication
Include the year of publication in parentheses, followed by a colon.

3b Page Numbers
Provide the page numbers on which the article begins and ends, separated by a hyphen. For numbers up to 99, include both digits. For higher numbers, include only the last two digits (145-57) unless doing so would be unclear (295-307). End with a period.

Malinowitz, Harriet. "Business, Pleasure, and the Personal Essay." *College English* 65.3 (2003): 305-22. Print.

Figure 36.3 Locating and citing sources from a journal article

25. Signed Article in a Monthly or Bimonthly Periodical—MLA

Fallows, James. "The $1.4 Trillion Question." *The Atlantic* Jan.-Feb. 2008: 36-48. Print.

26. Unsigned Article in a Weekly or Monthly Periodical—MLA

"The Price Is Wrong." *Economist* 2 Aug. 2003: 58-59. Print.

27. Article in a Scholarly Journal

Adler-Kassner, Linda, and Heidi Estrem. "Rethinking Research Writing: Public
    Literacy in the Composition Classroom." *WPA: Writing Program
    Administration* 26.3 (2003): 119-31. Print.

28. Article in a Collection of Reprinted Articles—MLA

First include the original publication information, then *Rpt.* and information
about the place the article was republished.

Brumberg, Abraham. "Russia after Perestroika." *New York Review of Books* 27
    June 1991: 53-62. Rpt. in *Russian and Soviet History*. Ed. Alexander Dallin.
    Vol. 14 of *The Gorbachev Era*. New York: Garland, 1992. 300-20. Print.

Textbooks used in college writing courses often collect previously printed articles.

Rothstein, Richard. "When Mothers on Welfare Go to Work." *New York Times*
    5 June 2002: A20. Rpt. in *Writing Arguments: A Rhetoric with Readings*. Ed.
    John D. Ramage, John C. Bean, and June Johnson. New York: Longman,
    2004. 263. Print.

29. Signed Article in a Daily Newspaper—MLA

Omit *A, An,* or *The* as the first word in a newspaper title. Give the day, month,
and year of the issue (and the edition, if applicable). If sections are designated,
give the section letter as well as the page number. If an article runs on noncon-
secutive pages, give the starting page number followed by a plus sign (for example, *23+* for an article that starts on page 23 and continues on a later page).

Green, Penelope. "The Slow Life Picks Up Speed." *New York Times* 31 Jan. 2008,
    natl. ed.: D1+. Print.

30. Unsigned Article in a Daily Newspaper—MLA

"Oscars Ready Plans to Deal with Strike." *Denver Post* 31 Jan. 2008: B3. Print.

If the city of publication is not part of the title, put it in square brackets after
the title, not italicized.

"Hackers Hit Northwestern Computer Net." *Pantagraph* [Bloomington] 26 Mar.
    2005: A5. Print.

31. Editorial, Letter to the Editor, or Review—MLA

After the author's name or title, provide information about the type of publication.

"Primary Considerations." Editorial. *Washington Post* 27 Jan. 2008: B6. Print.

Finanger, Emily. Letter. *Outside* Feb. 2008: 14. Print.

Shenk, David. "Toolmaker, Brain Builder." Rev. of *Beyond Big Blue: Building
    the Computer That Defeated the World Chess Champion*, by Feng-Hsiung
    Hsu. *American Scholar* 72 (Spring 2003): 150-52. Print.

32. Article in a Looseleaf Collection of Reprinted Articles—MLA

Give the citation for the original publication first, followed by the citation for the collection.

Hayden, Thomas. "The Age of Robots." *US News and World Report* 23 Apr. 2001:
44+. Print. *Applied Science* 2002. Ed. Eleanor Goldstein. Boca Raton: SIRS,
2002. Art. 66.

33. Abstract in a Collection of Abstracts—MLA

To cite an abstract, first give information for the full work: the author's name, the title of the article, and publication information about the full article. If a reader could not know that the cited material is an abstract, write the word *Abstract,* not italicized, followed by a period. Give publication information about the collection of abstracts. For abstracts identified by item numbers rather than page numbers, use the word *item* before the item number.

Marcus, Hazel R., and Shinobu Kitayamo. "Culture and the Self: Implications
for Cognition, Emotion, and Motivation." *Psychological Review* 88 (1991):
224-53. *Psychological Abstracts* 78 (1991): item 23878. Print.

PERIODICALS—ONLINE VERSIONS FROM SUBSCRIPTION SERVICES

A large (and increasing) number of periodicals are available in digital versions online, as well as in print; some periodicals are available only online. Online periodicals fall into two categories: (1) periodicals you access through a DATABASE or **subscription service** paid for by your library or company, such as EBSCO or FirstSearch, or through an online service to which you personally subscribe (examples 34–38); and (2) periodicals you directly access by entering a specific URL (examples 39–44). Articles you access through a subscription service are the most important for academic research. Of course, many other online sources are not from periodicals; we explain them in examples 45–75.

⚠ **ALERT:** Online periodical articles are frequently available in both "HTML" (hypertext mark-up language) and "PDF" (portable document format) versions. The PDF versions are almost always preferable for research because they present an image of articles exactly as they appear in print. This means the PDF version of an article has page numbers, images and graphics, side-bar stories, headings, and so on. As a result, PDFs are easier to cite. The HTML version of an article does include all of the text; however, because it has been formatted to work efficiently in databases, it contains no page numbers or graphics. HTML versions load more quickly on your computer, but citing them is less precise. If you have a choice, always use the PDF version. ●

34. Subscription Service: Article with a Print Version—MLA

Jackson, Gabriel. "Multiple Historic Meanings of the Spanish Civil War."
    Science and Society 68.3 (2004): 272-76. *Academic Search Elite*. Web.
    7 Mar. 2005.

VandeHei, Jim. "Two Years after White House Exit, Clinton Shaping Democratic
    Party." *Washington Post* 21 June 2003, final ed.: A1. *Academic Universe*.
    Web. 5 May 2005.

Figure 36.4 illustrates citing an article that has a print version but has been accessed through a subscription service.

35. Subscription Service: Material with No Print Version—MLA

Siemens, Raymond G. "A New Computer-Assisted Literary Criticism?"
    Computers and the Humanities 36.3 (2002). *America Online*. Web.
    12 Nov. 2002.

36. Subscription Service: Abstract—MLA

The example below is for the same abstract shown in item 33, but here it is accessed from an online database (*PsycINFO*) by means of a library subscription service. The name of the library shows where the source was accessed, and *10 Apr. 2004* is the date it was accessed.

Marcus, Hazel R., and Shinobu Kitayamo. "Culture and the Self: Implications
    for Cognition, Emotion, and Motivation." *Psychological Abstracts* 78 (1991).
    PsycINFO. Web. 10 Apr. 2004.

37. Subscription Service Access with a Keyword: Article in a Periodical with a Print Version—MLA

Electronic versions of sources that also appear in print start with information about the print version. Here's an entry for a journal article accessed through a computer service; it also has a print version.

Wynne, Clive D. L. "'Willy' Didn't Yearn to Be Free." Editorial. *New York Times*
    27 Dec. 2003: *New York Times Online*. America Online. Web. 29 Dec. 2003.
    Keyword: nytimes.

Information applying to the print version of this article in the *New York Times* ends with the publication date and information about the online version starts with the title of the database, *New York Times Online*. *America Online* is the service through which the database was accessed, and *29 Dec. 2003* is the access date. The keyword *nytimes* was used to access *New York Times Online*.

MLA

1 AUTHOR INFORMATION

Name of Author
Write the author's last name, followed by a comma, the author's first name, and the middle initial (if given). End with a period.

2 TITLE INFORMATION

Article Title
State the full title of the article, enclosed in quotation marks. Use a period before the closing quotation mark.

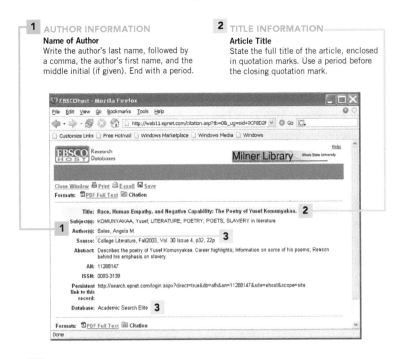

3 PUBLICATION INFORMATION

3a **Name of Periodical**
Provide the journal title (italicized).

3b **Volume and Issue Numbers**
Leave one space after the journal title and provide the volume and issue numbers, separated by a period.

3c **Date of Publication**
Provide the year of publication, in parentheses, followed by a colon.

3d **Page Numbers**
Provide the inclusive page numbers for the complete article, not just the portion you used. End with a period.

3e **Title of Database**
Italicize the name of the database. End with a period.

3f **Medium of Publication**
Provide the medium of publication consulted (*Web*), followed by a period.

3g **Date of Access**
Provide the day, month, and year that you accessed the article online. End with a period.

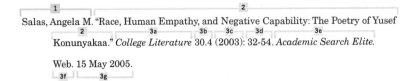

Salas, Angela M. "Race, Human Empathy, and Negative Capability: The Poetry of Yusef Konunyakaa." *College Literature* 30.4 (2003): 32-54. *Academic Search Elite.*

Web. 15 May 2005.

Figure 36.4 Locating and citing source information for a journal found in an online database

38. Subscription Service Access Showing a Path—MLA

When you access a source by choosing a series of keywords, menus, or topics, end the entry with the "path" of words you used. Use semicolons between items in the path, and put a period at the end.

Futrelle, David. "A Smashing Success." *Money.com* 23 Dec. 1999. America Online. Web. 26 Dec. 1999. Path: Personal Finance; Business News; Business
Publications; Money.com.

PERIODICALS—ONLINE VERSIONS ACCESSED DIRECTLY

You can access some online versions of periodicals directly, without going through a paid subscription service. Newspapers and magazines often publish some of their articles from each issue online this way. Often, however, you can't access every single article—or any older articles—without being a subscriber.

39. Online Version of a Print Magazine Article—MLA

The example below is for the online version of the same article cited in 25, above. In addition to the print information, include the date you accessed the online version. (If the page numbers from the print version are available, include them, too, before the access date.)

Fallows, James. "The $1.4 Trillion Question." *The Atlantic.com*. Atlantic
Monthly Group, Jan.-Feb. 2008. Web. 2 May 2008.

If the article is unsigned, begin with the title.

"Too Smart to Marry." *The Atlantic.com*. Atlantic Monthly Group, 14 Apr. 2005.
Web. 7 Mar. 2005.

40. Online Version of a Print Journal Article—MLA

Hoge, Charles W., et al. "Mild Traumatic Brain Injury in U.S. Soldiers
Returning from Iraq." *New England Journal of Medicine* 358.5 (2008):
453-63. Web. 10 Sept. 2008.

41. Periodical Article Published Only Online—MLA

Many periodicals are published only online; others have "extra" online content that doesn't appear in print. Figure 36.5 illustrates how to cite an article that appears only online.

Ramirez, Eddy. "Comparing American Students with Those in China and
India." *U.S. News and World Report*. U.S. News and World Report, 30 Jan.
2008. Web. 4 Mar. 2008.

Shipka, Jody. "This Was (Not!!) an Easy Assignment." *Computers and
Composition Online*. Computers and Composition Online, Fall 2007.
Web. 2 May 2008.

1 AUTHOR INFORMATION

Name of Author
Write the author's last name, followed by a comma, the author's first name, and the middle initial (if given). End with a period.

2 TITLE INFORMATION

Article Title
State the full title of the article, enclosed in quotation marks. Unless the title contains its own closing punctuation (question mark), use a period before the closing quotation mark.

3 PUBLICATION INFORMATION

3a **Title of the Overall Web Site**
Provide the title of the Web site (italicized), followed by a period.

3b **Publisher or Sponsor of the Web Site**
Leave one space after the title of the overall Web site and provide the publisher or sponsor of the Web site. If this information is not available, use "n.p." End with a comma.

3c **Date of Publication**
Provide the day, month, and year of publication, followed by a period. If no date is available, use "n.d."

3d **Medium of Publication**
Provide the medium of publication consulted (Web), followed by a period.

3e **Date of Access**
Provide the day, month, and year that you accessed the article online. End with a period.

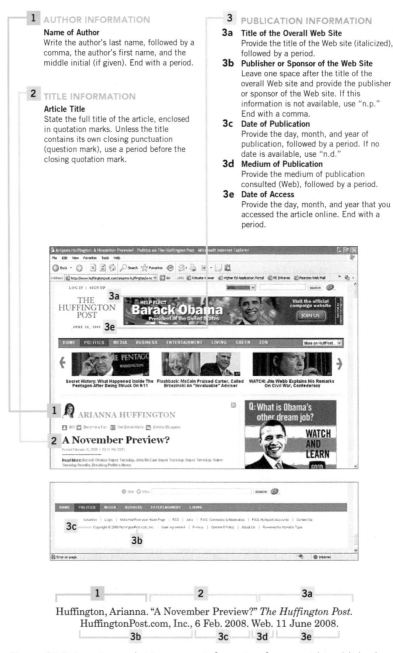

Huffington, Arianna. "A November Preview?" *The Huffington Post.*
HuffingtonPost.com, Inc., 6 Feb. 2008. Web. 11 June 2008.

Figure 36.5 Locating and citing source information for an article published only online

42. Online Version of a Print Newspaper Article—MLA

If the article is signed, begin with the author's name, last name first.

Wilson, Janet. "EPA Fights Waste Site near River." *Los Angeles Times*. Los
Angeles Times, 5 Mar. 2005. Web. 7 Mar. 2005.

If the article is unsigned, begin with the article title.

"Remnant of Revolutionary War Washes Ashore." *CNN.com*. Cable News
Network, 28 Mar. 2005. Web. 29 Mar. 2005.

43. Online Editorial or Letter to the Editor—MLA

"Garbage In, Garbage Out." Editorial. *Los Angeles Times*. Los Angeles
Times, 2 Feb. 2008. Web. 22 Mar. 2008.

Ennis, Heather B. Letter to the Editor. *U.S. News and World Report*. U.S. News
and World Report, 20 Dec. 2007. Web. 22 Dec. 2007.

44. Online Material from a Newspaper or News Site Published Only Online—MLA

Harris, Edward. "Rain Forests Fall at 'Alarming' Rate." *denverpost.com*.
Denver Post, 3 Feb. 2008. Web. 3 Feb. 2008.

OTHER INTERNET SOURCES

This section shows models for online sources. For such sources, provide as
much of the following information as you can.

- The author's name, if given.

- In quotation marks, the title of a short work (Web page, brief document,
  essay, article, message, and so on); or italicized, the title of a book.

- Publication information for any print version, if it exists.

- The name of an editor, translator, or compiler, if any, with an abbreviation
  such as *Ed., Trans.,* or *Comp.* before the name.

- The italicized title of the Internet site (scholarly project, database, online
  periodical, professional or personal Web site). If the site has no title, describe it: for example, *Home page.*

- The date of electronic publication (including a version number, if any) or
  posting or the most recent update.

- The name of a sponsoring organization, if any.

- The medium of publication.

- The date you accessed the material.

- The URL in angle brackets (< >), only when the reader probably could not locate the source without it. If you must break a URL at the end of a line, break only after a slash and do not use a hyphen.

45. Online Book—MLA

Chopin, Kate. *The Awakening.* 1899. *PBS Electronic Library.* 10 Dec. 1998. PBS. Web. 13 Nov. 2008.

46. Online Book in a Scholarly Project—MLA

Herodotus. *The History of Herodotus.* Trans. George Rawlinson. 1947. *Internet Classics Archive.* Ed. Daniel C. Stevenson. 11 Jan. 1998. MIT. Web. 15 May 2006.

47. Online Government-Published Book—MLA

Start with the name of the government or government body, and then name the government agency, the title, the work's author (if known), the publication date, the access date, and the URL, if the reader needs it.

United States. Cong. Research Service. *Space Stations.* By Marcia S. Smith. 12 Dec. 1996. Web. 4 Dec. 2007.

MLA also permits an alternative format, with the author's name first, then title, then government body.

Huff, C. Ronald. *Comparing the Criminal Behavior of Youth Gangs and At-Risk Youths.* United States. Dept. of Justice. Natl. Inst. of Justice. Oct. 1998. Web. 5 Aug. 2008.

48. Professional Home Page—MLA

Provide as much of the following information as you can find.

- If available, include the name of the person who created or put up the home page. If first and last names are given, reverse the order of the first author's name.
- For a professional home page, include the name of the sponsoring organization.
- Include the date you accessed the material.

Association for the Advancement of Artificial Intelligence. Web. 17 Mar. 2008.

49. Personal Home Page—MLA

Follow guidelines for professional home pages, with the following changes. Give the name of the person who created the page, last name first. Include the page's title, if there is one, italicized; if there is no title, add the description *Home page,* not italicized, followed by a period.

Hesse, Doug. Home page. Web. 1 Nov. 2007. <http://portfolio.du.edu/dhesse>.

1 TITLE

Title of the Work
State the full title of the work cited, enclosed in quotation marks. Use a period before the closing quotation mark.

2 PUBLICATION INFORMATION

2a **Title of the Overall Web Site**
Provide the title of the Web site (italicized), followed by a period.

2b **Publisher or Sponsor of the Web Site**
Leave one space after the title of the overall Web site and provide the publisher or sponsor of the Web site. If this information is not available, use "n.p." End with a comma.

2c **Date of Publication**
Provide the available date (day, month, and year) of publication, followed by a period. If no date is available, use "n.d."

2d **Medium of Publication**
Provide the medium of publication consulted (Web), followed by a period.

2e **Date of Access**
Provide the day, month, and year that you accessed the article online. End with a period.

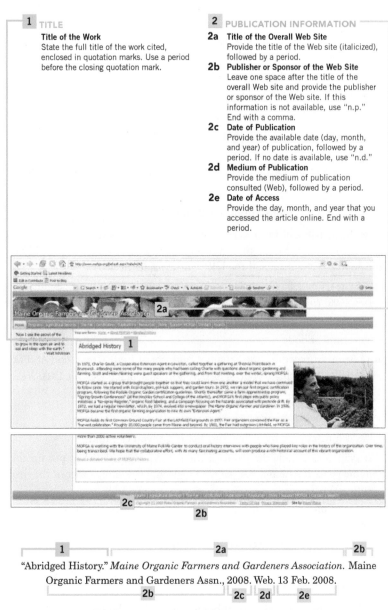

1   **2a**   **2b**

"Abridged History." *Maine Organic Farmers and Gardeners Association.* Maine Organic Farmers and Gardeners Assn., 2008. Web. 13 Feb. 2008.

2b   **2c**   **2d**   **2e**

Figure 36.6 Locating and citing source information for a Web page with no author

50. Page from a Web Site—MLA

Provide as much information as you can (see Figure 36.6).

"Protecting Whales from Dangerous Sonar." *National Resources Defense
Council.* NRDC, 9 Nov. 2005. Web. 12 Dec. 2005.

"Abridged History." *Maine Organic Farmers and Gardeners Association.*
Maine Organic Farmers and Gardeners Assn., 2007. Web. 13 Dec. 2007.

51. Entire Internet Site—MLA

WebdelSol.Com. Ed. Michael Neff. 2008. Web. 11 Nov. 2008.

52. Academic Department Home Page—MLA

Write the name of the academic department, followed by the words *Dept. home
page.* (Do not put any words in quotations or in italics.) Also include the name
of the institution and the date you accessed the page.

Writing. Dept. home page. Grand Valley State U. Web. 26 Feb. 2008.

53. Course Home Page—MLA

St. Germain, Sheryl. Myths and Fairytales: From *Inanna* to *Edward Scissorhands.*
Course home page. Summer 2003. Dept. of English, Iowa State U. Web. 20
Feb. 2005. <http://www.public.iastate.edu/~sgermain/531.homepage.html>.

54. Government or Institutional Web Site—MLA

Home Education and Private Tutoring. Pennsylvania Department of Education,
2005. Web. 15 Dec. 2005.

55. Online Poem—MLA

Browning, Elizabeth Barrett. "Past and Future." *Women's Studies Database
Reading Room.* U of Maryland. Web. 9 June 2003.

56. Online Work of Art—MLA

Provide artist, title of work, creation date (optional), the museum or individual who owns it, the place and the access date.

van Gogh, Vincent. *The Starry Night.* 1889. Museum of Mod. Art, New York.
Web. 5 Dec. 2003. Keyword: Starry Night.

In this example, the keyword "Starry Night" is what a researcher types into a
search box on the museum's Web site.

1 TITLE

Title of the Work
State the full title of the work cited, enclosed in quotation marks. Use a period before the closing quotation mark.

2 PUBLICATION INFORMATION

2a **Title of the Overall Web Site**
Provide the title of the Web site (italicized), followed by a period.

2b **Publisher or Sponsor of the Web Site**
Leave one space after the title of the overall Web site and provide the publisher or sponsor of the Web site. If this information is not available, use "N.p." End with a comma.

2c **Date of Publication**
Provide the day, month, and year of publication, followed by a period. If no date is available, use "n.d."

2d **Medium of Publication**
Provide the medium of publication consulted (*Web*), followed by a period.

2e **Date of Access**
Provide the day, month, and year that you accessed the article online. End with a period.

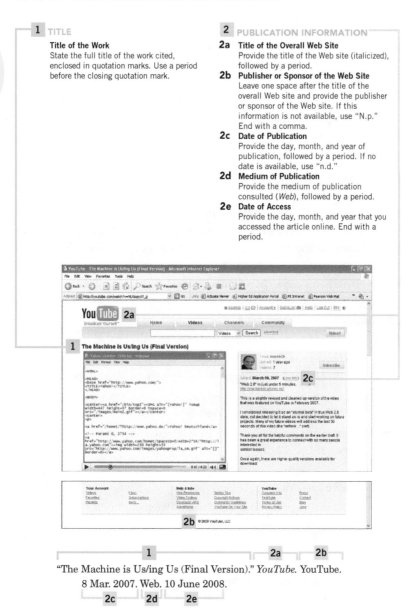

"The Machine is Us/ing Us (Final Version)." *YouTube*. YouTube. 8 Mar. 2007. Web. 10 June 2008.

Figure 36.7 Locating and citing source information for an online video

57. Online Image or Photograph—MLA

As with images from print publications (see item 88), include information about the photographer and title, if known. Otherwise, describe the photograph briefly and give information about the Web site and the access date.

Bourke-White, Margaret. "Fort Peck Dam, Montana." 1936. Gelatin silver print. Metropolitan Museum of Art, New York. Web. 5 Aug. 2008.

58. Online Interview—MLA

Pope, Carl. Interview by Amy Standen. *Salon.com*. Salon Media Group, 29 Apr. 2002. Web. 27 Jan. 2005.

59. Online Video or Film Clip—MLA

See Figure 36.7.

Reeves, Matt, dir. *Cloverfield*. Trailer. Bad Robot, 2008. Web. 18 Jan. 2008.

60. Online Cartoon—MLA

Harris, Sidney. "We have lots of information technology." Cartoon. *New Yorker* 27 May 2002. Web. 9 Feb. 2007.

61. Online Television or Radio Program—MLA

Chayes, Sarah. "Concorde." *All Things Considered*. Natl. Public Radio. 26 July 2000. Web. 7 Dec. 2001.

"The Beginning of the End." *Lost*. ABC. 30 Jan. 2008. Web. 1 Feb. 2008.

62. Online Discussion Posting—MLA

To cite an online message, give the author's name (if any), the title of the message in quotation marks, and then *Online posting*. Give the date of the posting and the name of the bulletin board, if any. Then give the access date and, in angle brackets, the URL if needed.

Firrantello, Larry. "Van Gogh on Prozac." Online posting. 23 May 2005. *Salon Table Talk*. Web. 7 June 2005. <http://tabletalk.salon.com/webx?50@931.xC34anLmwOq.1@.773b2ad1>.

Be cautious about using online postings as sources. Some postings contain cutting-edge information from experts, but some contain trash. Unfortunately, it is nearly impossible to find out whether people online are who they claim to be.

63. Real-Time Communication—MLA

Give the name of the speaker or writer, a title for the event (if any), the forum, date, and access date.

Berzsenyi, Christyne. Online discussion of "Writing to Meet Your Match: Rhetoric, Perceptions, and Self-Presentation for Four Online Daters." *Computers and Writing Online*. 13 May 2007. AcadianaMoo. Web. 13 May 2007.

64. E-Mail Message—MLA

Start with the name of the person who wrote the e-mail message. Give the title or subject line in quotation marks. Then describe the source (*e-mail*) and identify the recipient. End with the date.

Pessin, Eliana. "Scottish Writers." Message to Georgia Dobyns. 11 Nov. 2007. Email.

65. Part of an Online Book—MLA

Teasdale, Sara. "Driftwood." *Flame and Shadow*. Ed. A. Light. N.p., 1920. *Project Gutenberg*. 1 July 1996. Web. 18 Aug. 2008.

66. Online Review—MLA

Travers, Peter. Rev. of *No Country for Old Men*, dir. Joel Coen and Ethan Coen. *Rollingstone.com*. Rolling Stone, 1 Nov. 2007. Web. 25 Nov. 2007.

67. Online Abstract—MLA

Avery, Christopher, et al. "A Revealed Preference Ranking of U.S. Colleges and Universities." NBER Working Paper No. W10803. Abstract. Web. 11 Oct. 2004.

68. Posting on a Blog—MLA

McLemee, Scott. "To Whom It May Concern." *Quick Study*. 1 Jan. 2008. Web. 14 May 2008.

69. Online Sound Recording or Clip—MLA

Komunyakaa, Yusef. "My Father's Love Letters." Poets.org Listening Booth. Academy of American Poets, 5 May 1993. Web. 27 Apr. 2005.

70. Online Advertisement—MLA

Samsung. Advertisement. *RollingStone*. 8 Nov. 2005. Web.

71. Online Manuscript or Working Paper—MLA

deGrandpre, Andrew. "Baseball Destined to Die in Hockey Town." 2002. Unpublished article. Web. 7 Mar. 2005.

72. Podcast—MLA

A podcast is an audio recording that is posted online. Include as much of the following information as you can identify: author, title, sponsoring organization or Web site, date posted, and date accessed.

"Business Marketing with Podcast: What Marketing Professionals Should Know." *Podblaze.com*. The Info Gurus, 13 Oct. 2005. Web. 19 Oct. 2005.

73. Online Slide Show—MLA

Erickson, Britta, narr. *Visionaries from the New China.* July 2007. Web. 11 Sept.
     2008.

74. Online Photo Essay—MLA

Nachtwey, James. "Crime in Middle America." *Time* 2 Dec. 2006. Web. 5 May 2007.

75. Online Map, Chart, or Other Graphic—MLA

"Hurricane Rita." Graphic. *New York Times Online.* New York Times. 24 Sept.
     2005. Web. 24 Sept. 2005.

OTHER PRINT, NONPRINT, AND ELECTRONIC SOURCES

76. Published or Unpublished Letter—MLA

Begin the entry with the author of the letter. Note the recipient, too.

Irvin, William. Letter to Lesley Osburn. 7 Dec. 2007. Print.

Williams, William Carlos. Letter to his son. 13 Mar. 1935. *Letters of the Century:
     America 1900-1999.* Ed. Lisa Grunwald and Stephen J. Adler. New York:
     Dial, 1999. 225-26. Print.

77. Microfiche Collection of Articles—MLA

A microfiche is a transparent sheet of film (a *fiche*) with microscopic printing
that needs to be read through a special magnifier. Each fiche holds several pages,
with each page designated by a grid position. A long document may appear on
more than one fiche.

Wenzell, Ron. "Businesses Prepare for a More Diverse Work Force." *St. Louis
     Post Dispatch* 3 Feb. 1990: 17. Microform. *NewsBank: Employment* 27 (1990):
     fiche 2, grid D12.

78. Map or Chart—MLA

Colorado Front Range Mountain Bike Topo Map. Map. Nederland: Latitude 40,
     2001. Print.

79. Report or Pamphlet—MLA

Use the format for books, to the extent possible.

National Commission on Writing in America's Schools and Colleges. *The
     Neglected "R": The Need for a Writing Revolution.* New York: College
     Board, 2003. Print.

80. Legal Source—MLA

Include the name of the case, the number of the case (preceded by *No.*), the
name of the court deciding the case, and the date of the decision.

Brown v. Board of Ed. No. 8. Supreme Ct. of the US. 8 Oct. 1952. Print.

MLA

81. Interview—MLA

Note the type of interview—for example, "Telephone," "Personal" (face-to-face), or "E-mail."

Friedman, Randi. Telephone interview. 30 Aug. 2008.

For a published interview, give the name of the interviewed person first, identify the source as an interview, and then give details as for any published source: title; author, preceded by the word *By;* and publication details.

Winfrey, Oprah. "Ten Questions for Oprah Winfrey." By Richard Zoglin. *Time*
15 Dec. 2003: 8. Print.

82. Lecture, Speech, or Address—MLA

Kennedy, John Fitzgerald. Greater Houston Ministerial Assn. Rice Hotel,
Houston. 12 Sept. 1960. Address.

83. Film, Videotape, or DVD—MLA

Give the title first, and include the director, the distributor, and the year. For older films that were subsequently released on tape or DVD, provide the original release date of the movie *before* the type of medium. For video downloads, include the download date and the source. Other information (writer, producer, major actors) is optional but helpful. Put first names first.

Shakespeare in Love. Screenplay by Marc Norman and Tom Stoppard. Dir.
John Maddon. Prod. David Parfitt, Donna Gigliotti, Harvey Weinstein,
Edward Zwick, and Mark Norman. Perf. Gwyneth Paltrow, Joseph
Fiennes, and Judi Dench. Miramax, 1998. Film.

It Happened One Night. Screenplay by Robert Riskin. Dir. and Prod. Frank Capra.
Perf. Clark Gable and Claudette Colbert. 1934. Sony Pictures, 1999. DVD.

It Happened One Night. Screenplay by Robert Riskin. Dir. and Prod. Frank
Capra. Perf. Clark Gable and Claudette Colbert. Columbia 1934. 2007.
4 Mar. 2008. MPEG file.

84. Musical Recording—MLA

Put first the name most relevant to what you discuss in your paper (performer, conductor, the work performed). Include the recording's title, the medium for any recording other than a CD (*LP, audiocassette*), the name of the issuer (*Vanguard*), and the year the work was issued.

Smetana, Bedrich. *My Country*. Czech Philharmonic Orch. Cond. Karel Anserl.
LP. Vanguard, 1975. CD.

Springsteen, Bruce. "Lonesome Day." *The Rising*. Sony, 2002. CD.

Radiohead. "Jigsaw Falling into Place." *In Rainbows*. Radiohead, 2007. MP3 file.

85. Live Performance (Play, Concert, etc.)—MLA

All My Sons. By Arthur Miller. Dir. Calvin McLean. Center for the Performing
     Arts, Normal, IL. 27 Sept. 2005. Performance.

86. Work of Art, Photograph, or Musical Composition—MLA

Cassatt, Mary. *La Toilette*. 1890. Oil on canvas. Art Institute of Chicago.

Mydans, Carl. *General Douglas MacArthur Landing at Luzon*, 1945. Gelatin sil-
     ver print. Soho Triad Fine Art Gallery, New York. 21 Oct.-28 Nov. 1999.

Don't underline or put in quotation marks music identified only by form, number, and key.

Schubert, Franz. Symphony no. 8 in B minor. Print.

Italicize any work that has a title, such as an opera or ballet or a named symphony.

Schubert, Franz. *Unfinished Symphony*. Print.

To cite a published score, use the following format.

Schubert, Franz. *Symphony in B Minor (Unfinished)*. Ed. Martin Cusid. New
     York: Norton, 1971. Print.

87. Television or Radio Program—MLA

Include at least the title of the program or series (underlined), the network,
the local station and its city, and the date of the broadcast.

*Not for Ourselves Alone: The Story of Elizabeth Cady Stanton and Susan B.
     Anthony*. Writ. Andrei Burns. Perf. Julie Harris, Ronnie Gilbert, and Sally
     Kellerman. Prod. Paul Barnes and Andrei Burns. PBS. WNET, New York.
     8 Nov. 1999. Television.

Supply the title of a specific episode (if any) in quotation marks before the title
of the program (italicized) and the title of the series (if any) neither italicized
nor in quotation marks.

"The Middle of Nowhere." *This American Life*. Prod. Ira Glass. Chicago Public
     Radio. KCFR-AM, Denver. 7 Dec. 2007. Radio.

Note that many radio programs also exist as podcasts (see item 72).

88. Image or Photograph in a Print Publication—MLA

To cite an image or a photograph that appears as part of a print publication (perhaps as an illustration for an article), give the photographer (if known), the
title or caption of the image, and complete publication information, as for an
article. If the image has no title, provide a brief description.

Greene, Herb. "Grace Slick." *Rolling Stone* 30 Sept. 2004: 102. Print.

89. Advertisement—MLA

American Airlines. Advertisement. ABC. 24 Aug. 2003. Television.

Canon Digital Cameras. Advertisement. *Time* 2 June 2003: 77. Print.

90. Video Game or Software—MLA

Guitar Hero III: Legends of Rock. Santa Monica: Activision, 2007.

91. Nonperiodical Publications on CD, DVD, or Magnetic Tape—MLA

Citations for publications on DVD, CD-ROM, or other recording formats follow guidelines for print publications, with two additions: list the publication medium (for example, *CD*), and give the vendor's name.

Perl, Sondra. *Felt Sense: Guidelines for Composing*. Portsmouth: Boynton, 2004.
    CD.

92. Materials on CD or DVD with a Print Version—MLA

Before the maturity of the Internet, many print materials were previously stored on CD-ROMs.

"The Price Is Right." *Time* 20 Jan. 1992: 38. *Time Man of the Year*. CD-ROM. New
    York: Compact, 1993.

Information for the print version ends with the article's page number, 38. The title of the CD-ROM is *Time Man of the Year,* its producer is the publisher Compact, and its copyright year is 1993. Both the title of the print publication and the title of the CD-ROM are italicized.

93. Materials on CD or DVD with No Print Version—MLA

"Artificial Intelligence." *Encarta 2003*. CD-ROM. Redmond: Microsoft, 2003.

Encarta 2003 is a CD-ROM encyclopedia with no print version. "Artificial Intelligence" is the title of an article in *Encarta 2003*.

94. Book in Digital Format—MLA

Many books are now available for downloading from the Internet in digital format, to be read on special players.

Gilbert, Elizabeth. *Eat, Pray, Love*. New York: Viking, 2007. Kindle Edition.

95. PowerPoint or Similar Presentation—MLA

Delyser, Ariel. "Political Movements in the Philippines." University of Denver.
    7 Apr. 2006. PowerPoint.

96. Work in More than One Publication Medium—MLA

For more information, log into:

MyCommunicationLab

Congratulations! You now have an organized prepared speech ready to present to your class on speech day. For many of you, delivering the speech is the part that gives you the most concern. Keep in mind that delivering a great speech is a learned skill. Each time you rehearse the speech, you will notice certain areas of strengths and weaknesses. Use this to identify areas where you need extra work and then proceed to work on those areas; as a result, during the presentation you can erase from your weaknesses list and add to your strengths list. This chapter will offer useful instruction regarding the delivery of your speech.

CHAPTER 4 CONTENTS—DELIVERING A SPEECH

Methods of Delivery

1 **Impromptu Speaking**
2 **Extemporaneous Speaking**
3 **Manuscript Speaking**
4 **Memorized Speaking**

There are four methods of delivering speeches: impromptu, extemporaneous, manuscript, and memorized. Your instructor will identify which method is required for the different types of speeches that you will be presenting in the public speaking course. While there is a place for all four types of speeches, it is important to realize that the occasion usually dictates the method of delivery.

1

Impromptu Speaking

On the first day of class you might have been asked to participate in impromptu speaking. This type of speech is probably the most familiar to you in a classroom situation. Perhaps you were asked a question by an instructor or colleague that required you to speak without prior preparation. Some people call this "thinking on your feet" because it is an informal way of making contact with your audience. Since you would not have had time to think of a clever answer or to rehearse what you plan to say, you will have to give a quick answer or response.

Tips for Impromptu Speaking:

- Be prepared! Always arrive to class on time and make sure that you have completed all homework assignments. You can bet the questions which will be asked of you would have been covered in the homework assignments.

- Be a good listener! Pay attention to the instructor so that you will not have to ask for the question to be repeated.

- Be patient! Take a moment to think about the question before you begin to answer. Use this time to acknowledge your audience. They'll think you are establishing good eye contact and rapport with the audience, when in reality you are thinking of a clever response. People who rush to answer usually end up stumbling over their answer.

- Be brief! Begin by restating the question and make sure that you only answer the question. Connecting the relevance of the question to your answer will allow the audience to know that you are offering information they need to know. It is also

important to stay with two or three clear points that cover the question. Expanding on the points too much may cause you to drift to other things that were not a part of the original question.

- Be personal! Can you include a personal story or example to add to your credibility as a speaker?

2

Extemporaneous Speaking

Most of the speeches (Introduction, Central Idea, Demonstration, Persuasion, Special Occasion, and Group Presentations) presented in a public speaking course will use the extemporaneous speaking method because it is audience centered speaking. This type of speech is organized speaking without the use of a full written speech. Generally, you will memorize the introduction and the conclusion; however, the body of your speech will not be memorized so that you do not follow an exact script or wording of the speech. The benefit of this type of speech is that your audience will get the impression that you are creating the speech as it is presented. In a drama class, this is called the "illusion of the first time." How does this happen? Simply, your speech will seem more conversational because you are not reciting a speech word for word, but telling the speech; that makes it more appealing for your audience. Through extemporaneous speaking, you will spend less time looking at your notes and more time establishing direct eye contact with your audience. Another benefit of extemporaneous speaking is discovered as you engage your audience and respond to them as they respond to you.

Tips for Extemporaneous Speaking

- Choose a topic you love! Enthusiasm is contagious. If you are excited about the topic, your audience will also be excited about the topic.

- Include research and supporting material to support the topic! Make sure that you verbally cite research used during the speech.

- Prepare visual aids! Not only will you prepare the visual aids, but you should

rehearse using them! If you need technical assistance with the visual aids, prepare a script and rehearse the presentation with anyone who will be assisting. Use caution to check all technology prior to the speech to make sure it is in good working order.

- Create useful notes and rehearse using your notes! Keep notes simple so that you are not tempted to read the notes, but can quickly find your place and stay on topic. The best advice is to create notes with only key words or phrases that will provide prompts to keep you on task.

- Rehearse, rehearse, rehearse! If you rehearse the speech a minimum of three times, you will be familiar enough with the content but would not have memorized the entire speech.

- Evaluate the rehearsal! Determine your strengths and weaknesses. Make adjustments to minimize the weaknesses and emphasize the strengths.

- Check timing requirements! During rehearsal, if your speech is shorter than the required time, add content; subsequently, if the speech is longer than the required time, reduce content.

- Determine what you will wear the day of your speech. Is it appropriate for the topic? Do you feel comfortable and confident in the outfit?

3

Manuscript Speaking

Most fundamental public speaking courses will not require the manuscript method of speaking, but it is important that you understand the dynamics involved. Typically, manuscript speaking involves reading a speech word-for word as it is written. This type of speech is used by politicians, executives, and broadcasters when they must be careful about the message they deliver and if the speech must be presented exactly as planned. Usually the message includes statistical information, details, or critical data. Due to this method, speakers usually do not *connect* with the audience; instead, they merely present information.

Tips for Manuscript Speaking

- Understand the process of using a teleprompter! Most manuscript speeches are delivered with the aid of a teleprompter. Rehearse with the teleprompter before the presentation.

- Be familiar with the script! Whether you have written the manuscript, or if you are presenting a manuscript which has been prepared for you, it is important to rehearse the script many times.

- Check and double-check pronunciations of names and places!

- Establish eye contact! Since you must read the manuscript word-for-word, it is important to have pauses where eye contact is strong and rapport with the audience can be maintained.

- Use large gestures! Since you will be standing behind a lectern and staying with the script, it is very important that you include gestures that reach beyond the lectern. Gestures will add interest to your manuscript speech.

- Add vocal variance to your speech! Reading a speech word-for-word can often lead to a monotone quality. Add variations in pitch, pace, rate, and volume to create added interest in your voice.

4
Memorized Speaking

Much like the manuscript method, the memorized speaking method involves delivering a speech exactly as it is written; although, it is memorized. This method is used when accuracy of information is of great importance, yet a rapport with the audience is equally as important.

It is not often that your instructor will ask you to memorize a speech to be presented in the public speaking course. This does afford the opportunity of having better eye contact because you will not be referring to notes; however, it also provides many problems. Memorized speeches are usually short and to the point - and for good reason! Most memorized speeches do not have the conversational aspect for which extemporaneous speeches are famous. The biggest problem occurs when you lose your place in the speech. It is often difficult to remember where you were and where you were going without notes to keep you organized. Another problem is that you will not be in a position to respond to the audience if something unplanned happens. Flexibility and adaptability are almost impossible with a memorized speech.

Tips for Memorized Speaking

- Memorize the speech! Well, that's why it's called a memorized speech! Follow whatever strategy that allows you to memorize things. Most people choose to memorize the speech in three sections, so they can keep on target with the speech.

- Rehearse, rehearse, rehearse! Yes, once again, the best advice to prepare for a memorized speech is to rehearse. Be completely confident and comfortable with the material. Rehearse so much that you commit the entire speech to memory.

- Keep it fresh! Although you have rehearsed it so many times that you have memorized it, the speech should be presented in a conversational tone and must sound like this is the first time that you have ever presented the speech.

- Establish eye contact! Although eye contact is easier with this speech, it must be sincere eye contact. Look directly at your audience as you deliver the message and notice their response to you, as a speaker.

Verbal Skills and Non-verbal Skills

"What you do speaks so loudly, I can't hear what you say."

UNKNOWN

1 **Paralanguage**
2 **Kinesics**
3 **Proxemics**
4 **Chronemics**
5 **Haptics**

Most of our discussion has centered on verbal communication. Actually, we should spend more time becoming aware of non-verbal communication!

Albert Mehrabian, a scholar who has conducted research involving non-verbal communication, reported his findings in a fascinating book entitled *Silent Messages*. Mehrabian has chosen to divide his research and the research of other investigators of non-verbal communication into three primary areas: verbal, vocal, and visual.

Mehrabian suggests that 7% of our communication consists of words (verbal), 38% of our communication is how we say what we say (vocal), and 55% of our communication is what we see (visual). Mehrabian's findings conclude that an astonishing 93% of all communication is non-verbal and 7% is verbal. In other words, we will believe what we **see** before we believe what we **hear** because people believe body language even when the words contradict it.

Watch what you don't say; your body is speaking volumes! Since body language is unconscious for the most part, it is the most honest form of communication we use. It is the body language that we use without realizing it that tells our true feelings about something. In essence, body language transmits feelings; whereas, verbal communication transmits words and thoughts.

Let's go back to the salesperson mentioned in the "Listening Skills" section of this book. While the successful salesperson is practicing active listening skills, he is also watching the body language of his customer. Simply paying attention to the pupils of his customer's eyes, he can tell whether or not the customer is interested. When people are excited or find something particularly interesting, the pupils of their eyes increase in size. Subtle body language cues read by the acute observer can mean the difference between a "sale" and a "no sale."

What are **body language cues?** They are signals given as communication to help us to read a person's thoughts and feelings. Are we mind readers? No. But we do learn to read body language cues over the years as we interact with others. When presenting a speech to your classmates, you should be aware of your own body language and the non-verbal message you might be sending. Mehrabian

continues his dialogue in the book *Silent Messages* to explain that feelings and attitudes also are an integral part of non-verbal communication. With this information in mind, it is important to realize there are actually five areas of non-verbal communication: paralanguage, kinesics, proxemics, chronemics, and haptics.

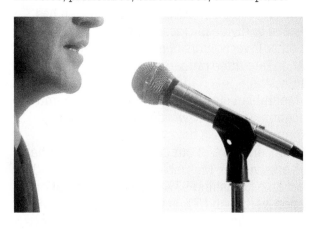

1
Paralanguage

Paralanguage, the vocal part of speech and its' nuances, is offered in the form of **vocal cues** and comprises 38% of our non-verbal communication (vocal). This is a study of how we say what we say. The use of your voice determines the audience's perception of your message. Often, you will hear your instructor mention the importance of adding **vocal variance** to your presentation. This means that she wants you to incorporate a variety of **volume, rate, pitch,** and **pauses or rhythm** to create effect.

VOLUME

Volume is crucial to good speech delivery. It is important to speak loudly enough that your audience can hear every word you say, but not so loud they feel you are shouting at them. A good rule of thumb is to project your voice so that the person in the back row can hear you. How do you do this? Just remember that the more air you project (push) through your **larynx,** also known as your voice box, the louder your sound. In comparison, the less air you push through your larynx, the softer your sound. You have worked so hard to prepare your speech; make sure that your audience can hear it!

In most classroom situations where you will be making a speech, the speech area is small enough for you to be able to project sound loudly enough for your audience to hear. However, sometimes you may be asked to speak in a larger arena. Perhaps you might even be asked to be the featured speaker for your graduation class on graduation day! If that should happen, you most certainly will be provided with a microphone which will amplify your voice. When using a microphone or speaking in an area that is unfamiliar to you, the best advice is to be prepared. You will want to visit the area where you will be speaking prior to the speech and become comfortable with it. You will also want to practice your speech using the microphone system that you will be using on the day of your speech. All sound systems are different and you will want to be familiar with the system that you will be using. Understanding this will also allow you to have more confidence in yourself on the day of your speech.

RATE

All too often, speakers tend to increase their **rate** of speaking when nervous. The rate of your speech will determine how fast or how slowly you are speaking. Rate can be used for vocal variance; you might choose to speed up during a certain point about which you are particularly excited or slow down your speech to emphasize a certain point. This is an effective use of rate. Basically, you will want to speak at a rate that is comfortable for your audience. If you speak too quickly, your audience will have trouble following your points and comprehending what you have said. If you speak too slowly, you just might put them to sleep. How do you find that happy medium? Rehearse your speech using a timer to make sure that you are speaking within the assigned time. Then record (either video or audio) your speech so that you can listen to it critically. If using a video, try turning your back on the screen so that you can concentrate on your voice. Try to take notes as you listen to your speech. Are you speaking too fast? Are you speaking too slowly?

PITCH

Vocal inflection is determined as you raise or lower the **pitch** of your voice. Pitch is defined by the high or low sounds produced by your voice and is caused by the vibration of your vocal cords. A faster vibration results in a higher pitch; a slower vibration results in a lower pitch. Some people talk with a particularly high pitch while others generally use a lower pitch. More often than not, women will have a higher pitch and men will have a lower pitch, but there are variances even within this scenario. One word of caution, maintaining a constant pitch, also known as a **monotone** voice, is sure to put your audience to sleep. You add variety and interest in your speech when you vary the level of your pitch throughout the speech.

PAUSE/RHYTHM

A **pause** skillfully inserted within your speech can be a powerful public speaking tool. Remember Martin Luther King's, "I Have a Dream" speech? If you do, then you most certainly will remember the very long pause he used following his initial opening statement. Here is the technique that he used: "I have a dream (long pause), that one day this nation will rise up and live out the true meaning of its creed." The pause that he used gave the audience an opportunity to stop and focus on the word, "dream." The effective use of pauses must be timed and used in such a manner that it delivers the impact of your message. Therefore, you must plan to rehearse the pause as strongly as you rehearse the speech.

Just as surely as a skillfully inserted pause can augment your speech, an awkward pause can harm your speech. It is usually at this time that you have lost your place in the speech and you are frantically searching your notes to find out where you are supposed to be. This is usually when speakers insert the famous "uh" or "uhm" into their speech. Too many of these are so distracting that the audience tends to quit listening to your content and begins to count the number of "uhs" or "uhms" they hear.

ARTICULATION AND PRONUNCIATION

Articulation is the process by which the speaker sounds out words so that the audience can understand everything that is being said. Usually errors in articulation are found when we speak too fast or when we get lazy with our speaking habits. The trick is to identify words or phrases that you have a habit of saying incorrectly. Once you have identified your trouble words, you can begin to work on them. If you are unsure about the proper **pronunciation** of a word, consult a dictionary where words are spelled phonetically, or you might ask your speech instructor for direction. Articulation actually refers to the clarity of sounds, and pronunciation refers to the way you use the sounds to form words. Bad habits in articulation and pronunciation can distract from your speech content and from your credibility as a speaker. For the purpose of the basic speech class, you will want to make sure you are always using Standard English. In other words, slang or off-color words are not acceptable. You will also want to avoid using contractions during your speech as these can often become slurred or chopped to the point that they are hard to comprehend.

DIALECT

Dialect is often used to refer to a speaker's accent which might be common to the geographic region where he/she was raised. It is certain that you can tell the dialectical difference between someone who is from the deep South of the United States from someone who was raised in England. Having an unusual dialect should not deter an audience from comprehending the message unless the dialect is so strong that the listeners cannot understand the speaker's words. If you have a strong dialect that is vastly different from the average dialect spoken within your class, you will want to spend extra time working on pronunciation. It is within this realm that most word meaning is lost. For this reason, the emphasis point of the word or the sounds of certain vowels might be said in such a way as to create word confusion. Another issue found with dialect happens to

be the rate of speaking. Some cultures speak at a faster rate; couple that with an unusual pronunciation of a word, and you can understand why audiences sometimes have trouble comprehending a foreign dialect.

VOICE SELF-ASSESSMENT

Are you concerned with the quality of your voice? Your voice reflects your personality. If it needs improvement, you can do it, but you must be willing to try. Practicing voice skills is no different than practicing a sport. If you stay at it, you are bound to improve. Often, people who do not enjoy speaking in public are more concerned with their vocal quality, than with the prospect of standing in front of a crowd and delivering a message. If this sounds like you, then read on.

What are the vocal aspects which cause you concern? Are you worried about your voice quality, pitch, pitch range, loudness, nasal resonance, stamina, or breathing techniques? If so, a brief evaluation can help you to pinpoint areas of concern so that you can begin working on improvements. A trip to a profes-sional speech therapist is one way to complete the evaluation; however, you can conduct your own evaluation, if you are so inclined.

Simply record your voice through an audio recorder or video record yourself. The important thing to remember is time. Give yourself enough time to get an adequate reading of your voice quality. One suggested activity is to read a passage from a book for a period of two to three minutes. Another strategy involves recording yourself in a three to five minute conversation with a friend or family member.

Once you have completed the recording, play it back and evaluate your voice. Have paper and a pencil handy so that you can jot down notes about your voice.

Here are vocal evaluation aspects to consider:

Vocal quality: normal, husky, hoarse, gravely, breathy, whispered, nasal, throaty;

Volume: loud, soft;

Rate/pace: normal, too fast, too slow;

Pitch: normal, high, low;

Rhythm/color: cadence, vocal variance normal, inadequate variability, excessive variability.

Rate Your Voice

Rate your voice using this self-evaluation.

Check characteristics that apply to you. Ask a family member or friend to help evaluate your responses. Decide if this is something that you can work on yourself or if you need expert help.

DESIRABLE (Voice Description)	UNDESIRABLE (Voice Description)
☐ My voice sounds pleasant.	☐ My voice sounds nasal.
☐ My voice has pitch variations.	☐ My voice sounds monotone.
☐ My voice is light.	☐ My voice sounds throaty/thick or coarse.
☐ My voice varies in volume.	☐ My voice is too soft/too loud.
☐ I articulate words clearly as I speak.	☐ I do not articulate words clearly.
☐ I sound like I am smiling.	☐ I sound bored with myself.
☐ My vocal quality is clear.	☐ My voice squeaks or cracks when I talk.
☐ My voice sounds forceful.	☐ My voice sounds weak.
☐ My accent is not distinguishable.	☐ My accent is heavy and hard to understand.
☐ I like hearing my voice.	☐ I do not like hearing my voice.

2

Kinesics

Kinesics, offered in the form of **physical cues,** comprises 55% of our non-verbal (visual) communication and is the most used aspect of summing up the speaker before the speaker has ever uttered the first word. Have you ever heard someone say, "You never get a second chance to make a first impression?" This is your opportunity to make a good first impression with your audience and it begins the moment you leave your seat to make your way to the stage area. To put it bluntly, your evaluation begins as you stand up and ends only after you are seated.

PHYSICAL APPEARANCE

It is certain that your instructor will have expectations of the way you present yourself the day of your speech. While there may not be a particular dress code in place for most college students, your **physical appearance** while in front of a group will send strong non-verbal cues regarding your credibility and the perceived success of your speech. In order to get you prepared for the world outside of the college campus, you will be expected to appear on speech day dressed as if you are going to a job interview. Men and women should wear conservative colors and business type clothing and accessories. Yes, that is right! No shorts, tennis shoes, muscle shirts, t-shirts, sunglasses, or hats! Colors that are too bright, over accessorized outfits, unusual styles, and improperly fitted garments are also distracting to the audience and will reduce your level of effectiveness. Avoid clothes that "show off" piercing or tattoos, and avoid distracting hair styles. On speech day, first impressions count, so make the most of your opportunities by dressing the part.

POSTURE AND POISE

Your **posture** will speak volumes about how you feel about yourself and your speech. Good posture also helps you breathe and project correctly and serves as a foundation for effective movement and gesturing. You will want to stand tall and straight with your chin up and eyes forward. As you stand from your place in the audience, plant your feet firmly on the ground and walk with a purpose to the stage area. Once you have arrived at the lectern and you have placed your folder or note card on the lectern surface, look proudly toward the audience to acknowledge them.

Poise is detected by the way you carry yourself. Shoulders drooping and eyes downcast send a strong non-verbal message that you lack confidence. In comparison, a speaker who walks confidently to the lectern with shoulders high, direct eye contact, and good facial expressions sends a strong non-verbal message that he/she is in control. Some people call this being comfortable in your own skin. Essentially, this is communicated by the way you carry yourself. Some things to avoid are leaning on the lectern, shifting from foot to foot, standing with your hands in your pockets or propped on your hip, standing with your hands behind you or folded against your chest, and handling your notes.

MOVEMENT

Movement plays a functional role for the speaker. Although there are a variety of movements used during a speech presentation, such as gestures, postural shifts, facial movements, and arm and hand movements, many students often wonder how they should plan movement from one area of the stage to the next. Understanding the area and space restrictions are important, but most students simply want to know, "Why should I move away from the lectern?"

The speech begins from the moment you get out of your chair and move toward the stage area. Walk confidently and acknowledge the audience. As you reach the lectern, do not use it as a barrier to hide behind; instead, use it to hold your notes and stand to the side. Standing still during part of your presentation is important, but remember that when you move, it forces your audience to focus on you and to follow you with their eyes. Movement adds energy and variety to your presentation, but it also makes you look more confident. Students who are extremely nervous will usually be frozen in one spot; whereas, students who are more confident tend to add movement while on the stage. Adding movement to your presentation will help you to feel more confident. The reason for this is because you are doing something with all of the extra adrenalin that is pumping through your system.

Movement is not pacing! Audiences may be distracted if the speaker paces up and down

or uses mindless, repetitive movements. Good advice would be to incorporate movement with moments of stillness in order to create more impact for your presentation.

In the theater world, directors plan different positions of movement for actors on a stage. This is called **blocking** and provides specific positions and movements for a character. Speakers also do this to block their presentation by choosing a primary beginning area where they state their key message; usually, this center stage and close to the audience. Think of your stage as divided into three areas: left, center, and right. Attempt to move into each of the areas as you present the speech.

Recently, I was at a Toastmasters International meeting and the mentor suggested that you draw an imaginary "M" on the floor of the stage. Here is a stage diagram and instructions to help you block the "M" approach:

1. Start at the base of the M to begin the speech at position #1. This will place you closer to the audience and center stage as you deliver your introduction step.

2. Move two steps up the letter to the top right (this is usually the place where a lectern has been placed—so that you can refer to your notes as you begin your first point)—position #2.

3. Travel down two steps until you are at the base of the "M"—position #3.

4. Retrace your steps until you are back at position #2 (again, you will be near the lectern and can refer to your notes as you begin your second point).

5. Move slowly down to position #1.

6. Move two steps up the letter to the top left and to position #4 (this is where you can begin your third and final point—if you need to refer to notes, it is not hard to move toward the lectern before settling in position #4).

7. Travel down the letter two steps and to position #5.

8. Retrace your steps until you are back at position #4.

9. As you begin your summary and closing statements, slowly move two steps back to position #1 in order to be closer to the audience as you deliver the speech conclusion.

10. Remember that you are only taking about two steps up or back each time that you move. This is not TOO much movement, but just enough to add interest to your presentation.

Hopefully, this will help with some of your questions regarding movement. If this seems too complicated, you can resort to the "V" approach, which uses the same type movements, but fewer steps and only involves positions #1, #2, #4. Some movement is good. Too much

movement can be distracting. As you make speech presentations, you will soon find a system that works best for you and will incorporate enough movement to keep your speech interesting for the audience!

GESTURES

Gestures are defined as the way we use our hands and bodies to communicate. Often you will think of gesturing as simply moving your hands around to emphasize a point. While this is one aspect of gesturing, it certainly is not the only means. Using your entire body in the gesturing process means that you will be alternating forms of gestures for more variety. For the purpose of the fundamental speech class, you will want to use gestures to augment your delivery. Gestures should never appear rehearsed, but should happen naturally in a way that emphasizes what you are saying. Remember how we said 55% of non-verbal communication is body language? You will want to make sure your gestures match the words you are saying. Otherwise, your audience will not listen to what you say, but they will listen to what they see.

FACIAL EXPRESSIONS

When rehearing your speech, consider standing in front of a mirror so that you can observe your **facial expressions.** Your thoughts, emotions, and attitudes are often seen through facial expressions; it is one of the first visual cues you give to your audience. If you are standing before your audience with a very stern facial expression, your audience will perceive that your topic will also be very stern. Use your face to help communicate to your audience through eye contact, smiling, and head tilting. As you do this, you will share your enthusiasm for the topic you have chosen.

EYE CONTACT

Eye contact is the most important aspect of speech delivery. When you establish good eye contact with your audience, you will be perceived as being more credible and knowledgeable about your subject. Looking directly into the eyes of your audience communicates that you are confident and ready to talk to them.

Once you have begun, continue good eye contact so that you will see how your audience is responding to your speech. Notice the feedback you receive in the form of returned eye contact, head nodding, and smiling. If you see quizzical looks, it will be an indication that you need to restate your point or clarify your point so they understand what you are saying. If you notice members turning their ears toward you, it might mean that they are having trouble hearing you. So you see, eye contact is not just effective in the delivery, but also in your ability to reach the audience.

If you are speaking in a room of between twenty to twenty five people, you will need to make sure that you lock eye contact with each member of your audience at some point during your speech. Start with panning the audience from left to right and then back to left—catching the gaze of each member before you move to the next. One word of advice, avoid looking only at the back wall or at just one audience member. Looking at each member of the audience will let them feel valued and included in your speech. If you tend to look at one person longer than another, you will often lose your place in the speech. It is only necessary to look at someone for just a second or two before you move to look at the next person. If you tend to favor one side of the audience more than another side, you will want to practice eye contact during rehearsal and make sure that your eyes are moving around the room in an equal manner.

SMILING

Smiling at your audience will allow them to know that you feel comfortable with them. Usually you will find that if you talk while you are smiling, your voice will reflect the smile. The interesting thing to discover is that if you are smiling at your audience, they will smile back at you. This act of reciprocal smiling will cause your anxiety to lesson and your body language to show you are at ease.

HEAD TILTING

Head tilting is another form of non-verbal body language. For the purpose of the speech class, this is mentioned so that you will be aware of the head tilting of your audience

members. Often when a listener tilts her head coupled with the brows furrowing, she is sending a non-verbal clue that she does not comprehend the point you just made. If you see much of this, you would be well advised to restate your point and make it clearer.

3
Proxemics

Proxemics is the study of a person's perception of space and is offered in the form of **spatial cues.** Your ability to control and use **movement** and the available stage space during your speech will help your audience to connect with you on a deeper level. Undoubtedly, you have many questions about what you are supposed to do while you are standing in the speaker's spotlight. You might wonder the following:

- Do I use the lectern? Do I not use the lectern?
- Do I sit on a stool in front of my audience?
- Do I walk around?
- Do I stand still?
- Do I move around my audience?

MOVEMENT

Movement during a speech involves the use of space in and around the lectern and stage area. Although a lectern is always front and center of a speech classroom, it is not a good idea to plant yourself behind the lectern and never move away from it. The reason? It creates a barrier between the speaker and the audience. Also, nervous speakers tend to hold on to the lectern, tap the lectern, and hide behind the lectern. A lectern should be used as a tool for the speaker. It usually houses the microphone equipment needed to project your voice, but it also provides a place for speech notes. Most instructors will suggest that you enter the stage, place your notes on the lectern, and then stand to the side of the lectern to present the speech. In doing so, you will have both hands available for gesturing and the audience will be able to observe your body movements during the speech.

Movement also involves the speaker's entrance to and exit from the stage. As mentioned in the opening remarks about kinesics, the audience evaluates the speaker from the moment he stands until he takes his seat at the conclusion of the speech. It is for this reason that speakers should briskly enter the stage using good posture, walking with confidence, and acknowledging the audience on the way to the lectern. Movement is one of the ways your audience will size up your credibility. With that being said, it is a good idea to rehearse your entrance and exit, just as you rehearse the presentation.

The study of proxemics reveals that using movement during a speech increases the audience's retention and level of understanding. The main thing to consider is that your movement should be natural and appear unrehearsed, even if you did rehearse your movements. Be aware of any obstructions or barriers to your movement. They might be in the form of a TV/VCR/DVD station, chairs, tables, desks, etc. You will want to maneuver around these things so that you will not trip or fall during your speech. Also, make sure that all of your movements are made with a specific purpose in mind. For example, you might want to move away from the lectern and over to an easel to point at a visual aid that you are using. Mindless walking around on the stage is distracting and causes your audience to focus on your movement instead of your message. Using well planned movement serves a purpose to augment your speech and causes your audience to feel more connected.

CHRONEMICS AND HAPTICS

The next two forms of non-verbal communication, Chronemics and Haptics, do not fall within the verbal, vocal, and visual categories that Albert Mehrabian discussed, but they do send very loud non-verbal messages that you should consider.

4
Chronemics

Have you wondered why some of your friends and co-workers are always chronically early or late for social and business gatherings? Many of you may explain it as a matter of culture, and for some people that is the truth; however, most of the time they are sending you a non-verbal signal.

Is a colleague always late? He's sending a message that his time is more important than your time, and that you should wait for him to arrive because he is so important. Do you know someone who is always early? That person is eager to arrive on time so that you will know they value your time and are eager to show their willingness to meet with you.

Chronemics is the study of how we use time in the communication process. The manner in which we respond to time signals will send a clear message. Ask yourself the following questions:

- What do you think about time?
- How do you structure and prioritize your time?
- Do you make time?
- Do you save time?
- Do you spend time?
- Do you buy time?

Often, our perception about time involves our own punctuality and our willingness to wait for people who are scheduled to see us. In addition to that, the speech class has time considerations as the required speeches are designed to last for a particular amount of time. Your instructor will tell you how much time you should spend when presenting a speech. Speech times are usually determined by the number of students in the classroom; however, they are also determined by how much time an audience is willing to invest in hearing a particular speech topic!

5
Haptics

Every day we send non-verbal communication through touch. When greeting people, we shake hands, hold hands or kiss loved ones, pat people on the back or the shoulder, and give high fives! As we say our goodbyes, we often do the same type of thing. **Haptics** is the study of communicating through touch. How we touch others and how we touch ourselves is another source of non-verbal communication that involves an understanding of culture. Depending upon where you are and with whom you are communicating, it is important to understand the culture of the person that you will be meeting and if the occasion calls for it, touching! Since touching is perceived differently, socially acceptable levels of touching will vary from one country, or one culture, to another.

As students give speeches, we notice if they are nervous by the way they touch themselves. Adjusting clothing, pushing back hair, crossing arms, holding their hands, scratching, touching their head or face, and licking their lips are indicators of the speaker's true feelings. What types of non-verbal messages do you send with your use of touch?

Rehearsal

You practice basketball; you practice piano; you even practice rollerblading, but when it comes to speeches—you **rehearse!** What is the difference? When you practice basketball, your goal is to get the ball into the basket so that you score. When you practice piano, your goal is to play a piano piece without hitting a wrong note. When you practice rollerblading, your goal is to move without falling and injuring yourself or the family pet. With speech-making and speech delivery, your goal is not about an object, or a talent, or about yourself—it is about connecting with an audience. Therefore, the difference is that your goal is people oriented not object oriented.

There is a direct correlation between the amount of time you spend crafting and re-hearsing a speech and the grade for your speech. In other words, if you want a higher speech grade, you should spend more time crafting and rehearsing.

Earlier in this book you were warned that a good speech is not written, researched, and rehearsed in just a couple of days. It is true when we say this process takes a great deal of time and effort. Here are some advantages for rehearsing your speech:

1. Allows time to create useful notes for your speech,
2. Allows you to become comfortable with your speech notes,
3. Allows greater retention of facts and sta-tistics to support your speech,
4. Allows the opportunity to add to your speech if it is too short,
5. Allows the opportunity to reduce content if your speech is too long,
6. Allows the opportunity to work with your visual aids and handouts,
7. Allows the opportunity to rehearse ges-tures and movements,
8. Allows the opportunity to rehearse with a stand-in audience,
9. Allows the opportunity to work on delivery skills,
10. Allows the opportunity to memorize the introduction and conclusion.

Delivery

You have done everything that you can to organize, research, craft, and rehearse your speech. Well, maybe not everything! Have you taken care of YOU? Did you know that the night before a speech should be treated the same way you treat the night before a big exam? Make sure that you do the following:

1. Ease your mind by packing all of your materials (speech notes, outline for your instructor, visual aids, handouts, bottle of water, etc.) the night before.
2. Get a good night's sleep.
3. Make sure that you eat, although a heavy meal or high sugar snacks are not advised.
4. Stay away from milk products within three hours of your speech as they may affect your voice quality.
5. Drink plenty of fluids the day before your speech, but avoid caffeine.
6. Warm up your voice prior to your speech.

The day of your speech, you will want to arrive early so that you have time to feel familiar with your surroundings. The last thing you will want to do is to plow into the parking lot at the last minute, frantically looking for a parking space, and then run to your building before the class starts. Arriving early will give you time to walk calmly inside, put your things down, get a drink of water, and relax.

Have your Speech Group/Tech Team meet you in the classroom a few minutes before class so that you can go over any last minute instructions. If you are expecting them to help with the visual aids or handouts, you should plan on providing them with a script several days prior to your speech, so they will know when to do the things you need.

If using a computer or video/DVD player, you will want to make sure they are in working order prior to your speech. If you find a problem, let your instructor know so that she can assist you.

If you still happen to be a bit jittery, you might want to use the rest of your time before class starts to try a few breathing exercises. Let's call them "Stress to Success Breathing Exercises."

STRESS RELIEVERS

Although you have spent time determining how to effectively deliver a speech, you might still be wondering about strategies to help relieve stress prior to the presentation. Let's face it! We all get nervous prior to presenting a speech. This fact was discussed during the first chapter in the section, "Overcoming the Fear of Public Speaking."

The first step to relieving public speaking stress is to acknowledge the fact that you are absolutely normal. Feeling stress prior to being introduced to the stage area is unavoidable. But, let's concentrate on the good stress. This is the feeling that you have as adrenaline rushes through your body and helps you rise to the challenge ahead. When you experience bad stress, you will feel fear and anxiety. This type of stress is harmful to your presentation.

How do you focus on the good stress and remove the bad stress? The best advice that I can offer, is to provide you with practical stress relieving tips which help you to become calm and take control of the speech making situation. Realizing that all of you are different and handle stress differently, it becomes important to examine a variety of stress relievers so that you can choose the strategy which works best for you. You'll notice that the strategies I suggest all involve the senses. Some strategies for relieving stress are aromatherapy, music therapy, meditation, and breathing exercises.

STRESS RELIEVING STRATEGIES	DEFINITION
Aromatherapy	**Aromatherapy** involves the sense of smell and is an ancient practice which uses scents to treat stress and improve mental health. Choose a scent that you find calming. As you inhale the scent, your brain interacts with the scent to cause a positive impact on your mood. Lavender, peppermint, and chamomile are soothing scents which might help to calm your nerves.
Music	**Music** therapy involves the sense of hearing and uses sounds and music to calm stress. Often soft music is combined with nature sounds, such as the ocean, waterfalls, birds singing, wind, or rain to create a composition which promotes a calming effect upon the listener.
Meditation	**Meditation** involves a thought process which utilizes imagery and visualization to relieve stress and promote relaxation. The key is to concentrate on positives and to remove negatives from the thought process. Prior to a speech, use imagery to imagine and visualize your success. Concentrate on the feeling of success and do not allow negative thoughts to compromise your goals.
Breathing	**Breathing** is a powerful function of the body which also can affect your state of mind. Through controlled breathing exercises, you can slow your heart beat and release tension which causes stress. As you practice the following *Stress to Success Breathing Exercises,* you will notice how this one strategy can release tension in your muscles, provide your body with needed oxygen, and positively influence your thoughts and feelings.

"Success is going from failure to failure without losing your enthusiasm."

ABRAHAM LINCOLN

Stress to Success Breathing Exercises

Use the following exercises to remain calm before your next speech presentation.

Sit in your chair
- ✓ Shoulders touching the back of your chair
- ✓ Legs not crossed
- ✓ Feet flat on the floor
- ✓ Hands folded in your lap

Close your eyes
Inhale
- ✓ Inhale slowly and deeply
- ✓ Fill your chest with air
- ✓ Count four seconds to yourself (one and two and three and four)—counting gives you a nice, easy, even pace
- ✓ Breathe as fully as you can without discomfort
- ✓ Imagine your chest slowly filling with air, from your diaphragm to your collar bone

Hold your breath
- ✓ Hold your breath for another four seconds (after you have taken a full breath)
- ✓ Count to yourself (one and two and three and four)

Exhale
- ✓ Exhale—but don't blow
- ✓ Let the air out through your mouth slowly counting to yourself (one and two and three and four)
- ✓ Feel your shoulders, chest, and diaphragm letting go
- ✓ As you exhale, think of the tension flowing out of you
- ✓ Feel yourself relaxing as you exhale

Now do as follows:
- ✓ Inhale—breathe in fully
- ✓ Hold breath—hold it very briefly
- ✓ Exhale—let the air out slowly and count with each exhalation

Repeat this cycle ten times. You will soon begin to feel a calm, thoroughly pleasurable feeling. Some say they experience warmth radiating from your chest throughout your body. Now allow yourself to breathe normally and tell yourself relaxing phrases: "I feel very relaxed . . . I can do this . . . I will be successful. . . "

For more information, log into:

MyCommunicationLab

Understanding Types of Speeches

There are three basic types of speeches: **informative, entertaining,** and **motivational.** While your instructor may require several types of speeches, you might notice that some speech types are not mutually exclusive of one another. In other words, your informative speech might also be entertaining; or, your persuasion speech might cause audience members to act upon information that you have supplied. The following information will help you gain a clearer understanding of the types of speeches as you consider which topic to choose.

Informative

The Introduction, Central Idea, and Demonstration Speech are good examples of an informative speech. This presentation provides interesting and useful information to your audience and may clarify the audience's understanding of material. The speaker assumes the role of an instructor and teaches or describes a topic, instructs a process, reports, or explains a concept or issue. It becomes the task of the speaker to convince the audience of the information's value or usefulness.

In order to be successful with the informative speech, the speaker should establish his/her own credibility with the topic. Adding scholarly research to support the topic will strengthen information presented.

Entertaining

Any type of speech may contain entertaining qualities; however, the Special Occasion Speech is the best example of an entertaining speech. Although a special occasion speech may be entertaining and informative, the ceremonial and social event categories almost always include entertaining aspects and have a potential for creating a bigger response than informative or motivational speeches. The reason? Entertaining speeches are usually delivered during social occasions that provide the opportunity to bond with an audience. The results? Well, you might be pleasantly surprised to see how this one speech could build relationships, create employment opportunities, and enhance networking possibilities.

Opportunities might present themselves at dinner parties, meetings, holidays, graduations, and other social functions. Many times they will be in the form of an impromptu speech as you are asked to "say a few words." Other times, you will have advance notice and the speech will be delivered extemporaneously. Very rarely would you be asked to deliver this type of speech using a manuscript or memorized speech.

In order to be successful with the entertaining speech, the speaker must first identify the purpose of the speech and craft the presentation accordingly. Light-hearted speeches are crafted with a specific audience and occasion in mind; therefore, it is critical to remember that the audience has gathered for the purpose of having a good time. If you always try to give the audience what they came for, they should be happy – and entertained! Keep the message light, optimistic, and clear, and as always, end the speech with a BANG!

Motivational

Motivational speeches can touch your heart, inspire you to act on information, and encourage you to move away from your comfort zone! The Special Occasion Speech and the Persuasion Speech are examples of motivational speeches.

Do you remember when you graduated from high school? It is without a doubt that the keynote speaker at your high school graduation delivered a motivational speech. However, we also hear motivational speeches from politicians, community organizers, and religious leaders.

Although most people think the purpose of a persuasion speech is to persuade the audience to do something or to think a specific way; ironically, the true purpose of a persuasion speech is to motivate! If you have the responsibility of delivering a motivational speech, first consider your task of motivating or influencing values, beliefs, attitudes, or behaviors of an audience.

Values	Values are defined as a person's perception of right or wrong; however, it could also include what a person considers good or bad.
Beliefs	Beliefs are the person's perception of that which is true or false.
Attitudes	Attitudes are formed as a person reacts favorably or unfavorably toward something.
Behaviors	Behaviors are the result of a person's values, beliefs, and attitudes. In other words, a person behaves the way they do due to their values, beliefs, and attitudes.

The success of a motivational speech is determined by the speaker's ability to motivate the audience to follow the speaker's suggestions and change behaviors which have been influenced by values, beliefs, and attitudes.

Topic choice for a motivational speech is crucial to the speaker's success. It is important for the speaker to remember that members of the audience will have definite values, beliefs, and attitudes either in favor of the topic, or against the topic. Your goal will be to generate positive behaviors as a result of your presentation and of your ability to motivate your audience. Without a strong credibility statement and equally strong research to support the topic, the speaker will have a difficult time motivating audience members who have formed an opinion against the topic.

Regardless of the purpose of your upcoming speech, understanding the three basic types of speeches, informative, entertaining, and motivational, will help you to choose a topic which will interest you and your audience.

Types of Speeches

1
Introduction Speech

An Introduction Speech may be conducted in one of two ways. Your instructor may ask you to introduce yourself, or you may be asked to introduce another student. In either case, the Introduction Speech is an **informative** speech because it provides your audience with new information. As with all speeches, you should begin by conducting an audience analysis to inform the audience of something they would like to know. Since this is the first speech students are usually required to present, it is safe to assume the audience would like to know about past experiences, the present situation, and future goals.

Ultimately, the purpose of the Introduction Speech is to supply the audience with information. Before constructing the outline, it will be important to consider the following:

- How do you plan to conduct the introduction?
- What is the setting for your speech?
- What type of feelings do you hope to invoke?

Lengthy introduction speeches are not recommended. Mention specific points and avoid too much detail. Consider points your instructor and your peers would like to know. This is a great time to include things which set the subject of your speech apart from the rest of the class. For example, has the subject traveled to an unusual place, taken up a challenging project, accomplished some amazing feat, or explored an innovative idea? Describe hobbies or personal interests of the subject. Try to think of things which will pique the interest of your audience.

Remember, this is your first opportunity to present yourself to the audience. Get the audience's attention, tell them why they need to hear your speech and why you are the person credible to deliver the speech, and finally, clearly state your thesis. You will enjoy introducing yourself or your classmate and you will also enjoy having an opportunity to learn about the interesting people in your class.

As you begin the brainstorming (clustering and webbing) process, think about the subject of your speech. Are you introducing yourself or a classmate? When you have determined WHO you are introducing, then

you should think about WHAT details would be interesting for the audience. Consider the following:

- Hopes and dreams
- Travel
- Marital status
- Family
- Trade/profession/business
- Hobbies
- Talents and gifts
- Likes and dislikes
- Strengths and weaknesses
- Life experiences

Select things that seem most significant and organize them into an oral presentation for the class. In a friendly and conversational way, deliver the introduction speech so that your presentation feels like a visit instead of a prepared, formal speech.

For the Introduction Speech, it is a good idea to use a chronological (time-ordered) pattern to organize your thoughts. Begin with the past, move to the present, and then project into the future.

1. **(Past)** If this is a speech about yourself, you will want to give the audience a brief biographical sketch of your past: When and where were you born? Where have you been? What have you done?

2. **(Present)** Tell something about your current situation: Are you married or single? Are you living with parents, in a dormitory/apartment, or in your own home? Are you employed? Are you a full-time or part-time student? What is your major course of study? What are your hobbies and special interests?

3. **(Future)** Share with the audience about your hopes and dreams for the future. When will you graduate from college? What is your dream job? Do you plan to have children? Where do you want to live? Anything else you want to share?

Write a **working outline** of things you plan to cover. Develop your format by using three main points and include sub-points. Refer back to Chapter Two – Organizing a Speech, for more information about creating the outline.

Speech Brainstorming Worksheet

Use the Speech Brainstorming Worksheet to help gather your thoughts prior to typing an outline. Additional copies of this worksheet are in your Tools for Success/MyCommunicationLab online portal!

Name: _____   **Class ID:** _____

Instructor's Name: _____   **Date:** _____

Speech Category: Introduction Speech

Speech Title: Give your speech a clever title.
_____

General Purpose: Write the general purpose (Is the purpose of the speech to Inform? Instruct? Entertain? Motivate?).
_____

Specific Purpose: Write the specific purpose in full sentence format (What do you plan to accomplish by presenting this speech?).
_____
_____
_____

Introduction:

Attention Step: Write all you plan to say in full sentence format. (How will you get the audience's attention?)
_____
_____
_____
_____
_____

Establish Need/Relevance: Establish why this topic should interest the listener (full sentence).
_____
_____
_____

Establish Speaker Credibility: Establish why **_you_** are qualified to speak about this topic (full sentence).

_____

_____

_____

Thesis (Preview) Statement: Clearly state the three main points you plan to cover (full sentences).

1. _____

2. _____

3. _____

(Transition: Transition from the Introduction Step to the First Main Point. Write the transition in full sentence format.)

_____

_____

_____

Body: _Be sure to parenthetically cite research used._

I. First Main Point: PAST (Share information about your past—you don't have to include everything—remember it is a short speech.)

    A. First Sub-Point _____

       1. First Sub-Sub-Point (_Note: Not all points will have Sub-Sub Points_).

         _____

       2. Second Sub-Sub-Point _____

    B. Second Sub-Point _____

       1. First Sub-Sub-Point _____

       2. Second Sub-Sub-Point _____

(Transition: Transition from the First Main Point to the Second Main Point. Write the transition in full sentence format.)

_____

_____

_____

II. Second Main Point: PRESENT (What are you doing currently?)

    A. First Sub-Point _____

       1. First Sub-Sub-Point _____

       2. Second Sub-Sub-Point _____

    B. Second Sub-Point _____

       1. First Sub-Sub-Point _____

       2. Second Sub-Sub-Point _____

(Transition: Transition from the Second Main Point to the Third Main Point. Write the transition in full sentence format.)

_____

_____

_____

III. Third Main Point: FUTURE (What are your future plans and goals?)

    A. First Sub-Point _____

        1. First Sub-Sub-Point _____

        2. Second Sub-Sub-Point _____

    B. Second Sub-Point _____

        1. First Sub-Sub-Point _____

        2. Second Sub-Sub-Point _____

(Transition: Transition from the Third Main Point to the Conclusion. Write the transition in full sentence format.)

_____

_____

_____

Conclusion:

Summary: Write in full sentence format. Summarize **ALL** main points.

1. _____

2. _____

3. _____

Appeal to Action: End with a **BANG**! Leave your audience thinking about your speech!

_____

_____

Speech Outline Checklist

Before each speech, follow this checklist to make sure your outline is in order.

The Outline:
- ☐ Typed
    - ☐ Uses correct outline format
    - ☐ Includes header (student's name, class ID, professor's name, date)
    - ☐ Includes headings (shown in bold letters on the example outline)
- ☐ Includes a Speech Category
- ☐ Includes a Title
- ☐ Includes a General Purpose and a Specific Purpose

Introduction:
- ☐ Written in a full sentence format
- ☐ Includes an Attention Step
- ☐ Establishes Need/Relevance
- ☐ Establishes Speaker Credibility
- ☐ Clearly stated Thesis/Preview Statement

Body:
- ☐ Uses Roman Numerals (I., II., III.), capitalized letters for Sub-Points (A., B., C.), and numbers for Sub-Sub-Points (1., 2., 3.)
- ☐ Develops three main points using key words or phrases
- ☐ Used transition sentences

Conclusion:
- ☐ Written in a full sentence outline format
- ☐ Summarizes all main points
- ☐ Uses an appropriate final appeal

Tech Team Checklist

Make use of your Tech Team during each of the speeches that require the use of visual aids. In order for your Tech Team to do a good job for you, there are some preliminary steps that you must take. After all, they will do a better job if they know what you expect. **Complete this form for your benefit** as you meet with your Tech Team prior to your speech, and then supply **each member with their individual assignments (Tech Team Member's Responsibility Form).** You may not need help with each category for every speech.

Speaker's Name: _____

Class ID: _____   **Date:** _____

Type of Speech (General Purpose): _____

Description of Visual Aids to be used:

1.

2.

3.

4.

Tech Team Member's Name: _____
Is assigned to help with Visual Aids by:

Tech Team Member's Name: _____
Is assigned to help with sound by:

Tech Team Member's Name: _____
Is assigned to help with lights by:

Tech Team Member's Name: _____
Is assigned to help with set up and break down by:

Tech Team Member's Name: _____
Is assigned to help with handouts by:
Other help needed during this speech:

Tech Team Member's Responsibility Worksheet

This form is to be provided to Tech Team Members who are assigned responsibilities for your speech.

Speaker's Name: _____

Class ID: _____ **Date:** _____

Tech Team Member's Name: _____

Speaker: _____

Type of Speech: _____

Date of Speech: _____

Description of Visual Aids to be used:

1.

2.

3.

4.

A copy of my speech outline is attached. I have highlighted and made notes in areas where I need help. Please help by:

_____

_____

_____

_____

_____

Example of an Introduction Speech Outline

Use this page as a worksheet to aid in the crafting of your first speech. The basic format of an introduction speech *preparation outline* should look like the template provided.

Student's Full Name
Professor Name
Course ID, Section
Day Month Year

Speech Category: Introduction Speech
Topic: (Title of the speech)
General Purpose: To Inform
Specific Purpose: (Full Sentence: The purpose of this speech is to introduce …)

INTRODUCTION:
Attention Step: (Full Sentence: How will you get the audience's attention?)
Establish Need/Relevance: (Full Sentence: Why does the audience need to hear this speech?)
Establish Credibility: (Full Sentence: Why are YOU credible to present this speech?)
Thesis: (Full Sentence: What are the three main points?)

Transition/Link: (Full Sentence: Transition from the introduction step to the first main point)

BODY:
I. Past
   A. Sub-point
   B. Sub-point

Transition/Link: (Full Sentence: Transition from the first main point to the second main point)

II. Present
   A. Sub-point
   B. Sub-point

Transition/Link: (Full Sentence: Transition from the second main point to the third main point)

III. Future
   A. Sub-point
   B. Sub-point

Transition/Link: (Full Sentence: Transition from the third point to the conclusion step)

CONCLUSION:
Summary: (Full Sentence: Clearly restate the three main points.)
Appeal to Action: (Full Sentence: End with a BANG!)

Introduction Speech Evaluation Worksheets

On the following pages you will find a Speech Evaluation Worksheet, Outline Evaluation Worksheet, Peer Evaluation Worksheet, and a Self-Evaluation Worksheet.

Instructions:

- Provide your instructor with a copy of the Speech Evaluation Worksheet and Outline Evaluation Worksheet for grading your speech.

- Make enough copies of the Peer Evaluation Worksheets so that you will have one for each classmate and bring the copies to class on the day of scheduled Introduction Speeches.

- Complete the Self-Evaluation Worksheet after your speech. Please view your speech video twice. Once with the sound to evaluate your verbal skills and once without the sound to evaluate your non-verbal skills.

Introduction Speech

Speech Evaluation Worksheet

Student's Name: _____

Grade Awarded: _____   **Time of Speech:** _____

ORGANIZATION/MATERIAL	5 Points EXCELLENT	4 Points GOOD	3 Points AVERAGE	2 Points FAIR	1 Point POOR
Introduction:					
1 Attention Step					
2. Established Need					
3. Established Credibility					
4. Stated Thesis (3 Main Points)					
Body:					
5. Point #1—Past					
6. Point #2—Present					
7. Point #3—Future					
8. Used Effective Transitions?					
Conclusion:					
9. Summary (3 Main Points)					
10. Appeal to Action (Ended with a BANG!)					
Delivery Techniques:					
11. Volume					
12. Rate of Speech					
13. Quality of Speech					
14. Language Skills					
15. Poise and Confidence					
16. Eye Contact					
17. Gestures					
18. Appearance					
19. Movement: Entrance Exit					
20. Stayed Within Time Limit?					

Comments for the Speaker:

Introduction Speech

Outline Evaluation Worksheet

Student's Name: _____

Grade Awarded: _____   **Time of Speech:** _____

POSSIBLE POINTS 100	POINTS EARNED	OUTLINE REQUIREMENTS—INTRODUCTION SPEECH
5 Points		Typed Outline
15 Points		Header Included: • Name, Class Identification, and Date • Speech Category • General Purpose • Specific Purpose (Full Sentence): • Title of Speech
40 Points		Introduction Step Included (Full Sentence): • Attention Step • Established Need • Established Credibility • Clearly Stated Thesis (3 Main Points)
15 Points		Body of the Speech Used Proper Outline Format • I, II, III—Roman Numerals • A, B, C • 1, 2
15 Points		Transitions (Full Sentence): • Between Introduction and Body • Between Each Main Point • Between Body and Conclusion
10 Points		Conclusion Included (Full Sentence): • Summary (Re-stated 3 Main Points) • Appeal to Action (Ended with a BANG!)

Introduction Speech

Peer-Evaluation Worksheet

Make a copy for each person in your class and evaluate their speeches using this form.

Student's Name: _____

Grade Awarded: _____   **Time of Speech:**_____

ORGANIZATION/MATERIAL	5 Points EXCELLENT	4 Points GOOD	3 Points AVERAGE	2 Points FAIR	1 Point POOR
Introduction:					
1 Attention Step					
2. Established Need					
3. Established Credibility					
4. Stated Thesis (3 Main Points)					
Body:					
5. Point #1—Past					
6. Point #2—Present					
7. Point #3—Future					
8. Used Effective Transitions?					
Conclusion:					
9. Summary (3 Main Points)					
10. Appeal to Action (Ended with a BANG!)					
Delivery Techniques:					
11. Volume					
12. Rate of Speech					
13. Quality of Speech					
14. Language Skills					
15. Poise and Confidence					
16. Eye Contact					
17. Gestures					
18. Appearance					
19. Movement: Entrance Exit					
20. Stayed Within Time Limit?					

Introduction Speech

Self-Evaluation Worksheet

Instructions: Complete this following your speech presentation.

Student's Name: _____

ORGANIZATION/MATERIAL	5 Points EXCELLENT	4 Points GOOD	3 Points AVERAGE	2 Points FAIR	1 Point POOR
Introduction:					
1 Attention Step					
2. Established Need					
3. Established Credibility					
4. Stated Thesis (3 Main Points)					
Body:					
5. Point #1—Past					
6. Point #2—Present					
7. Point #3—Future					
8. Used Effective Transitions?					
Conclusion:					
9. Summary (3 Main Points)					
10. Appeal to Action (Ended with a BANG!)					
Delivery Techniques:					
11. Volume					
12. Rate of Speech					
13. Quality of Speech					
14. Language Skills					
15. Poise and Confidence					
16. Eye Contact					
17. Gestures					
18. Appearance					
19. Movement: Entrance Exit					
20. Stayed Within Time Limit?					

IDENTIFY THREE AREAS TO IMPROVE BEFORE THE NEXT PRESENTATION.	WHY DO THESE AREAS NEED IMPROVEMENT? (PROBLEM)	HOW DO YOU PLAN TO IMPROVE THESE AREAS? (SOLUTION)
1.		
2.		
3.		

2
Central Idea Speech

A **Central Idea Speech,** often called a Key Idea Speech, is presented with the purpose of informing your audience or sharing information with them. For the fundamental speech class, you will need to **share with your audience something valuable that you have learned in school, work, or in your community.** The topic you choose might well be something with which your audience is already familiar. In that event, your job will be to enhance their knowledge of the subject by offering supplemental information and elaborating on the content. Often students will research the topic in order to provide a humorous quote, or startling statistics for the attention step and conclusion of their speech. Whether you rely on your personal experiences or if you choose to supplement your subject with researched material, you will need to make sure that you are connecting with your audience and gaining their confidence. With this speech, you will need to establish the audience's **need** to know what you plan to share. You already have the audience's attention through the attention step, now you will have the opportunity to make the speech personal for them. In other words, you will make them want to listen to your content because it will benefit them.

Do not be afraid to share a part of yourself during this speech. Audiences will enjoy hearing stories or illustrations referring to how you learned this subject that you are sharing. Let us see your personality and your passion regarding the subject. Becoming comfortable with your audience and "telling" us your speech will be much more effective than reciting scads of information that we will forget before the next day. Generally, this speech lasts only a few minutes, so make every minute count.

Your instructor may require a visual aid and research to support the topic. As you present this informative speech, you will assume the role of a teacher and the audience will be your class. Often, this is the type of speech that you will be asked to make in your college classes where a presentation is a part of your required coursework. It is for this reason that the Central Idea Speech is an important element in a basic fundamentals of speech class.

Study the example outline provided in this chapter and use it as a model for preparing your own outline. Notice the sidebar of information on the example and make sure that you include it as you type the outline.

Speech Brainstorming Worksheet

Use the Speech Brainstorming Worksheet to help gather your thoughts prior to typing an outline. Additional copies of this worksheet are in your Tools for Success/MyCommunicationLab online portal!

Name: _____   Class ID: _____

Instructor's Name: _____   Date:_____

Speech Category: Introduction Speech

Speech Title: Give your speech a clever title.

_____

General Purpose: Write the general purpose (Is the purpose of the speech to Inform? Instruct? Entertain? Motivate?).

_____

Specific Purpose: Write the specific purpose in full sentence format (What do you plan to accomplish by presenting this speech?).

_____

_____

_____

Introduction:

Attention Step: Write all you plan to say in full sentence format. (How will you get the audience's attention?)

_____

_____

_____

_____

_____

Establish Need/Relevance: Establish why this topic should interest the listener (full sentence).

_____

_____

_____

Establish Speaker Credibility: Establish why *you* are qualified to speak about this topic (full sentence).

_____

_____

_____

Thesis (Preview) Statement: Clearly state the three main points you plan to cover (full sentences).

1. _____

2. _____

3. _____

(Transition: Transition from the Introduction Step to the First Main Point. Write the transition in full sentence format.)

_____

_____

_____

Body: *Be sure to parenthetically cite research used.*

I. First Main Point _____
  A. First Sub-Point _____
    1. First Sub-Sub-Point (*Note: Not all points will have Sub-Sub Points*).

    _____
    2. Second Sub-Sub-Point _____
  B. Second Sub-Point _____
    1. First Sub-Sub-Point _____
    2. Second Sub-Sub-Point _____

(Transition: Transition from the First Main Point to the Second Main Point. Write the transition in full sentence format.)

_____

_____

_____

II. Second Main Point: _____
  A. First Sub-Point _____
    1. First Sub-Sub-Point _____
    2. Second Sub-Sub-Point _____
  B. Second Sub-Point _____
    1. First Sub-Sub-Point _____
    2. Second Sub-Sub-Point _____

(Transition: Transition from the Second Main Point to the Third Main Point. Write the transition in full sentence format.)

_____

_____

_____

III. Third Main Point _____
    A. First Sub-Point _____
        1. First Sub-Sub-Point _____
        2. Second Sub-Sub-Point _____
    B. Second Sub-Point _____
        1. First Sub-Sub-Point _____
        2. Second Sub-Sub-Point _____

(Transition: Transition from the Third Main Point to the Conclusion. Write the transition in full sentence format.)

_____

_____

_____

Conclusion:

Summary: Write in full sentence format. Summarize **ALL** main points.

1. _____

2. _____

3. _____

Appeal to Action: End with a **BANG**! Leave your audience thinking about your speech!

_____

_____

Speech Outline Checklist

Before each speech, follow this checklist to make sure your outline is in order.

The Outline:
- ☐ Typed
    - ☐ Uses correct outline format
    - ☐ Includes header (student's name, class ID, professor's name, date)
    - ☐ Includes headings (shown in bold letters on the example outline)
- ☐ Includes a Speech Category
- ☐ Includes a Title
- ☐ Includes a General Purpose and a Specific Purpose

Introduction:
- ☐ Written in a full sentence format
- ☐ Includes an Attention Step
- ☐ Establishes Need/Relevance
- ☐ Establishes Speaker Credibility
- ☐ Clearly stated Thesis/Preview Statement

Body:
- ☐ Uses Roman Numerals (I., II., III.), capitalized letters for Sub-Points (A., B., C.), and numbers for Sub-Sub-Points (1., 2., 3.)
- ☐ Develops three main points using key words or phrases
- ☐ Used transition sentences

Conclusion:
- ☐ Written in a full sentence outline format
- ☐ Summarizes all main points
- ☐ Uses an appropriate final appeal

Presentation Aids (*Note: Visual Aids are not required for ALL speeches*):
- ☐ Includes a separate Visual Aid Explanation Page
- ☐ PowerPoint Slides follow outline and are effectively designed
- ☐ Handout is usable, effectively designed, and one for each audience member

Research:
- ☐ Follows MLA Guidelines
- ☐ Required number of sources are included
- ☐ Uses reliable research
- ☐ Uses various types of research (magazines, journals, books, interviews)
- ☐ Uses timely research (less than five years old)
- ☐ Includes parenthetical citations within the document
- ☐ Includes a Works Cited page

Tech Team Checklist

Make use of your Tech Team during each of the speeches that require the use of visual aids. In order for your Tech Team to do a good job for you, there are some preliminary steps that you must take. After all, they will do a better job if they know what you expect. **Complete this form for your benefit** as you meet with your Tech Team prior to the speech, and then **supply each member with their individual assignments (Tech Team Member's Responsibility Form).** You may not need help with each category for every speech.

Speaker's Name: _____

Class ID: _____   **Date:** _____

Type of Speech (General Purpose): _____

Description of Visual Aids to be used:

1.

2.

3.

4.

Tech Team Member's Name: _____
Is assigned to help with Visual Aids by:

Tech Team Member's Name: _____
Is assigned to help with sound by:

Tech Team Member's Name: _____
Is assigned to help with lights by:

Tech Team Member's Name: _____
Is assigned to help with set up and break down by:

Tech Team Member's Name: _____
Is assigned to help with handouts by:
Other help needed during this speech:

Tech Team Member's Responsibility Worksheet

This form is to be provided to Tech Team Members who are assigned responsibilities for your speech.

Speaker's Name: _____

Class ID: _____ **Date:** _____

Tech Team Member's Name: _____

Speaker: _____

Type of Speech: _____

Date of Speech: _____

Description of Visual Aids to be used:

1.

2.

3.

4.

A copy of my speech outline is attached. I have highlighted and made notes in areas where I need help. Please help by:

_____

_____

_____

_____

_____

Example of a Central Idea Outline

Student's Full Name
Professor Name
Course ID, Section
Day Month Year

Speech Category: Central Idea Speech
Topic: Manage Your Time
General Purpose: Inform
Specific Purpose: The purpose of this speech is to teach the audience how to manage time.

INTRODUCTION:

Attention Step: (Hold up alarm clock and set off the alarm) Does the sound of a ringing alarm clock chill you?

Establish Need/Relevance: When you hear that sound, do you just want to roll over and pretend it was a bad dream?

Establish Credibility: There is probably no one in this room who hates that sound more than I, but now that has changed!

Thesis: During my career as a student, I've learned three helpful strategies for handling time. I've learned how to (1) organize time, (2) save time, and (3) make time for myself.

Transition/Link: The first strategy I have developed is to organize time.

BODY:

I. Organize time (Pausch)
   A. Establish goals
      1. Explain daily, short term, and long term goals
      2. Show chart on PowerPoint and explain how it works
   B. Use a tickler file
      1. Define a tickler file
      2. Show visual – tickler file

Transition/Link: Once I learned how to organize my time, I realized I had to manage my time more effectively. This led to my second strategy. I had to practice saving time!

II. Save time
   A. Limit telephone use
      1. Show visual – egg timer
      2. Explain cluster calls
   B. Set priorities
      1. Make minor decisions quickly
      2. Set deadlines

Transition/Link: The first two strategies proved to be very successful; however, I found my third strategy the most difficult to achieve. I had to learn the fine art of making time for myself.

III. Make time
    A. Make time a priority
        1. Say "No" when I need to
        2. Set times that work best for me
    B. Delegate to others (Covey)
        1. Trade duties with friends or family
        2. Ask for help

Transition/Link: I have shared with you strategies for handling time during my career as a student.

CONCLUSION:

Summary: Learning how to (1) organize time, (2) save time, and (3) make time for myself has been the key to my success. (Hold up the alarm clock)

Appeal to Action: Now, when the alarm goes off, I don't hate it as much because I feel in control of my time. (Alarm goes off again and the speaker raises her arm into the air holding the alarm clock with a big smile)…You might try it yourself!

Add a separate page:

VISUAL AID EXPLANATION

Table Display:
    Wind-up alarm clock
    Tickler file
    Egg timer

PowerPoint Presentation:
    Slide #1: Picture/cluster of clocks
    Slide #2: Picture of clock and three headings (Organize Time, Save Time, Make Time)
    Slide #3: Picture of a clock with a smiley face

Add a separate page:

Works Cited

Covey, Stephen R. *The 7 Habits of Highly Effective People* (15th ed.). New York: Free
    Press. 2004. Print.

Pausch, Randy. "Time Management." 2008. Web. 17 Sept. 2008.

For more information, log into:

MyCommunicationLab

Central Idea/ Informative Speech Evaluation Worksheets

On the following pages you will find a Speech Evaluation Worksheet, Outline Evaluation Worksheet, Peer Evaluation Worksheet, and a Self-Evaluation Worksheet.

Instructions:

- Provide your instructor with a copy of the Speech Evaluation Worksheet and Outline Evaluation Worksheet for grading your speech.

- Make enough copies of the Peer Evaluation Worksheets so that you will have one for each classmate and bring the copies to class on the day of scheduled Central Idea Speeches.

- Complete the Self-Evaluation Worksheet after your speech. Please view your speech video twice. Once with the sound to evaluate your verbal skills and once without the sound to evaluate your non-verbal skills.

Central Idea Speech

Speech Evaluation Worksheet

Student's Name: _____

Grade Awarded: _____   **Time of Speech:** _____

ORGANIZATION/MATERIAL	5 Points EXCELLENT	4 Points GOOD	3 Points AVERAGE	2 Points FAIR	1 Point POOR
Introduction:					
1 Attention Step					
2. Established Need					
3. Established Credibility					
4. Stated Thesis (3 Main Points)					
Body:					
5. Point #1 (Organized and Informative?)					
6. Point #2 (Organized and Informative?)					
7. Point #3 (Organized and Informative?)					
8. Used Effective Transitions?					
Conclusion:					
9. Summary (3 Main Points)					
10. Appeal to Action (Ended with a BANG!)					
Delivery Techniques:					
11. Visual Aids: Design Use					
12. Research Used? Sources Verbally Cited?					
13. Voice: Volume/Rate/Quality of Speech					
14. Language Skills					
15. Poise and Confidence Enthusiasm for Topic					
16. Gestures					
17. Eye Contact					
18. Appearance					
19. Movement: Entrance Exit					
20. Stayed Within Time Limit?					

Central Idea Speech

Outline Evaluation Worksheet

Student's Name: _____

Grade Awarded: _____ **Time of Speech:** _____

POSSIBLE POINTS 100	POINTS EARNED	OUTLINE REQUIREMENTS—INTRODUCTION SPEECH
5 Points		Typed Outline
10 Points		Header Included: • Name, Class Identification, and Date • Speech Category • General Purpose • Specific Purpose (Full Sentence): • Title of Speech
20 Points		Introduction Step Included (Full Sentence): • Attention Step • Established Need • Established Credibility • Clearly Stated Thesis (3 Main Points)
10 Points		Body of the Speech Used Proper Outline Format • I, II, III • A, B, C • 1, 2, 3
15 Points		Transitions (Full Sentence): • Between Introduction and Body • Between Each Main Point • Between Body and Conclusion
10 Points		Conclusion Included (Full Sentence): • Summary (Re-stated 3 Main Points) • Appeal to Action (Ended with a BANG!)
10 Points		Visual Aid Explanation Page: • Separate Page Detailing Visual Aids and/or Handouts Used
20 Points		Research: • Followed MLA Guidelines • Parenthetical Citations Found in Outline • Separate Page for "Works Cited" • Included Copies of All Required Research

Central Idea Speech

Peer-Evaluation Worksheet

Make a copy for each person in your class and evaluate their speeches using this form.

Student's Name: _____

Grade Awarded: _____   **Time of Speech:** _____

ORGANIZATION/MATERIAL	5 Points EXCELLENT	4 Points GOOD	3 Points AVERAGE	2 Points FAIR	1 Point POOR
Introduction:					
1. Attention Step					
2. Established Need					
3. Established Credibility					
4. Stated Thesis (3 Main Points)					
Body:					
5. Point #1 (Organized and Informative?)					
6. Point #2 (Organized and Informative?)					
7. Point #3 (Organized and Informative?)					
8. Used Effective Transitions?					
Conclusion:					
9. Summary (3 Main Points)					
10. Appeal to Action (Ended with a BANG!)					
Delivery Techniques:					
11. Visual Aids: Design Use					
12. Research Used? Sources Verbally Cited?					
13. Voice: Volume/Rate/Quality of Speech					
14. Language Skills					
15. Poise and Confidence Enthusiasm for Topic					
16. Gestures					
17. Eye Contact					
18. Appearance					
19. Movement: Entrance Exit					
20. Stayed Within Time Limit?					

Central Idea Speech

Self-Evaluation Worksheet

Instructions: Complete this following your speech presentation.

Student's Name: _____

ORGANIZATION/MATERIAL	5 Points EXCELLENT	4 Points GOOD	3 Points AVERAGE	2 Points FAIR	1 Point POOR
Introduction:					
1 Attention Step					
2. Established Need					
3. Established Credibility					
4. Stated Thesis (3 Main Points)					
Body:					
5. Point #1 (Organized and Informative?)					
6. Point #2 (Organized and Informative?)					
7. Point #3 (Organized and Informative?)					
8. Used Effective Transitions?					
Conclusion:					
9. Summary (3 Main Points)					
10. Appeal to Action (Ended with a BANG!)					
Delivery Techniques:					
11. Visual Aids: Design Use					
12. Research Used? Sources Verbally Cited?					
13. Voice: Volume/Rate/Quality of Speech					
14. Language Skills					
15. Poise and Confidence Enthusiasm for Topic					
16. Gestures					
17. Eye Contact					
18. Appearance					
19. Movement: Entrance Exit					
20. Stayed Within Time Limit?					

IDENTIFY THREE AREAS TO IMPROVE BEFORE THE NEXT PRESENTATION.	WHY DO THESE AREAS NEED IMPROVEMENT? (PROBLEM)	HOW DO YOU PLAN TO IMPROVE THESE AREAS? (SOLUTION)
1.		
2.		
3.		

3
Demonstration Speech

Why present a demonstration speech? Other speeches are accomplished as the speaker explains a process to the audience; however, sometimes it is necessary for an audience to see the process. The demonstration speech allows the speaker an opportunity to show the audience how something works. Through the demonstration speech, the audience may actively take part in the process. New information presented to an audience will be comprehended and retained at a greater rate if the audience is able to hear about the process, watch as the process is completed, and ultimately participate in the process.

Now that you are familiar with how to outline your speech and create visual aids, it is time to start involving your audience in the presentations. The demonstration speech provides you with an opportunity to develop a variety of presentational techniques, to create effective handouts and visual aids, and involve your audience in the demonstration. In this speech, you will assume the role of an instructor. You will incorporate visual aids and handouts to illustrate and support your topic, and you will create an environment that will encourage audience participation.

The most effective presentations are creative, informative, useful, and focus on the needs and interests of the audience. You could choose to demonstrate something that has to do with your major in college. Some successful presentations have involved crafts, food preparation, sports, automotive concerns, horticulture, interior design, financial concerns, and home repairs.

One final note, these presentations can be informative and fun. The key to a successful demonstration speech is preparation. Practice with a group of friends or your family so that you can get an accurate timing of your entire presentation. Finally, pay attention to the small details, (i.e. the supplies and their distribution, the handouts, the room arrangement, etc.). Your audience will appreciate your preplanning strategies, and you will feel a sense of accomplishment when you and your audience are successful.

Speech Brainstorming Worksheet

Use the Speech Brainstorming Worksheet to help gather your thoughts prior to typing an outline. Additional copies of this worksheet are in your Tools for Success/MyCommunicationLab online portal!

Name: _____   **Class ID:** _____

Instructor's Name: _____   **Date:** _____

Speech Category: Demonstration Speech

Speech Title: Give your speech a clever title.

_____

General Purpose: Write the general purpose (Is the purpose of the speech to Inform? Instruct? Entertain? Motivate?).

_____

Specific Purpose: Write the specific purpose in full sentence format (What do you plan to accomplish by presenting this speech?).

_____

_____

_____

Introduction:

Attention Step: Write all you plan to say in full sentence format. (How will you get the audience's attention?)

_____

_____

_____

_____

Establish Need/Relevance: Establish why this topic should interest the listener (full sentence).

_____

_____

_____

Establish Speaker Credibility: Establish why *you* are qualified to speak about this topic (full sentence).

_____

_____

_____

Thesis (Preview) Statement: Clearly state the three main points you plan to cover (full sentences).

1. _____

2. _____

3. _____

(Transition: Transition from the Introduction Step to the First Main Point. Write the transition in full sentence format.)

_____

_____

_____

Body: *Be sure to parenthetically cite research used.*
I. First Main Point _____ .
  A. First Sub-Point _____
    1. First Sub-Sub-Point (*Note: Not all points will have Sub-Sub Points*).

      _____
    2. Second Sub-Sub-Point _____
  B. Second Sub-Point _____
    1. First Sub-Sub-Point _____
    2. Second Sub-Sub-Point _____

(Transition: Transition from the First Main Point to the Second Main Point. Write the transition in full sentence format.)

_____

_____

_____

II. Second Main Point: _____
  A. First Sub-Point _____
    1. First Sub-Sub-Point _____
    2. Second Sub-Sub-Point _____
  B. Second Sub-Point _____
    1. First Sub-Sub-Point _____
    2. Second Sub-Sub-Point _____

(Transition: Transition from the Second Main Point to the Third Main Point. Write the transition in full sentence format.)

_____

_____

_____

III. Third Main Point _____
    A. First Sub-Point _____
        1. First Sub-Sub-Point _____
        2. Second Sub-Sub-Point _____
    B. Second Sub-Point _____
        1. First Sub-Sub-Point _____
        2. Second Sub-Sub-Point _____

(Transition: Transition from the Third Main Point to the Conclusion. Write the transition in full sentence format.)

_____

_____

_____

Conclusion:

Summary: Write in full sentence format. Summarize **ALL** main points.

1. _____

2. _____

3. _____

Appeal to Action: End with a **BANG**! Leave your audience thinking about your speech!

_____

_____

Speech Outline Checklist

Before each speech, follow this checklist to make sure your outline is in order.

The Outline:
- ☐ Typed
    - ☐ Uses correct outline format
    - ☐ Includes header (student's name, class ID, professor's name, date)
    - ☐ Includes headings (shown in bold letters on the example outline)
- ☐ Includes a Speech Category
- ☐ Includes a Title
- ☐ Includes a General Purpose and a Specific Purpose

Introduction:
- ☐ Written in a full sentence format
- ☐ Includes an Attention Step
- ☐ Establishes Need/Relevance
- ☐ Establishes Speaker Credibility
- ☐ Clearly stated Thesis/Preview Statement

Body:
- ☐ Uses Roman Numerals (I., II., III.), capitalized letters for Sub-Points (A., B., C.), and numbers for Sub-Sub-Points (1., 2., 3.)
- ☐ Develops three main points using key words or phrases
- ☐ Used transition sentences

Conclusion:
- ☐ Written in a full sentence outline format
- ☐ Summarizes all main points
- ☐ Uses an appropriate final appeal

Presentation Aids (*Note: Visual Aids are not required for ALL speeches*):
- ☐ Includes a separate Visual Aid Explanation Page
- ☐ PowerPoint Slides follow outline and are effectively designed
- ☐ Handout is usable, effectively designed, and one for each audience member

Research:
- ☐ Follows MLA Guidelines
- ☐ Required number of sources are included
- ☐ Uses reliable research
- ☐ Uses various types of research (magazines, journals, books, interviews)
- ☐ Uses timely research (less than five years old)
- ☐ Includes parenthetical citations within the document
- ☐ Includes a Works Cited page

Tech Team Checklist

Make use of your Tech Team during each of the speeches that require the use of visual aids. In order for your Tech Team to do a good job for you, there are some preliminary steps that you must take. After all, they will do a better job if they know what you expect. **Complete this form for your benefit** as you meet with your Tech Team prior to the speech, and then **supply each member with their individual assignments (Tech Team Member's Responsibility Form)**. You may not need help with each category for every speech.

Speaker's Name: _____

Class ID: _____   **Date:** _____

Type of Speech (General Purpose): _____

Description of Visual Aids to be used:

1.

2.

3.

4.

Tech Team Member's Name: _____

Is assigned to help with Visual Aids by:

Tech Team Member's Name: _____

Is assigned to help with sound by:

Tech Team Member's Name: _____

Is assigned to help with lights by:

Tech Team Member's Name: _____

Is assigned to help with set up and break down by:

Tech Team Member's Name: _____

Is assigned to help with handouts by:

Other help needed during this speech:

Tech Team Member's Responsibility Worksheet

This form is to be provided to Tech Team Members who are assigned responsibilities for your speech.

Speaker's Name: _____

Class ID: _____   **Date:** _____

Tech Team Member's Name: _____

Speaker: _____

Type of Speech: _____

Date of Speech: _____
Description of Visual Aids to be used:

1.

2.

3.

4.

A copy of my speech outline is attached. I have highlighted and made notes in areas where I need help. Please help by:

_____

_____

_____

_____

_____

Example of a Demonstration Speech Outline

Student's Name
Professor's Name
Course ID, Section
Day Month Year

Speech Category: Demonstration Speech

Topic: Let's Make Ice Cream

General Purpose: Inform/Instruct

Specific Purpose: The purpose of this speech is to demonstrate how to make home-made ice cream.

INTRODUCTION:

Attention Step: (Sing out loud to the class. . . ." I SCREAM, You SCREAM, We All SCREAM for ICE CREAM!"

Establish Need/Relevance: Remember being a kid, and just hearing that little jingle made you want to make a mad dash for the freezer?

Establish Credibility: Well, all too often, there was no ice cream in the freezer. That used to be the scenario until I learned how to make ice cream just like the kind you buy at the grocery store—only better! Want to learn how?

Central Idea/Thesis: Today you are going to learn how we came to have this yummy confection, how to make homemade ice cream, and how to make it a special treat for holidays and events!

Transition/Link: Before you can really enjoy a nice, cold bowl of homemade ice cream, you should understand something about its history.

BODY:

I. The history of ice cream (Bellis 2)
    A. Where it first began
    B. When it first began
    C. How it came to America

Transition/Link: Now that you know about the history of ice cream, would you like to learn how to make ice cream?

II. How to make ice cream (Luchetti & Giblin)
    A. Ingredients
        1. 4 egg yolks
        2. 1/2 cup of sugar
        3. 1 tsp. of cornstarch
        4. 1 3/4 cups of scalded milk
        5. 1 tsp. pure vanilla extract
    B. Equipment

1. Electric mixer
2. 1 quart sauce pan
3. Wooden spoon
4. A fine mesh strainer
5. Ice cream maker

C. Procedures
1. Beat egg yolks in mixer on medium-high
2. Reduce to low speed and add cornstarch
3. Heat milk in sauce pan until hot
4. Slowly pour hot milk into eggs
5. Pour custard mixture into sauce pan
6. Cook over low heat
   a. Stir constantly with wooden spoon
   b. Don't cook above 180 degrees
7. Add vanilla
8. Freeze in the ice cream maker
9. Transfer to plastic container
10. Store in freezer until use

Transition/Link: Wasn't that fun? The next time you have a birthday party for someone in your family, you can add some of these variations to make it a special treat!

III. How to make it special!
   A. Fresh fruit
   B. Toppings (chocolate, caramel, pineapple, sprinkles)
   C. Don't forget the whipped cream and a cherry!

Transition/Link: Who would have ever thought something that tastes so good could be so much fun to make?

CONCLUSION:

Summary: As we wipe our sticky faces and dream of the next time we have homemade ice cream, don't forget that now you know the history of ice cream, you can actually make your own ice cream and add special variations for future holidays or events!

Appeal to Action: Remember that little jingle I sang at the beginning of this demonstration??? Why don't you sing it along with me. . . . "I SCREAM, You SCREAM, We All SCREAM for ICE CREAM!" . . . YUM, YUM!

Note to Students: The following information should be included with the outline as a separate page.

Visual Aid Explanation

VISUAL AIDS

- PowerPoint Presentation:
    — Slide #1: Picture of ice cream cones
    — Slide #2: History
    — Slide #3: Recipe
    — Slide #4: Picture of an ice cream maker/ice/electrical outlet
    — Slide #5: Picture of ice cream in bowls
    — Slide #6: Picture of fresh fruit
    — Slide #7: Picture of ice cream sundae— with sprinkles, cherry, whipped cream
    — Slide #8: Words. . . . I SCREAM, You SCREAM, We All SCREAM for ICE CREAM!—And picture of an ice cream cone
- Table display
- Ice cream maker filled with homemade vanilla ice cream
- Ice cream scoops (3 or 4)
- Table cloth for demonstration table
- Bowls, napkins, and spoons for each of the audience members
- Serving bowls filled with fresh berries, bottles of ice cream syrups (chocolate, caramel, pineapple, and strawberry), sprinkles, canned whipped cream and long stemmed cherries.

HANDOUT

The handout is a brochure with Homemade Ice Cream Recipes using yellow card stock paper. Handouts will be given to the class following the demonstration.

Let's Make Homemade Ice Cream!

Note to Students: The following information should be included with the outline as a separate page.

Works Cited

Bellis, Mary. *History of Ice Cream.* 2008. Web. 17 Sept. 2008.

Luchetti, Emily, and Sheri Giblin. *A Passion for Ice Cream: 95 Recipes for Fabulous Desserts.* Chronicle Books, 2006. Print.

Demonstration Speech Evaluation Worksheets

On the following pages you will find a Speech Evaluation Worksheet, Outline Evaluation Worksheet, Peer Evaluation Worksheet, and a Self-Evaluation Worksheet.

Instructions:

- Provide your instructor with a copy of the Speech Evaluation Worksheet and Outline Evaluation Worksheet for grading your speech.

- Make enough copies of the Peer Evaluation Worksheets so that you will have one for each classmate and bring the copies to class on the day of scheduled Demonstration Speeches.

- Complete the Self-Evaluation Worksheet after your speech. Please view your speech video twice. Once with the sound to evaluate your verbal skills and once without the sound to evaluate your non-verbal skills.

Demonstration Speech

Speech Evaluation Worksheet

Student's Name: _____

Grade Awarded: _____ **Time of Speech:** _____

ORGANIZATION/MATERIAL	5 Points EXCELLENT	4 Points GOOD	3 Points AVERAGE	2 Points FAIR	1 Point POOR
Introduction:					
1. Attention Step					
2. Established Need					
3. Established Credibility					
4. Stated Thesis (3 Main Points)					
Body:					
5. Point #1—History/Background Information (Organized and Informative)					
6. Point #2—Clear Instructions/Process (Organized and Informative)					
7. Point #3—Additional Information (Organized and Informative)					
8. Used Effective Transitions?					
Conclusion:					
9. Summary (3 Main Points)					
10. Appeal to Action (Ended with a BANG!)					
Visual Aids:					
PowerPoint Presentation/Table Display 11. Design/Visibility/Clarity Use Setting Up Handling Timing of Aids					

12. Handouts:
    Design and Use
    Relevant to Speech
    Ease of Distribution					

Delivery Techniques:					
13. Research Used? Sources Verbally Cited?					

14. Voice:
    Volume
    Rate
    Quality of Speech					

15. Language Skills
    Vocabulary
    Sentence Structure					

16. Poise and Confidence Enthusiasm for Topic					
17. Gestures					
18. Eye Contact					
19. Appearance					

20. Movement:
    Entrance
    Exit					

Stayed Within Time Limit? (Points will be deducted if student is under or over time.)					

Comments for the Speaker:

Demonstration Speech

Outline Evaluation Worksheet

Student's Name: _____

Grade Awarded: _____   **Time of Speech:** _____

POSSIBLE POINTS 100	POINTS EARNED	OUTLINE REQUIREMENTS—INTRODUCTION SPEECH
15 Points		Header Included: • Name, Class Identification, and Date • Speech Category • General Purpose • Specific Purpose (Full Sentence): • Title of Speech
20 Points		Introduction Step Included (Full Sentence): • Attention Step • Established Need • Established Credibility • Clearly Stated Thesis (3 Main Points)
15 Points		Body of the Speech Used Proper Outline Format • I, II, III • A, B, C • 1, 2, 3
15 Points		Transitions (Full Sentence): • Between Introduction and Body • Between Each Main Point • Between Body and Conclusion
10 Points		Conclusion Included (Full Sentence): • Summary (Re-stated 3 Main Points) • Appeal to Action (Ended with a BANG!)
5 Points		Visual Aid Explanation Page: • Separate Page Detailing Visual Aids and/or Handouts Used
20 Points		Research: • Followed MLA Guidelines • Parenthetical Citations Found in Outline • Separate Page for "Works Cited" • Included Copies of All Required Research

Demonstration Speech

Peer-Evaluation Worksheet

Make a copy for each person in your class and evaluate their speeches using this form.

Student's Name: _____

Grade Awarded: _____   **Time of Speech:** _____

ORGANIZATION/MATERIAL	5 Points EXCELLENT	4 Points GOOD	3 Points AVERAGE	2 Points FAIR	1 Point POOR
Introduction:					
1 Attention Step					
2. Established Need					
3. Established Credibility					
4. Stated Thesis (3 Main Points)					
Body:					
5. Point #1—History/Background Information (Organized and Informative)					
6. Point #2—Clear Instructions/Process (Organized and Informative)					
7. Point #3—Additional Information (Organized and Informative)					
8. Used Effective Transitions?					
Conclusion:					
9. Summary (3 Main Points)					
10. Appeal to Action (Ended with a BANG!)					
Visual Aids:					
PowerPoint Presentation/Table Display 11. Design/Visibility/Clarity Use Setting Up Handling Timing of Aids					

12. Handouts:
    Design and Use
    Relevant to Speech
    Ease of Distribution					

Delivery Techniques:					
13. Research Used? Sources Verbally Cited?					

14. Voice:
    Volume
    Rate
    Quality of Speech					

15. Language Skills
    Vocabulary
    Sentence Structure					

16. Poise and Confidence Enthusiasm for Topic					
17. Gestures					
18. Eye Contact					
19. Appearance					

20. Movement:
    Entrance
    Exit					

Stayed Within Time Limit?					

Comments for the Speaker:

1.

2.

3.

Demonstration Speech

Self-Evaluation Worksheet

Instructions: Complete this following your speech presentation.

Student's Name: _____

ORGANIZATION/MATERIAL	5 Points EXCELLENT	4 Points GOOD	3 Points AVERAGE	2 Points FAIR	1 Point POOR
Introduction:					
1 Attention Step					
2. Established Need					
3. Established Credibility					
4. Stated Thesis (3 Main Points)					
Body:					
5. Point #1—History/Background Information (Organized and Informative)					
6. Point #2—Clear Instructions/Process (Organized and Informative)					
7. Point #3—Additional Information (Organized and Informative)					
8. Used Effective Transitions?					
Conclusion:					
9. Summary (3 Main Points)					
10. Appeal to Action (Ended with a BANG!)					
Visual Aids:					
PowerPoint Presentation/Table Display 11. Design/Visibility/Clarity Use Setting Up Handling Timing of Aids					
12. Handouts: Design and Use Relevant to Speech Ease of Distribution					

Delivery Techniques:				
13. Research Used? Sources Verbally Cited?				
14. Voice: Volume Rate Quality of Speech				
15. Language Skills Vocabulary Sentence Structure				
16. Poise and Confidence Enthusiasm for Topic				
17. Gestures				
18. Eye Contact				
19. Appearance				
20. Movement: Entrance Exit				
Stayed Within Time Limit?				

IDENTIFY THREE AREAS TO IMPROVE BEFORE THE NEXT PRESENTATION.	WHY DO THESE AREAS NEED IMPROVEMENT? (PROBLEM)	HOW DO YOU PLAN TO IMPROVE THESE AREAS? (SOLUTION)
1.		
2.		
3.		

4
Persuasion Speech

Whether you would like to admit it or not, you use persuasion skills all day long every day. You might be persuading your dog to eat the new dog food you recently bought on sale; you might be persuading your three year old to eat her vegetables, or you might try to persuade a teacher to change a project due date—but you will be using your persuasive skills somehow this very day. You can also bet that someone else will be using their persuasion skills to persuade you. How? Just count the number of billboards you passed on the way to class today! Or, better yet, count how many commercials you heard on your favorite radio station between your home and the school. Been shopping lately? What does the salesperson know about changing your way of thinking? Just plan a dinner out with your family and listen to the amount of persuading going on as each member makes strong suggestions for a different restaurant. Let's face it, knowing how to present an effective persuasion speech affects your life in many ways. It will certainly benefit your career as you move from college to the corporate world.

You have learned how to present an informative speech, now you have the opportunity to think about speaking in a different way. Building on the principles you have already learned from previous speeches, you now have the opportunity to combine information with research to alter the purpose of your speech.

"There is no failure except in no longer trying. There is no defeat except from within, no insurmountable barrier except our own inherent weakness of purpose."

ELBERT HUBBARD

As you consider the purpose of a persuasion speech, it is important to remember that you will be providing information and supporting research which will answer questions the audience would want to know. Your purpose is to answer the questions of fact, value, and policy.

QUESTIONS OF FACT

This is the point where research is critical to the success of a persuasion speech. Your audience will want to know the facts. In other words, you must support your topic choice by including information which makes your argument solid. For any argument, you will find research that will support it. Due to this reason, you must only provide points and research for one side of the argument. Otherwise, your audience will not know which position you support. The audience wants to know if your position is true or not true. They want to know whether or not the problem you describe exists. Also, you should give facts about actions that result from the problem. In other words, questions of fact involve whether or not something is true or false.

QUESTIONS OF VALUE

Value is different from fact, in that it is a moral argument. This is a great place to add a personal story or research that describes someone's personal experience. Your audience will want to know if the topic you are discussing is moral or immoral. Is it good or bad? Is the topic just or unjust? Since this type of argument involves morality, you will need to strengthen the audience's attitudes, beliefs, or values. This was discussed earlier in Chapter Five as you first learned about the persuasion strategy of presenting information and influencing behaviors. As you discuss value, you might be tempted to branch off into several different directions, but too much information could confuse the audience. Since you only have a few minutes to present the persuasion speech, focus on one particular value. Is the most important value social? Is it financial? Is it intellectual? Is it humane? Is it justifiable? Choose the moral argument that you plan to make and offer emotional appeals that will answer your audience's questions of value.

QUESTIONS OF POLICY

Different from questions of fact and questions of value, the purpose of answering questions of policy will clarify for the audience what should be done to solve the problem that you are introducing. This might involve changing laws, reversing rulings, defining processes, or revising procedures. You will answer questions of policy in the satisfaction/solutions step of a persuasion speech. After you've defined the problem involved with your topic, the next step is to answer questions of policy through offering solutions to solve the problem. Again, with only a few minutes to present a persuasion speech, the speaker will not have time to introduce several policies which might remedy a problem. Consequently, the speaker should focus on a specific policy and offer points and sub-points to support the recommended solution. Introducing scholarly research makes the argument stronger and increases the effectiveness of a persuasion speech.

When presenting a persuasion speech, the speaker could offer information which would strengthen the listener's commitment to the topic, weaken the listener's commitment to the topic, convert the listener from one side to the other, or move the listener from belief to action. Each of the strategies mentioned above will invoke varying degrees of acceptance or rejection. Depending upon skills used, the speaker may be more, or less, effective. While speaking to a group of people, never forget that you have the opportunity to persuade each person individually. As a result, each individual's attitudes may be impacted in various degrees.

Reasoning with the audience is one way to achieve persuasive results; however, this is made stronger by including scholarly research to support your points. A personal story may help you to add an emotional appeal to the speech. Combine reasoning, logic, and emotion for a stronger case.

The problem-solution organization principle is the best course of action. This method of organization follows Monroe's Motivated Sequence, an organizational schema used to satisfy the audience's needs and to motivate the audience to become an active part of the solution. Monroe's Motivated Sequence consists of five steps.

Using Monroe's Motivated Sequence, as the organizational tool, will help you to present a persuasive speech instead of an informative speech. The following information should help as you plan the persuasion speech:

STRATEGY	PURPOSE	SUGGESTED METHODS
INTRODUCTION		
Attention step	Get the audience's attention.	Refer to topic; Ask a rhetorical question; Make a startling statement or provide startling statistics; Use a quote, story, imagery, or illustration.
Establish Need/Relevance	Why does the audience NEED to hear this speech?	Tie topic to the audience;
Establish Credibility	Why are YOU credible to present this speech?	Support statement with evidence;
Central Idea/Thesis Statement:	Preview three points: Need, Satisfaction, and Visualization.	Prepare audience for the topic;
BODY		
I. Need/Problem	Describe the problem. Determine why there is a NEED to change attitudes. Use scholarly research to support your position.	Make audience aware a problem exists; describe the problem, offer signs, symptoms, and effects of the problem; use vivid images and startling disclosures to pique audience interest; provide narrative, testimony, or story.
II. Satisfaction/Solution	Offer sound solutions, backed by research, to correct the problem.	Describe solutions to the problem; explain how the solution satisfies the problem; give plan of action details, and offer steps of the plan.
III. Visualization	Use imagery to paint a picture for your audience. Have the audience visualize results. You could say, "Imagine a world where the problem does not exist."	Describe expected results of the plan. Describe consequences if the plan is not followed.
CONCLUSION		
Summary	Offer a summary of three points.	Remind audience there is a problem which could be solved by implementing the solution.
Appeal to Action	Motivate audience to do something about the problem.	Offer final remarks which call for action.

One final note—try to avoid speech topics that deal with fixed beliefs like abortion, capital punishment, religion, and politics. People have spent many years deciding what they think about these topics, and you are not likely to change their minds during a short speech. Don't set yourself up to fail. A Persuasion Speech Contract and a Brainstorming Worksheet, found on the next couple of pages, will help as you organize the upcoming Persuasion Speech. Not all instructors will require a Persuasion Speech Contract, but it is a good idea to complete this so that your instructor will know how you plan to develop your topic.

Persuasion Speech Topic Information/Contract

Speaker's Name: _____

Class ID: _____ **Date:** _____

Persuasion Speech Topic: _____

I. **Problem:** Briefly describe the need/problem. Identify three areas to be discussed.

   A. Area #1

   B. Area #2

   C. Area #3

II. **Solution/Satisfaction:** Briefly discuss the recommended solutions to satisfy the problem/need.

III. **Visualization of Results:** Briefly describe the positive results that could occur if your solution is implemented, or discuss the consequences if your solution is not implemented.

Works Cited
Identify the research you have gathered (Use MLA Guidelines to cite sources).

Please sign and date the following disclaimer:
I understand that this is my final topic choice for the Persuasion Speech, and that I cannot, under any circumstances, change my topic.

Signature: _____

Date: _____

Persuasion Speech
Brainstorming Worksheet

Student's Name
Professor's Name
Course ID, Section
Day Month Year

Speech Category: Persuasion Speech
Topic: (Give your speech a TITLE)
General Purpose: Motivational
Specific Purpose: (Full sentence: The purpose of this speech is to motivate the audience to...)

INTRODUCTION:

Attention Step: (Full sentence: How will you get the audience's attention?)
Establish Need/Relevance: (Full sentence: Why would this topic interest your audience?)
Establish Credibility: (Full sentence: Why are you qualified to speak about this topic?)
Thesis: (Full sentence: What are your three main points?)
Transition/Link: (Full sentence: Transition from the Introduction to Point #1)

BODY:

I. Description of the Need/Problem
    A. Discuss the problem as it exists today
    B. Does it answer questions of fact?
    C. Include both personal facts and researched data to highlight a need for change
    D. Include documentation of research (parenthetically cite research)
    E. Use logical and emotional appeals

Transition/Link: (Full sentence: Transition from Point #1 to Point #2)

II. Satisfaction/Solution
    A. Offer a realistic, detailed solution which satisfies the need/problem
    B. Does it answer questions of policy?
    C. Support satisfaction/solution with facts and documentation (parenthetically cite research)

Transition/Link: (Full sentence: Transition from Point #2 to Point #3)

III. Visualization of Results
    A. Does it answer questions of value?
    B. Use vivid descriptions to paint a picture
    C. Use imagery to help the audience imagine what would happen if solution is implemented or not implemented
    D. Support with facts and documentation (parenthetically cite research)

Transition/Link: (Full sentence: Transition from Point #3 to the Conclusion)

CONCLUSION:

Summary: Write a full sentence summarizing the three main points (Need/Problem, Satisfaction/Solution/ and Visualization of Results).

Appeal to Action: Write a full sentence and provide a strong appeal which motivates the audience to DO something with the information that you have provided.

Works Cited

Note: Include citations for all sources of research used in the outline. Use current documentation guidelines

Persuasion Speech
Outline Example

Student's Full Name
Professor's name
Course ID, Section
Day Month Year

Speech Category: Persuasion Speech

Topic: Breast Cancer: Be Aware

General Purpose: Motivational

Specific Purpose: The purpose of this speech is to motivate others by discussing the problem with breast cancer, offering solutions to the problem, and visualizing a world where breast cancer does not exist.

INTRODUCTION:

Attention Step: "Two hundred and fifty thousand women are living with breast cancer. One thousand women will be between the ages of 20 and 30 years of age when diagnosed. And 1,700 men will learn that they have breast cancer each year" ("What You Should Know about Breast Cancer" 1).

Establish Need/Relevance: You have just heard staggering breast cancer statistics for both genders. Clearly there is a need for us to be aware of this disease. What is breast cancer? What can we do to prevent it; more importantly, what is being done to stop breast cancer in its tracks?

Establish Credibility: Unfortunately, I have close family members whose lives are affected by breast cancer. My father's sister had breast cancer. Although she suffered a mastectomy and had to endure chemotherapy treatments, loss of hair, and months of recovery, it was her family – husband and daughters – who suffered the most. Conducting research about this topic and watching my family members live through this terrible disease qualifies me to share information with you.

Thesis Statement: We must take time to identify the problem of breast cancer. Understanding this disease can help us embrace solutions such as screenings and treatment options. It is only after we identify the problem and possible solutions that we can find ways to achieve a cure that can lead to a world without breast cancer.

Transition/Link: First, let us identify the problems associated with breast cancer.

BODY:

I. Description of the Problem (Need):
   A. Breast cancer
      1. Problems associated with breast cancer (Martini 1073)
      2. Statistics in females and in males (" We're Taking Care of Our Lives" 2)
   B. Risk factors ("What You Should Know About Breast Cancer")
   C. Family history and personal history
   D. Knowing the symptoms ("Anatomy of Breast Cancer" 4)

Transition/Link: Now that you know about the problem of breast cancer, it is important that you know ways to solve the problem.

II Solution (Satisfaction)
   A. Screening and diagnosing the problem ("What You Should Know About Breast Cancer")
      1. Mammogram
      2. Self-examinations
   B. Treatments
      1. Surgery
      2. Chemotherapy
      3. Radiation

Transition/Link: Treatments for breast cancer are just that, treatments that for thousands of women have been successful. But, is not a cure for the disease. In order to achieve a world without breast cancer, research is continuously being done through efforts of such foundations as the *Susan G. Komen Foundation.*

III. Visualization of Results
   A. Continued charitable efforts of Susan G. Komen Foundation
      1. Race for the Cure
      2. Research
   B. Support for those diagnosed with breast cancer
      1. *Susan G. Komen Foundation* ("About Us" 2)
      2. *The National Cancer Institute*
      3. Local physician and support groups

Transition/Link: As you can see the world will be a brighter place as we all work towards a cure for breast cancer.

CONCLUSION:

Summary: You now know that breast cancer is a significant problem. Through screenings and treatment options we now know there are solutions. But there is no greater solution to this disease than education and awareness in order for us to ever see a world without breast cancer.

Appeal to Action: To continue the awareness and possibly prevent you or a loved one from the devastating effects of this disease, I will have a member of my team pass out bags which contain educational information provided by the *Susan G. Komen Foundation* and local *Susan G. Komen Foundation Affiliates* with instructions for performing a self-breast exam along with other information that you can share with your friends and family. In the beginning of my speech, I told you about my father's sister who had breast cancer. I'm happy to report that my aunt is cancer free at the age of 82! With your help, we can all become ONE step closer to finding a cure.

Works Cited

"About Us." *The Susan G. Komen for the Cure.* 2012. Web. 30 March 2012.

"Anatomy of Breast Cancer." *The Susan G. Komen for the Cure.* 2012. Web. 30 March 2012.

Martini, Frederic, et al. *Fundamentals of Anatomy & Physiology.* San Francisco: Pearson, 2009. Print.

"We're Taking Care of Our Lives." *The Susan G. Komen Foundation for the Cure.* 2008. Print.

"What You Should Know About Breast Cancer." *The National Cancer Institute.* 2012. Web. 30 March 2012.

For more information, log into:

MyCommunicationLab

Persuasion Speech Evaluation Worksheets

On the following pages you will find a Speech Evaluation Worksheet, Outline Evaluation Worksheet, Peer Evaluation Worksheet, and a Self-Evaluation Worksheet.

Instructions:

- Provide your instructor with a copy of the Speech Evaluation Worksheet and Outline Evaluation Worksheet for grading your speech.

- Make enough copies of the Peer Evaluation Worksheets so that you will have one for each classmate and bring the copies to class on the day of scheduled Persuasion Speeches.

- Complete the Self-Evaluation Worksheet after your speech. Please view your speech video twice. Once with the sound to evaluate your verbal skills and once without the sound to evaluate your non-verbal skills.

Persuasion Speech

Speech Evaluation Worksheet

Student's Name: _____

Grade Awarded: _____   **Time of Speech:** _____

ORGANIZATION/MATERIAL	5 Points EXCELLENT	4 Points GOOD	3 Points AVERAGE	2 Points FAIR	1 Point POOR
Introduction:					
1 Attention Step					
2. Established Need					
3. Established Credibility					
4. Stated Thesis (3 Main Points)					
Body:					
5. Point #1 (Organized and Informative)					
6. Point #2 (Organized and Informative)					
7. Point #3 (Organized and Informative)					
8. Used Effective Transitions?					
Conclusion:					
9. Summary (3 Main Points)					
10. Appeal to Action (Ended with a BANG!)					
Visual Aids:					
PowerPoint Presentation/Table Display					
11. Design/Visibility/Clarity Use Setting Up Handling Timing of Aids					
12. Handouts: Design and Use Relevant to Speech Ease of Distribution					

Delivery Techniques:					
13. Research Used? Sources Verbally Cited?					
14. Voice: Volume Rate Quality of Speech					
15. Language Skills Vocabulary Sentence Structure					
16. Poise and Confidence Enthusiasm for Topic					
17. Gestures					
18. Eye Contact					
19. Appearance					
20. Movement: Entrance Exit					
Did the Speaker Stay Within Time Limit?	Yes?	No? Points will be deducted.			

Comments for the Speaker:

Persuasion Speech

Outline Evaluation Worksheet

Student's Name: _____

Grade Awarded: _____   **Time of Speech:** _____

POSSIBLE POINTS 100	POINTS EARNED	OUTLINE REQUIREMENTS—INTRODUCTION SPEECH
15 Points		Header Included: • Name, Class Identification, and Date • Speech Category • General Purpose • Specific Purpose (Full Sentence): • Title of Speech
20 Points		Introduction Step Included (Full Sentence): • Attention Step • Established Need • Established Credibility • Clearly Stated Thesis (3 Main Points)
15 Points		Body of the Speech Used Proper Outline Format • I, II, III • A, B, C • 1, 2, 3
10 Points		Transitions (Full Sentence): • Between Introduction and Body • Between Each Main Point • Between Body and Conclusion
10 Points		Conclusion Included (Full Sentence): • Summary (Re-stated 3 Main Points) • Appeal to Action (Ended with a BANG!)
10 Points		Visual Aid Explanation Page: • Separate Page Detailing Visual Aids and/or Handouts Used and an EXAMPLE of the Handout
20 Points		Research: • Followed MLA Guidelines • Parenthetical Citations Found in Outline • Separate Page for "Works Cited" • Included Copies of All Required Research

Persuasion Speech

Peer-Evaluation Worksheet

Make a copy for each person in your class and evaluate their speeches using this form.

Student's Name: _____

Grade Awarded: _____   **Time of Speech:** _____

ORGANIZATION/MATERIAL	5 Points EXCELLENT	4 Points GOOD	3 Points AVERAGE	2 Points FAIR	1 Point POOR
Introduction:					
1 Attention Step					
2. Established Need					
3. Established Credibility					
4. Stated Thesis (3 Main Points)					
Body:					
5. Point #1 (Organized and Informative)					
6. Point #2 (Organized and Informative)					
7. Point #3 (Organized and Informative)					
8. Used Effective Transitions?					
Conclusion:					
9. Summary (3 Main Points)					
10. Appeal to Action (Ended with a BANG!)					
Visual Aids:					
PowerPoint Presentation/Table Display 11. Design/Visibility/Clarity Use Setting Up Handling Timing of Aids					

12. Handouts: Design and Use Relevant to Speech Ease of Distribution					
Delivery Techniques:					
13. Research Used? Sources Verbally Cited?					
14. Voice: Volume Rate Quality of Speech					
15. Language Skills Vocabulary Sentence Structure					
16. Poise and Confidence Enthusiasm for Topic					
17. Gestures					
18. Eye Contact					
19. Appearance					
20. Movement: Entrance Exit					
Stayed Within Time Limit?					

Comments for the Speaker:

1.

2.

3.

Persuasion Speech

Self-Evaluation Worksheet

Instructions: Complete this following your speech presentation.

Student's Name: _____

	5 Points	4 Points	3 Points	2 Points	1 Point
ORGANIZATION/MATERIAL	**EXCELLENT**	**GOOD**	**AVERAGE**	**FAIR**	**POOR**
Introduction:					
1 Attention Step					
2. Established Need					
3. Established Credibility					
4. Stated Thesis (3 Main Points)					
Body:					
5. Point #1 (Organized and Informative)					
6. Point #2 (Organized and Informative)					
7. Point #3 (Organized and Informative)					
8. Used Effective Transitions?					
Conclusion:					
9. Summary (3 Main Points)					
10. Appeal to Action (Ended with a BANG!)					
Visual Aids:					
PowerPoint/Table Display					
11. Design/Visibility/Clarity Use Setting Up Handling Timing of Aids					
12. Handouts: Design and Use Relevant to Speech Ease of Distribution					

Delivery Techniques:					
13. Research Used? Sources Verbally Cited?					

14. Voice:
    Volume
    Rate
    Quality of Speech					

15. Language Skills
    Vocabulary
    Sentence Structure					

16. Poise and Confidence Enthusiasm for Topic					
17. Gestures					
18. Eye Contact					
19. Appearance					

20. Movement:
    Entrance
    Exit					

Stayed Within Time Limit?					

IDENTIFY THREE AREAS TO IMPROVE BEFORE THE NEXT PRESENTATION.	WHY DO THESE AREAS NEED IMPROVEMENT? (PROBLEM)	HOW DO YOU PLAN TO IMPROVE THESE AREAS? (SOLUTION)
1.		
2.		
3.		

5
Special Occasion Speech

The purpose of the fundamentals of speech course is to provide you with a foundation and experience for public speaking. Many of you will be surprised how often you will use your public speaking skills. In this section, you will learn about the many types of speeches which are often grouped into the category of special occasion speeches. Much of the speech crafting tools that you have learned will prepare you for constructing a special occasion speech. You will need to determine the purpose for the speech, analyze your audience, and construct a speech according to the time restraints. Research is needed as you plan for a special occasion speech so that you will be able to speak intelligently about the subject. It will also be important to use good presentations skills in order to effectively deliver your speech.

Since the special occasion speech is usually short, it needs to pack a punch. Words should be carefully chosen and special attention must be paid to the attention step and to the final appeal to action. Many of the special occasion speeches are offered as a type of tribute and should be delivered with dignity, grace, and sincerity. Other special occasion speeches are lighter and can be adapted or personalized in order to include humor. Still others are informational in nature and should be delivered in a manner appropriate to the occasion. With the exception of work related speeches, most of the speeches found in the table below should be delivered in less than seven minutes.

CEREMONIAL SPEECHES

- **Commencement.** The occasion for a commencement speech revolves around graduation and the opportunity to congratulate students on their academic achievements. This speech often includes motivational and inspirational points for the graduates and should last between ten and fifteen minutes.

- **Commemorative.** Special ceremonies often include a commemorative speech in which the speaker celebrates some past event. This usually is a tribute and emphasizes people or history involved with the ceremony; therefore, the speaker must be careful to include accurate data. The speaker should also take great care in

pronouncing correctly the person's name and the event which is being celebrated. Again, this is a short speech that can range between five and fifteen minutes, depending on the nature of the subject.

- **Dedication.** We often think of dedication ceremonies for new buildings, parks, or monuments; however, many religious groups include a dedication ceremony for the children and for programs endorsed by the group. The dedication speech should be short, specific, and to the point so that the honor can be given to the object of the dedication.

- **Eulogy.** This type of speech is given for the purpose of paying respects or offering a tribute to someone who died. The length of this speech will vary according to culture and circumstances surrounding the occasion.

- **Presenting an Award.** The speaker who accepts this responsibility must understand that in a short time span he should refer to the occasion, acknowledge the contributions of the recipient, and present the award with dignity and sincerity. Care must be taken in order to correctly pronounce the name of the recipient.

- **Accepting an Award.** This type of speech typically lasts between five to seven minutes and is given for the purpose of expressing appreciation for an award. It should be delivered with sincerity and dignity. The speaker should always acknowledge the organization that is presenting the award along with any other people who helped the recipient achieve the award. A person accepting an award may not always know ahead of time that they will be receiving an award. It is for this reason that an acceptance speech is usually delivered impromptu making the task even more difficult. If the recipient is called to the stage prior to the presentation of the award, the recipient should stand attentive and be aware of non-verbal signals that he/she might send. More often than not, the speaker will not call the recipient's name until the concluding comments of his speech. At that point, the recipient

should walk confidently to the stage and acknowledge the audience with positive non-verbal cues which might include smiling, waving, head nodding, or bowing to the crowd. This speech is usually very short and the speaker should, above all, be sincere by showing gratitude for the award and for recognizing the group or agency presenting the award. Gratitude should also be shown for people who helped you to accomplish the tasks which lead to the award. If informed about the award ahead of time, the recipient will have the luxury of adding personal stories or anecdotes to make the acceptance speech one that audience members will remember long after the award ceremony is over.

WORK RELATED OR POLITICAL SPEECHES

- **Announcement.** Occasions often present themselves when announcements must be made. The speaker should deliver the brief message regarding the information. This type of speech must be short and specific. Notes should be made in order for the speaker to remember all of the pertinent information. This avoids having to make a second announcement.

- **Installation.** Although this type of speech might also fall under the ceremonial speech headline, it is being placed here due to the fact that many of the installation speeches are offered by politicians who have been elected to public office. The purpose of the speech is to thank those who voted for the speaker and helped with the campaign. This speech should not exceed seven minutes.

- **Keynote.** This type of speech is offered at the beginning of a meeting or conference. The keynote speaker accepts the responsibility to inform the audience of the purpose for the meeting. Depending upon the occasion for the meeting or the conference, the keynote speech should last between five and thirty minutes. With this in mind, it is a good idea to establish the required time frame prior to the speech so the you can plan accordingly.

- **Nomination.** Historically, this type of speech is offered to nominate or propose that a person be considered as a nominee for an elected office; people may also be nominated to receive a particular award. The nomination speech should be concise and to the point.

- **Public Relations.** This speech is informative in nature and usually centers on aspects which will improve a problem. The speaker must first discuss the problem before presenting possible solutions to the problem. Following this protocol will allow the speaker to adequately address the issue and motivate the audience. Some may also call this a speech of goodwill in which the speaker must build a positive atmosphere so that the audience will be in a position to accept a product, idea, or service.

- **Reports.** You can count on having to use this skill in the workplace. The purpose in presenting a report is to communicate information. These speaking occasions should also be kept to a minimum and should be concise. Your employer will usually give you a time frame required for the report, depending on how extensive the report needs to be. Audience members will appreciate the opportunity to see a visual report in the form of charts or graphs. Keep the visual aids simple, yet include all necessary material.

SOCIAL EVENT SPEECHES

- **Farewell.** This can be offered in two different ways. The speaker could be the person who is leaving and is offering a farewell to those left behind. On the other hand, the speaker could be a person who is remaining and chooses this opportunity to honor the person who is leaving. In either event, it should be a short speech, conducted in five to seven minutes.

- **Inspirational.** Some people have a talent for inspiring others or motivating them to action. The inspirational speaker does this by stimulating the audience to feel encouraged or excited about the topic. An inspirational speech may last between ten and thirty minutes.

- **Retirement.** As with the farewell speech, this could be delivered by the person who is retiring or delivered by a member of the organization from which someone is retiring. Again, this is a short speech and should be delivered in five to seven minutes.

- **Roast.** Over the years, this has become a popular event as people gather together in good humor to "roast" a member of their group. It usually involves a dinner gathering and is delivered as an "after-dinner" segment of the program. A roast involves several speakers; each speaker taking three to five minutes to talk about the guest of honor and with the intention of invoking laughter.

- **Toast.** A toast is another tribute speech which may be offered on many different types of occasions. Some of the more recognized occasions may fall within the realm of ceremonial speeches as they involve engagement parties, wedding parties, birthdays, Bar Mitzvah and Bat Mitzvah celebrations, the birth of a baby, sweet 16 parties, retirements, reunions, installations, presentations, and announcements. A toast is very short, usually a sentence or two, in which the speaker offers a meaningful and sincere sentiment. This is accompanied by audience members lifting their drinks and clinking together their glasses as an acknowledgement of the words offered.

- **Welcome.** Ironically this speech, which is listed last as a special occasion speech, is given at the beginning of an event. The speaker's purpose is to make the group feel welcomed and appreciated. A welcome speech should be brief and to the point.

Special Occasion Speech Brainstorming Worksheet

Student's Name
Professor's Name
Course ID, Section
Day Month Year

Speech Category: Special Occasion Speech
Topic: (Give your speech a TITLE)
General Purpose: (Choose purpose that is appropriate: Inform, Entertain, Motivate)
Specific Purpose: (Full sentence: The purpose of this speech is to...)

INTRODUCTION:

Attention Step: (Full sentence: How will you get the audience's attention?)
Establish Need/Relevance: (Full sentence: What is the occasion? Why does the audience need to hear this speech?)
Establish Credibility: (Full sentence: Why are you qualified to speak about this topic?)
Thesis: (Full sentence: What are your three main points?)

Transition/Link: (Full sentence: Transition from the Introduction to Point #1)

BODY:
I. Main Point
  A. Sub-Point
  B. Sub-Point

Transition/Link: (Full sentence: Transition from Point #1 to Point #2)

II. Main Point
  A. Sub-Point
  B. Sub-Point

Transition/Link: (Full sentence: Transition from Point #2 to Point #3)

III. Main Point
  A. Sub-Point
  B. Sub-Point

Transition/Link: (Full sentence: Transition from Point #3 to the conclusion)

CONCLUSION:
Summary: Write a full sentence summarizing the three main points.
Appeal to Action: Write a full sentence: Make it memorable – end with a BANG!

Works Cited

Note: Include citations for all sources of research used in the outline. Use current documentation guidelines

Special Occasion Speech
Example—Presenting an Award

Student's Name:
Professor's Name:
Course ID, Section
Day Month Year

Speech Category: Special Occasion Speech: Presenting an Award
Topic: Annual Community Service Award
General Purpose: Informative/Motivational
Specific Purpose: The purpose of this speech is to present a community service award to Jane Doe for her outstanding work as a volunteer for the past forty-five years.

INTRODUCTION:

Attention-Step: According to research conducted by The James Irvine Foundation and issued as a report on a statewide dialogue on service and volunteerism in California, "More than 80% of people who volunteer agree with the statement that it is within my power to do things that improve the welfare of others" ("Why Youth Service Matters").

Barbara Bush said, "Giving frees us from the familiar territory of our own needs by opening our minds to the unexplained worlds occupied by the needs of others" ("Community Service Quotes").

Establish Need/Relevance: We are gathered on this occasion to offer our appreciation to Jane Doe, who has tirelessly served our community for the past forty five years, often neglecting her own needs so that she could improve the welfare of others.

Establish Credibility: As a member of this community and chairman of the Community Service Award Committee, it is my honor and pleasure to stand on the same platform with Ms. Doe and to present her with the 2011 Community Service Award.

Thesis: Today, I would like to remind you of the reason we began this award, provide you with a few of the many contributions made by Ms. Doe over the past forty-five years, and present the award.

Transition/Link: First, let's remember how this award came to be.

BODY:
I. Refer to the Occasion—The Annual Community Service Award
  A. Began in 1975
  B. Based upon community service involvement
    1. Have over 50 hours service
    2. Not have been compensated for work

C. Awarded to one person in the community each year
D. Accept nomination's three months prior to the award ceremony
E. Determine which person is most deserving of the award
F. Winner of the award receives
    1. $1,000 gift certificate to the charity of their choice
    2. Framed certificate of appreciation
    3. Name on Community Service Award plaque in city hall

Transition/Link: Earning this award requires a person who thinks of others before they think of themselves. At this time, I have the honor of presenting to you the 2011 Community Service Award nominee—Ms. Jane Doe

II. Acknowledge the contributions of the recipient—Jane Doe
    A. Contributions since 1961
        1. Church and community
        2. School system
    B. Contributions at the County Jail
        1. Library for inmates
        2. Father's Day cakes

Transition/Link: Without further delay, we would like to present the 2011 Community Service Award to Ms. Jane Doe for her outstanding work with her community for the past forty five years.

III. Present the award

Transition/Link: When we attend events like this one and we have the opportunity to honor someone within our community who has made a difference in the lives of others, we might find ourselves thinking that we would like to be a great community leader, such as Ms. Doe.

CONCLUSION:

Summary: In the past few minutes, you have become acquainted with our community tradition of the annual Community Service Award, you've met Ms. Doe, and you have celebrated with all of us as she was presented with this prestigious award.

Appeal to Action: I would like to challenge you to become more like Ms. Jane Doe, serving others within our community—and remember the words of Martin Luther King, Jr. when he said, "Everyone can be great because everyone can serve" ("Community Service Quotes").

Works Cited

"Community Service Quotes." Lycoming College. 2010. Web. 28 Oct. 2012.

"Why Youth Service Matters: Important Statistics and Facts." California Youth Service. 2009. Web. 28 Oct. 2012.

Special Occasion Speech
Example—Roast and a Toast

Student's Name:
Professor's Name:
Course ID, Section
Day Month Year

Speech Category: Special Occasion Speech: Roast and Toast
Topic: Roasting My Classmates
General Purpose: Entertaining
Specific Purpose: The purpose of this speech is to roast my classmates for the last day of class!

INTRODUCTION:

Attention-Step: Have you ever thought of suing your brain for non-support? I have many times, especially when I have to give speeches in the Public Speaking course. To be quite honest, registering for this class TERRIFIED me! I have never enjoyed speaking in front of groups and to realize that I would be presenting several speeches this semester was enough to send me over the edge!
Establish Need/Relevance: Today is our last day of class and we all need to laugh as we remember the past weeks of speech class. So I will try to share with you some fond memories and some not-so fond memories to help you remember.
Establish Credibility: As a member of this class for the past 16 weeks, I feel qualified to roast certain classmates!
Thesis: Today, I will be roasting my Speech Group/Tech Team and sharing some of my favorite and not-so-favorite moments with Sharon, Michael, and Christine.

Transition/Link: First, I'll start with Sharon. You've heard of fashionistas? Sharon is a fashionista!

BODY:

I. Sharon
   A. References to my age
      1. Over 40 is not too old to be back in school
      2. No, I am not old enough to be your mother
   B. Helped me decide which suit to wear for speech day
      1. Yes, blue is a better color for me
      2. Staple machine for a hem malfunction
   C. Comments about my shoes
      1. Comfort vs. style
      2. Yes, they do call them "sensible shoes"
      3. Invitation to go shopping with Sharon for a new shoe wardrobe

Transition/Link: Now that you have laughed with me and Sharon about my age and my "old lady" shoes, I'd like to share a few memories that I have made with Michael.

II. Michael
    A. Tech Team assistance for speech presentations
        1. Do you know the definition of rehearsal?
        2. Can you spell rehearsal?
        3. Expertise with PowerPoint and Prezi
    B. Blue Jeans for speech presentations?
        1. Remember to dress for success
        2. Not your dress-up blue jeans

Transition/Link: Truthfully, I could not have made it through any of my speeches that required visual aids, if it had not been for Michael. By the way, do any of you remember Christine? You know, she was the blonde who sat in the back row and was a member of our class and my speech group for about—oh, maybe 45 minutes!

III. Christine
    A. Dropped class after the second week
    B. Absent for first Speech Group meeting—should have known . . .
    C. What was her last name, anyway?

Transition/Link: At least I had Sharon and Michael to work with me this semester and to be my greatest cheerleaders as I faced one of my biggest fears—Public Speaking!

CONCLUSION:

Summary: Today we have all had a great time sharing memories of past speech classes with each other and roasting our classmates. I have enjoyed having the opportunity to roast my Speech Group/Tech Team members: Sharon, Michael, and Christine.

Closing Comments: Do you remember earlier when I asked you if you ever thought of suing your brain for non-support? George Jessel, an American actor, singer, and songwriter said that "The human brain starts working the moment you are born and never stops; until you stand up to speak in public" ("George Jessel Quotes").

Toast: Please raise your glass and join me in this toast to all of my classmates in Public Speaking 1101: you always kept your foot to the pedal, your shoulder to the wheel, and your nose to the grindstone. How you ever stood here and presented a speech in that position, I'll never know! Cheers!

Works Cited

"George Jessel Quotes." ThinkExist Quotations. 2012. Web. 10 May 2012.

Special Occasion Speech Evaluation Worksheets

On the following pages you will find a Speech Evaluation Worksheet, Outline Evaluation Worksheet, Peer Evaluation Worksheet, and a Self-Evaluation Worksheet.

Instructions:

- Provide your instructor with a copy of the Speech Evaluation Worksheet and Outline Evaluation Worksheet for grading your speech.

- Make enough copies of the Peer Evaluation Worksheets so that you will have one for each classmate and bring the copies to class on the day of scheduled Special Occasion Speeches.

- Complete the Self-Evaluation Worksheet after your speech. Please view your speech video twice. Once with the sound to evaluate your verbal skills and once without the sound to evaluate your non-verbal skills.

Special Occasion Speech

Speech Evaluation Worksheet

Student's Name: _____

Grade Awarded: _____   **Time of Speech:** _____

ORGANIZATION/MATERIAL	5 Points EXCELLENT	4 Points GOOD	3 Points AVERAGE	2 Points FAIR	1 Point POOR
Introduction:					
1. Attention Step					
2. Established Need					
3. Established Credibility					
4. Stated Thesis (3 Main Points)					
Body:					
5. Point #1 (Organized and Informative?)					
6. Point #2 (Organized and Informative?)					
7. Point #3 (Organized and Informative?)					
8. Used Effective Transitions?					
Conclusion:					
9. Summary (3 Main Points)					
10. Appeal to Action (Ended with a BANG!)					
Delivery Techniques:					
11. Visual Aids: Design Use					
12. Research Used? Sources Verbally Cited?					
13. Voice: Volume/Rate/Quality of Speech					
14. Language Skills					
15. Poise and Confidence Enthusiasm for Topic					
16. Gestures					
17. Eye Contact					
18. Appearance					
19. Movement: Entrance Exit					
20. Stayed Within Time Limit?					

Special Occasion Speech

Outline Evaluation Worksheet

Student's Name: _____

Grade Awarded: _____   **Time of Speech:** _____

POSSIBLE POINTS 100	POINTS EARNED	OUTLINE REQUIREMENTS—INTRODUCTION SPEECH
15 Points		Header Included: • Name, Class Identification, and Date • Speech Category • General Purpose • Specific Purpose (Full Sentence): • Title of Speech
20 Points		Introduction Step Included (Full Sentence): • Attention Step • Established Need • Established Credibility • Clearly Stated Thesis (3 Main Points)
10 Points		Body of the Speech Used Proper Outline Format • I, II, III • A, B, C • 1, 2, 3
15 Points		Transitions (Full Sentence): • Between Introduction and Body • Between Each Main Point • Between Body and Conclusion
10 Points		Conclusion Included (Full Sentence): • Summary (Re-stated 3 Main Points) • Appeal to Action (Ended with a BANG!)
10 Points		Visual Aid Explanation Page: • Separate Page Detailing Visual Aids and/or Handouts Used
20 Points		Research: • Followed MLA Guidelines • Parenthetical Citations Found in Outline • Separate Page for "Works Cited" • Included Copies of All Required Research

Special Occasion Speech

Peer-Evaluation Worksheet

Make a copy for each person in your class and evaluate their speeches using this form.

Student's Name: _____

Grade Awarded: _____   **Time of Speech:** _____

ORGANIZATION/MATERIAL	5 Points EXCELLENT	4 Points GOOD	3 Points AVERAGE	2 Points FAIR	1 Point POOR
Introduction:					
1. Attention Step					
2. Established Need					
3. Established Credibility					
4. Stated Thesis (3 Main Points)					
Body:					
5. Point #1 (Organized and Informative?)					
6. Point #2 (Organized and Informative?)					
7. Point #3 (Organized and Informative?)					
8. Used Effective Transitions?					
Conclusion:					
9. Summary (3 Main Points)					
10. Appeal to Action (Ended with a BANG!)					
Delivery Techniques:					
11. Visual Aids: Design Use					
12. Research Used? Sources Verbally Cited?					
13. Voice: Volume/Rate/Quality of Speech					
14. Language Skills					
15. Poise and Confidence Enthusiasm for Topic					
16. Gestures					
17. Eye Contact					
18. Appearance					
19. Movement: Entrance Exit					
20. Stayed Within Time Limit?					

Special Occasion Speech

Self-Evaluation Worksheet

Instructions: Complete this following your speech presentation.

Student's Name: _____

Grade Awarded: _____   **Time of Speech:** _____

ORGANIZATION/MATERIAL	5 Points EXCELLENT	4 Points GOOD	3 Points AVERAGE	2 Points FAIR	1 Point POOR
Introduction:					
1 Attention Step					
2. Established Need					
3. Established Credibility					
4. Stated Thesis (3 Main Points)					
Body:					
5. Point #1 (Organized and Informative?)					
6. Point #2 (Organized and Informative?)					
7. Point #3 (Organized and Informative?)					
8. Used Effective Transitions?					
Conclusion:					
9. Summary (3 Main Points)					
10. Appeal to Action (Ended with a BANG!)					
Delivery Techniques:					
11. Visual Aids: Design Use					
12. Research Used? Sources Verbally Cited?					
13. Voice: Volume/Rate/Quality of Speech					
14. Language Skills					
15. Poise and Confidence Enthusiasm for Topic					
16. Gestures					
17. Eye Contact					
18. Appearance					
19. Movement: Entrance Exit					
20. Stayed Within Time Limit?					

IDENTIFY THREE AREAS TO IMPROVE BEFORE THE NEXT PRESENTATION.	WHY DO THESE AREAS NEED IMPROVEMENT? (PROBLEM)	HOW DO YOU PLAN TO IMPROVE THESE AREAS? (SOLUTION)
1.		
2.		
3.		

Visual Aid Explanation

Table Display:

Black tablecloth

Community Service Award Plaque – displayed on an upright brass bookholder

PowerPoint Presentation:

Slide #1: Community Service Award

Slide #2: Picture of Jane Doe volunteering

Slide #3: Martin Luther King, Jr. quote: "Everyone can be great because everyone can serve!"

For more information, log into:

MyCommunicationLab

6
Group Presentation

Mention the task, "Group Presentation," and you can watch those around you as they start showing obvious signs of stress. Most of us are more comfortable making our presentations solo because we know that we can count on ourselves to get an assignment completed according to the specifications listed in a syllabus. Anxiety often occurs as students realize they will have to depend on other students to complete the assigned task.

Why do college courses often require group presentations? The reality is that those who work well in a group have the skills most employers need! Incorporating group presentations into the curriculum allows students to have first-hand knowledge and experience with group work. The interesting thing to remember with group presentations is that everyone within a group is unique. It is important for each member of the group to participate and to make contributions according to their own personalities, experiences, and depth of knowledge. There are advantages and disadvantages of working in groups.

The advantages and disadvantages of group presentations are:

ADVANTAGES	DISADVANTAGES
Adds to the knowledge base;	Disagreements regarding the division of labor;
Builds teamwork among members;	Lack of collaboration;
Utilizes effective brainstorming techniques;	Domination of the discussion by one group member;
Encourages active participation in discussions;	Lack of teamwork;
Sparks creative ideas;	Inconvenience in scheduling group work sessions.
Includes different voices, speech styles, and presentation skills;	
Creates more satisfaction with the end results.	

While there may be obvious challenges involved with group presentations, you can take the initiative to build upon the advantages of group work and be aware of disadvantages so that they can be addressed at the onset. In some respects, group presentations and solo presentations are similar. The differences, however, represent a separate set of challenges. Both will require you to follow the same principles as you:

- Conduct an audience analysis;
- Determine a purpose;
- Brainstorm and choose a topic;
- Develop the topic;
- Research for materials to support the topic;
- Choose an appropriate visual aid and handout;
- Prepare for the presentation.

Group Presentation Steps

STEP #1: THE GROUP

A group presentation provides you with opportunities to do much more than a solo presenter can hope to do. Your instructor will divide you into groups consisting of three to five members. Since you have the benefit of several group members, you will be able to utilize the talents of each member. For example, if one person is particularly savvy with technical matters, that person can manage or design the audio-visual aids, run the video clips, or manage the PowerPoint presentations; the group member who is crafty or artistically inclined can design the handouts required for the presentation; the group member who enjoys research can conduct research to support the topic. Another way of dividing responsibilities would be to divide the topic into areas and have each person completely responsible for everything needed to cover that one area. The beauty of a group presentation is that you have a choice regarding the division of labor and the assignment of job responsibilities within the presentation.

Here are some tips to remember:

Know group members;	Exchange names, physical addresses, e-mail addresses and phone numbers
	Determine dates and times that work well with each member's schedule
	Record the information and distribute it among members
Discuss group expectations	Do not assume that the group presentation directions are clear to everyone
	Ask questions
	Answer questions
Respect diversity and individuality of group members;	Encourage group members to speak openly
	Keep an open mind regarding other members' contributions
Communicate;	Do not get caught up in your own work and neglect to assess the status of your group members
	Use effective listening skills when working with your group

STEP #2: THE TASK

As you begin to work on the presentation, you will need to define and establish the task as presented by your instructor. Every group presentation will operate within its own set of rules, so it becomes necessary to be familiar with the objectives of the task. The time allotted for the group presentation should be considered. This will give you a base-line idea of how many minutes each person in the group will be involved. For example, a group consisting of five members who plan to construct a 15–20 minute presentation could assign each group member between three and four minutes of presentation time.

If each group member will be presenting a separate segment within the presentation, it will be the presenter's role to introduce and wrap up his or her own segment, then transition or connect the thoughts leading to the next presenter. Utilizing good transitions will allow the presenter to move the audience's attention from one segment to the next segment. The following presenter will appreciate the transition and should seamlessly pick up the presentation and carry it through to the next segment. This action creates a sense of unity and teamwork. Each group member should make occasional references to the key points which have been made by the other group members, but careful not to restate or expound on the information which was the other group member's responsibility.

Although most group presentations occur with each group member taking a turn, the entire group should realize that from the moment the presentation begins, the entire group is on stage and is being critiqued. The audience will place most of their attention on the group member who is speaking, but they will also look at other members of the group. This increases your responsibility as a member of the group. Even though you are not presenting, you should remain interested and involved in the presentation—giving your full attention to the speaker and offering non-verbal cues to support the presentation. It should go without saying, that as a group member, you should never disagree with something that another presenter within your group may be saying. If you disagree with them during the presentation, your group will lose all credibility, and you will lose the respect of the other group members. Teamwork! It is important that the audience sees you all working as a team from the beginning to the very end. Here are some tips to help you as you divide the task:

- Look at the "big picture";
- Divide the presentation into a series of manageable segments;

- Determine a time frame for each segment;
- Determine an order which should be followed;
- Decide which group member will be responsible for each segment;
  — Opening
  — Segment #1
  — Segment #2
  — Segment #3
  — Closing
  — Visual aid construction
  — Handout construction
  — Research
  — Other
- Determine a time table for completion of certain job responsibilities;
- Agree on specific duties for each person;
- Decide what should be done about members who do not participate or complete their responsibilities;
- Set a time to meet and discuss the progress made,
- Assess the balance to be completed,
- Establish a plan to complete the presentation;
- Plan a rehearsal date;
- Evaluate the rehearsal presentation and make adjustments as needed prior to the actual in-class presentation.

STEP #3: THE PLAN

If you happen to be the first speaker in the group presentation, you will need to follow the same techniques that you learned in the introduction, central idea, demonstration, persuasion, and special occasion speeches. You will start with an attention step. Once you have the attention of the audience, you will need to introduce the various members of your group and give a brief description of the content which will follow. In the other

speeches, we called this the central idea/thesis statement and it allows you the opportunity to tell the audience what you plan to tell them.

If you happen to be the last speaker in the group presentation, you will also follow the same speech construction techniques that you learned in the other speeches. You will need to summarize the main points that were discussed during the presentation and wrap-up on a strong note.

Often your instructor will allow the groups to host a question and answer period directly following the presentation. If this is the case in your classroom, you should be prepared to answer questions that dealt with your particular segment and allow the other group members to answer questions that dealt with their segment. If you notice a group member struggling with an answer, it is appropriate to add to their response or relate it to the topic. Many times the audience will ask questions that are controversial or that spark debate among the group members and the audience. If so, please realize that your responsibility as a group member is to answer the questions and attempt to keep order throughout the time that your group is still "on stage." Group presentations begin when the first person stands and walks to the front and is not over until the last group member sits down. Consequently, you should be aware that the entire team is being scrutinized and studied from the beginning until the end. Keeping the conversation cordial and congenial should be one of your group membership goals.

As you can see, group presentations may offer challenges that you never had to deal with when making a solo presentation. With this in mind, remember that it is especially important that everyone within the group works closely to coordinate their presentations to make it one coherent presentation instead of a conglomeration of several presentations rolled into one package.

STEP #4: THE PRESENTATION

You have established your group, you understand the task, and you have made a plan. Now, it is time to work on the presentation. Your instructor will give you the time guidelines that are required for the speech, but I am sure you are wondering about the process involved with creating a group outline.

Some instructors may ask you to complete a separate outline for each group member, just as you would have completed for any of the other required speeches. Other instructors may ask for an individual outline and for a One Point Outline. This type of outline was not discussed in Chapter Two – Organizing a Speech because this outline is only used during group presentations. As you examine the example below, you will see the beauty of having a One Point Outline for a group presentation. It helps the group to be more cohesive and to transition seamlessly from one group member to the next.

STEPS FOR SUCCESS

- Work as a team to present one presentation
- Choose a topic
- Make a plan
- Decide on audio/visual aids and handout materials
- Divide tasks according to group members' expertise
- Set a time-line for completion of tasks
- Work individually on identified tasks
- Include research
- Use MLA guidelines to cite research in the outline
- Meet to evaluate progress
- Rehearse the group presentation
- Present the group presentation

Speech Brainstorming Worksheet

Use the Speech Brainstorming Worksheet to help gather your thoughts prior to typing an outline. Additional copies of this worksheet are in your Tools for Success/MyCommunicationLab online portal!

Name: _____

Class ID: _____

Instructor's Name: _____

Date: _____

Speech Category: Group Presentation

Speech Title: Give your speech a clever title.

_____

General Purpose: Write the general purpose (Is the purpose of the speech to Inform? Instruct? Entertain? Motivate?).

_____

Specific Purpose: Write the specific purpose in full sentence format (What do you plan to accomplish by presenting this speech?).

_____

_____

_____

Introduction: (Who will present the Introduction?)

Attention Step: Write all you plan to say in full sentence format. (How will you get the audience's attention?)

_____

_____

_____

_____

_____

Establish Need/Relevance: Establish why this topic should interest the listener (full sentence).

_____

_____

_____

Establish Speaker Credibility: Establish WHO is in the group and WHY they are qualified to speak about this topic (full sentence).

_____

_____

_____

Thesis (Preview) Statement: Clearly state the three main points you plan to cover (full sentences).

1. _____

2. _____

3. _____

(Transition: Transition from the Introduction Step to the First Main Point SPEAKER. Write the transition in full sentence format.)

_____

_____

_____

Body: _Be sure to parenthetically cite research used._
I. First Main Point (Who will present Point #1?) _____
   A. First Sub-Point _____
     1. First Sub-Sub-Point (_Note: Not all points will have Sub-Sub Points_).

       _____
     2. Second Sub-Sub-Point _____
   B. Second Sub-Point _____
     1. First Sub-Sub-Point _____
     2. Second Sub-Sub-Point _____

(Transition: Transition from the First Main Point to the Second Main Point SPEAKER. Write the transition in full sentence format.)

_____

_____

_____

II. Second Main Point: (Who will present Point #2?) _____
   A. First Sub-Point _____
     1. First Sub-Sub-Point _____
     2. Second Sub-Sub-Point _____
   B. Second Sub-Point _____
     1. First Sub-Sub-Point _____
     2. Second Sub-Sub-Point _____

(Transition: Transition from the Second Main Point to the Third Main Point SPEAKER. Write the transition in full sentence format.)

_____

_____

_____

III. Third Main Point (Who will present Point #3?) _____
    A. First Sub-Point _____
        1. First Sub-Sub-Point _____
        2. Second Sub-Sub-Point _____
    B. Second Sub-Point _____
        1. First Sub-Sub-Point _____
        2. Second Sub-Sub-Point _____

(Transition: Transition from the Third Main Point to the Conclusion SPEAKER. Write the transition in full sentence format.)

_____

_____

_____

Conclusion: (Who will present the Conclusion?)

Summary: Write in full sentence format. Summarize **ALL** main points.

1. _____

2. _____

3. _____

Appeal to Action: End with a **BANG**! Leave your audience thinking about your speech!

_____

_____

Speech Outline Checklist

Before each speech, follow this checklist to make sure your outline is in order.

The Outline:
- ☐ Typed
    - ☐ Uses correct outline format
    - ☐ Includes header (student's name, class ID, professor's name, date)
    - ☐ Includes headings (shown in bold letters on the example outline)
- ☐ Includes a Speech Category
- ☐ Includes a Title
- ☐ Includes a General Purpose and a Specific Purpose

Introduction:
- ☐ Written in a full sentence format
- ☐ Includes an Attention Step
- ☐ Establishes Need/Relevance
- ☐ Establishes Speaker Credibility
- ☐ Clearly stated Thesis/Preview Statement

Body:
- ☐ Uses Roman Numerals (I., II., III.), capitalized letters for Sub-Points (A., B., C.), and numbers for Sub-Sub-Points (1., 2., 3.)
- ☐ Develops three main points using key words or phrases
- ☐ Used transition sentences

Conclusion:
- ☐ Written in a full sentence outline format
- ☐ Summarizes all main points
- ☐ Uses an appropriate final appeal

Presentation Aids (*Note: Visual Aids are not required for ALL speeches*):
- ☐ Includes a separate Visual Aid Explanation Page
- ☐ PowerPoint Slides follow outline and are effectively designed
- ☐ Handout is usable, effectively designed, and one for each audience member

Research:
- ☐ Follows MLA Guidelines
- ☐ Required number of sources are included
- ☐ Uses reliable research
- ☐ Uses various types of research (magazines, journals, books, interviews)
- ☐ Uses timely research (less than five years old)
- ☐ Includes parenthetical citations within the document
- ☐ Includes a Works Cited page

Tech Team Checklist

Make use of your Tech Team during each of the speeches that require the use of visual aids. In order for your Tech Team to do a good job for you, there are some preliminary steps that you must take. After all, they will do a better job if they know what you expect. **Complete this form for your benefit** as you meet with your Tech Team prior to the speech, and then **supply each member with their individual assignments (Tech Team Member's Responsibility Form).** You may not need help with each category for every speech.

Speaker's Name: _____

Class ID: _____   **Date:** _____

Type of Speech (General Purpose): _____

Description of Visual Aids to be used:

1.

2.

3.

4.

Tech Team Member's Name: _____
Is assigned to help with Visual Aids by:

Tech Team Member's Name: _____
Is assigned to help with sound by:

Tech Team Member's Name: _____
Is assigned to help with lights by:

Tech Team Member's Name: _____
Is assigned to help with set up and break down by:

Tech Team Member's Name: _____
Is assigned to help with handouts by:

Other help needed during this speech:

Tech Team Member's Responsibility Worksheet

This form is to be provided to Tech Team Members who are assigned responsibilities for your speech.

Speaker's Name: _____

Class ID: _____   **Date:** _____

Tech Team Member's Name: _____

Speaker: _____

Type of Speech: _____

Date of Speech: _____
Description of Visual Aids to be used:

1.

2.

3.

4.

A copy of my speech outline is attached. I have highlighted and made notes in areas where I need help. Please help by:

_____

_____

_____

_____

_____

Group Presentation
One Point Outline Example

Alphabetically List Students' Names
Professor's Name
Course ID, Section
Day Month Year

Speech Category: Group Presentation: One Point Outline

Topic: Watch What You Watch

General Purpose: Informative

Specific Purpose: The purpose of this speech is to inform the audience about the negative effects of violence through video games, television, and movies.

INTRODUCTION: (Presented by: Student's Name)

Attention Step: The American Psychiatric Association reports that "By age 18, a U.S. youth will have seen 16,000 simulated murders and 200,000 acts of violence" ("Facts and TV Statistics" 3).

Establish Need/Relevance: The alarming fact is that "Children younger than 8 cannot uniformly discriminate between real life and fantasy/entertainment…They quickly learn that violence is an acceptable solution to resolving even complex problems, particularly if the aggressor is the hero" ("Voluntary Movie Rating System").

Establish Credibility: Lt. Colonel David Grossman said, "Violence is like the nicotine in cigarettes. The reason why the media has to pump ever more violence into us is because we've built up a tolerance. In order to get the same high, we need ever-higher levels…the television industry has gained its market share through an addictive and toxic ingredient" ("Facts and TV Statistics" 3). My name is (_____) and I would like to introduce you to the members of our group: (Student's Name…. Student's Name…. Student's Name….). Together we have researched violence in media and its effects on our children and we are prepared to present relevant information to you about this topic.

Thesis: During the next few minutes, our group will inform you about violence through (1) video games, (2) television, and (3) movies.

Transition/Link: First, let's begin with (Student's Name) as she describes for us the effects of violence in the media through video games.

BODY:

I. (Presented by: Student's Name) – Violence in the media through video games
   NOTE: In addition to the One Point Outline, each student will need to supply their own personal outline which details the points they plan to cover and the research they used. Each student must cite the sources they will use and must include a Works Cited page which follows MLA Guidelines.

Transition/Link: Now that you understand violence in the media delivered through video games, let's hear from (Student's Name) and look at the way that television is involved.

II. (Presented by: Student's Name) – Violence in the media through television
  NOTE: In addition to the One Point Outline, each student will need to supply their own personal outline which details the points they plan to cover and the research they used. Each student must cite the sources they will use and must include a Works Cited page which follows MLA Guidelines.

Transition/Link: As you can see, video games and television play a huge role in the way that violence is portrayed through the media, but now, (Student's Name) will explore the way that movies are involved.

III. (Presented by: Student's Name) – Violence in the media through movies
  NOTE: In addition to the One Point Outline, each student will need to supply their own personal outline which details the points they plan to cover and the research they used. Each student must cite the sources they will use and must include a Works Cited page which follows MLA Guidelines.

Transition/Link: It is alarming to realize that the things we consider entertainment are also the vehicles used to incorporate violence into our daily lives!

CONCLUSION: (Presented by: Student's Name)

Summary: Today, our group has supplied research and statistics to inform you of the negative effects of violence through video games, television, and movies.

Closing Appeal: We have also discussed the media ratings procedure. However, you should realize that according to the Kaiser Family Foundation, "Many parents don't understand what the various rating guidelines mean…For example…only 12% of parents of young children (2-6 years old) know what the rating TV-Y7 means" ("Facts and TV Statistics" 2). Do you know what it means? Are you familiar with the rating, FV? It actually means "fantasy violence" and is related to violent content. "8% of our public thinks it means "Family Viewing" ("Voluntary Movie Rating System"). Make it your business to understand the rating system. Our group will be providing you with a handout for your next evening at home watching television. Refer to the ratings card that is attached to your treat bag. Become informed! Know the content BEFORE you watch the show!

Open Question/Answer Time from Audience: At this time, we would like to invite the audience to ask questions or initiate discussion regarding our presentation.

Works Cited

"Facts and TV Statistics: It's Just Harmless Entertainment, Oh really?" <u>Parents Television Council</u> 2007. 5 Nov. 2012 <http://www.parentstv.org/PTC/facts/mediafacts.asp>.

"Voluntary Movie Rating System." <u>The Classification and Rating Administration</u> 2010. 20 Oct. 2012 <http://www.filmratings.com/guide.htm>.

Visual Aid Explanation

PowerPoint Presentation:

Slide #1: Title Slide – Watch What You Watch

Slide #2: Video – graphic of child playing a video game

Slide #3: Television – graphic of children watching television

Slide #4: Movies – graphic of family at the movie theater buying tickets

Slide #5: Watch What You Watch – graphic of family watching TV

Handout:

Paper pop-corn box

Pkg. of microwave popcorn

Ratings card

Group Presentation Evaluation Worksheets

On the following pages you will find a Speech Evaluation Worksheet, Outline Evaluation Worksheet, Peer Evaluation Worksheet, and a Self-Evaluation Worksheet.

Instructions:

- Provide your instructor with a copy of the Speech Evaluation Worksheet and Outline Evaluation Worksheet for grading your speech.

- Make enough copies of the Peer Evaluation Worksheets so that you will have one for each classmate and bring the copies to class on the day of scheduled Group Presentations.

- Complete the Self-Evaluation Worksheet after your speech. Please view your speech video twice. Once with the sound to evaluate your verbal skills and once without the sound to evaluate your non-verbal skills.

Group Presentation

Speech Evaluation Worksheet

Group Member's Names: _____

Grade Awarded: _____   **Time of Speech:** _____

ORGANIZATION/MATERIAL	5 Points EXCELLENT	4 Points GOOD	3 Points AVERAGE	2 Points FAIR	1 Point POOR
Introduction: Presented by: _____					
1 Attention Step					
2. Established Need					
3. Established Credibility Introduced Group Members					
4. Stated Thesis (3 Main Points) Identified Group Member/Point					
Body:					
5. Point #1 (Organized and Informative?) Presented by: _____ Transitioned to next presenter?					
6. Point #2 (Organized and Informative?) Presented by: _____ Transitioned to next presenter?					
7. Point #3 (Organized and Informative?) Presented by: _____ Transitioned to next presenter?					
Conclusion: Presented by: _____					
8. Summary (3 Main Points) Recognized Group Member/Point					
9. Appeal to Action (Ended with a BANG!)					
Delivery Techniques:					
10. Visual Aids: Design Use					
11. Research Used? Sources Verbally Cited?					
12. Voice: Volume/Rate/Quality of Speech					
13. Language Skills					
14. Poise and Confidence					

15. Enthusiasm for Topic					
16. Gestures					
17. Eye Contact					
18. Appearance					

19. Movement:
    Entrance
    Exit					

20. Stayed Within Time Limit?					
Was the group cohesive? Did the group work well together? Did the group achieve the purpose?					
Question and Answer Session:					

Group Presentation

Outline Evaluation Worksheet

Student's Name: _____

Grade Awarded: _____ **Time of Speech:** _____

POSSIBLE POINTS 100	POINTS EARNED	TYPED OUTLINE REQUIREMENTS FOR INDIVIDUAL STUDENT RESPONSIBILITIES
15 Points		Header Included: • Name, Class Identification, and Date • Speech Category • General Purpose • Specific Purpose (Full Sentence): • Title of Speech
20 Points		Introduction Step Included (Full Sentence): • Attention Step • Established Need • Established Credibility • Clearly Stated Thesis (Point/Points Covered by Individual)
15 Points		Body of the Speech Used Proper Outline Format • I, II, III • A, B, C • 1, 2, 3
15 Points		Transitions (Full Sentence): • Between Introduction and Body • Between Each Main Point • Between Body and Conclusion
10 Points		Conclusion Included (Full Sentence): • Summary (Re-stated Points Covered by Individual) • Appeal to Action (Ended with a BANG!)
5 Points		Visual Aid Explanation Page: • Separate Page Detailing Visual Aids and/or Handouts Used
20 Points		Research: • Followed MLA Guidelines • Parenthetical Citations Found in Outline • Separate Page for "Works Cited" • Included Copies of All Required Research

Group Presentation

Peer-Evaluation Worksheet

Make a copy for each person in your class and evaluate their speeches using this form.

Group Member's Names: _____

Grade Awarded: _____   **Time of Speech:** _____

	5 Points EXCELLENT	4 Points GOOD	3 Points AVERAGE	2 Points FAIR	1 Point POOR
ORGANIZATION/MATERIAL					
Introduction: Presented by: _____					
1. Attention Step					
2. Established Need					
3. Established Credibility Introduced Group Members					
4. Stated Thesis (3 Main Points) Identified Group Member/Point					
Body:					
5. Point #1 (Organized and Informative?) Presented by: _____ Transitioned to next presenter?					
6. Point #2 (Organized and Informative?) Presented by: _____ Transitioned to next presenter?					
7. Point #3 (Organized and Informative?) Presented by: _____ Transitioned to next presenter?					
Conclusion: Presented by: _____					
8. Summary (3 Main Points) Recognized Group Member/Point					
9. Appeal to Action (Ended with a BANG!)					
Delivery Techniques:					
10. Visual Aids: Design Use					
11. Research Used? Sources Verbally Cited?					
12. Voice: Volume/Rate/Quality of Speech					

13. Language Skills					
14. Poise and Confidence					
15. Enthusiasm for Topic					
16. Gestures					
17. Eye Contact					
18. Appearance					
19. Movement: Entrance Exit					
20. Stayed Within Time Limit?		.			
Stayed Within Time Limit?					
Question and Answer Session:					

Group Presentation

Self-Evaluation Worksheet

Instructions: Complete this following your speech presentation.

Student's Name: _____

Group Member's Names: _____

Grade Awarded: _____ **Time of Speech:** _____

ORGANIZATION/MATERIAL	5 Points EXCELLENT	4 Points GOOD	3 Points AVERAGE	2 Points FAIR	1 Point POOR
Introduction:					
1 Attention Step					
2. Established Need					
3. Established Credibility (Personal)					
4. Stated Thesis					
Body:					
5. Sub-Point #1 (Organized and Informative?)					
6. Sub-Point #2 (Organized and Informative?)					
7. Sub-Point #3 (Organized and Informative?)					
8. Used Effective Transitions Between Points					
Conclusion:					
9. Summary (Main Point and Sub-Point Breakdown)					
10. Appeal to Action (Ended with a BANG!) Introduced Speaker for Next Point?					
Delivery Techniques:					
11. Visual Aids: Design Use					
12. Research Used? Sources Verbally Cited?					
13. Voice: Volume/Rate/Quality of Speech					
14. Language Skills					

15. Poise and Confidence					
16. Cohesive Presentation Worked Well Within Group					
17. Gestures					
18. Eye Contact					
19. Appearance					
20. Movement: Entrance Exit					
Stayed Within Time Limit?					
Question and Answer Session:					

IDENTIFY THREE AREAS TO IMPROVE BEFORE THE NEXT PRESENTATION.	WHY DO THESE AREAS NEED IMPROVEMENT? (PROBLEM)	HOW DO YOU PLAN TO IMPROVE THESE AREAS? (SOLUTION)
1.		
2.		
3.		

For more information, log into:

MyCommunicationLab

Glossary

adrenaline: a chemical released by the adrenal gland to the body producing a sudden rush of energy which includes a feeling of joy, exuberance, and excitement.

APA: disciplines that deal with psychology, sociology, social work, criminology, education, business, and economics are cited using the American Psychological Association guidelines.

appreciative listening: a listening skill which involves the audience member exhibiting non-verbal cues to show that he/she is enjoying the speaker and the content of the speech.

articulation: to speak, express oneself, and to provide clear communication through the use of sound.

attitudes: formed as a person reacts favorably or unfavorably toward something.

audience: a group of listeners or spectators gathered together for a specific purpose.

audience analysis: a procedure conducted by the speaker prior to the speech in order to determine and examine information about the audience who will be hearing the speech.

behaviors: result of a person's values, beliefs, and attitudes.

beliefs: a person's perception of that which is true or false.

blocking: the process of planning where, when, and how speakers will move about the stage area during a speech presentation.

body language: a type of communication through which the communicator uses his body in gesturing, movement, and mannerisms.

body language cues: cues or signals given with knowledge or
inadvertently to share the true feelings of the person sending the cues.

boolean search: advanced Web search which is specific and allows the computer operator to narrow the number of Web sites at his
disposal. The process includes adding various requirements to communicate narrowing the subject.

chronemics: the study of how we use time in the communication process.

clustering and webbing: an organizational process by which the writer will segment thoughts together, separating, and grouping ideas that belong together.

CMS: disciplines that deal with the history of art and humanities are cited using Chicago Manual of Style guidelines.

connectors: words, known also as transitions, which connect one thought to another.

credibility: the quality or power of inspiring belief in the speaker as being knowledgeable and worthy of speaking on a specified subject.

critical listening: a listening skill which involves the audience member listening to the speaker's message, mentally reviewing what the speaker says, and thinking of ways to apply what has been said.

CSE: disciplines that deal with natural sciences are cited using the Council of Science Editors guidelines.

cues: signals, whether verbal or non-verbal, to signify a certain response.

delivery: the act or manner of delivering communication to an audience.

delivery outline: an outline tool created to be used by the speaker during the presentation.

dialect: the manner of speaking which includes pronouncing words using sounds and nuances central to the speaker's ethnic, cultural, or religious background, often referred to as an accent.

drafting: the second stage of writing which allows the writer the opportunity to focus on the content he or she plans to share.

editing and proofreading: the fourth stage of writing in which a peer editing group will edit a written draft.

empathetic listening: a listening skill which involves the audience member actively working to understand the speaker's meaning and offering support for the speaker.

entertain: providing amusement for the enjoyment of an audience.

evaluation: a process of gathering information and making decisions regarding the worth or quality of something.

extemporaneous speaking: a method of organized speaking in which the speaker does not memorize the speech word for word. The speaker uses an outline or notes as a means of support.

eye contact: the process by which a speaker connects with the audience by maintaining eye contact with his audience.

facial expressions: non-verbal communication signals sent using the face. They will include eye contact, eye movements, mouth movements, crinkling the nose, head tilting, and a combination of all the above.

figure/ground: a design principle in which the most important information is thrust, visually, in front of the audience. As the audience sees the larger, bolder information, they perceive that particular information as being important and worthy of consideration.

free-writing: a part of the drafting stage of the writing process in which the writer can write freely without concern for mechanics.

gestalt: a design principle based upon a German word which means the whole is greater than the sum of many parts.

gestures: communication by movement of the body, arms, legs, and head to express an attitude, sentiment, or to emphasize a point.

goal: the end result toward which an effort is directed.

handout: a supplement provided to the audience by the speaker which provides support and additional information regarding the speech. It can be in the form of an object, brochure, or booklet.

haptics: the study of communicating through touch.

hierarchy: a design principle which utilizes bar graphs, diagrams, directional arrows, line graphs, lists, maps, outlines, pie charts, and tables to draw the audience's attention.

impromptu speaking: a method of speaking in which the speaker presents a speech without advance preparation.

inform: to make known or communicate knowledge to a listener.

informative listening: a listening skill which involves the audience member making notes of the main points, sub-points, and noting evidence or research that supports the points. This type of listening is known as informative listening because the listener is hoping to learn something from the speaker.

Internet: a worldwide system of interconnected information and communication networks.

kinesics: the study of the body's physical movements.

larynx: also called a "voice box", the larynx is the upper part of the trachea and is used in the creation of sound.

manuscript speaking: a method of speaking in which the speaker delivers the speech by reading word-for-word from a prepared manuscript.

mapping: the process of using shapes as an organizational tool to plan the introduction, main points, sub-points, sub-sub-points, supporting material, and conclusion of a speech.

memorized speaking: a method of speaking in which the speaker delivers the speech word-for-word having memorized all parts of the speech.

MLA: disciplines that deal with language and literature cite research using the Modern Language Association guidelines.

monotone: speaking while using a constant pitch results in a monotone voice.

motivate: to cause one to act upon information presented.

movement: the act or process of changing a place, position, or posture.

non-verbal communication: communication that is delivered without the written or spoken language.

outline: the principal features or the different parts of a speech.

paralanguage: the vocal part of speech and its nuances.

paraphrase: restate or summarize a source's research in the writer's own words and offering a statement, either before or after the summarization, to give credit to the source.

parenthetical documentation: placing the source information in parenthesis within written documents.

pause: a brief break or suspension of the voice used to emphasize a point or cause the listener to concentrate on something specific.

peer: one who is of equal standing with another.

persuade: the process by which someone will attempt to change or reinforce another's attitudes or beliefs regarding a certain topic.

pitch: the process by which a speaker can raise or lower vocal sounds.

plagiarism: when the writer uses someone else's ideas and claims them as his own.

poise: the process by which a speaker will hold or carry himself in a particular way.

posture: the position of the body assumed for a specific purpose.

preparation outline: a formal outline which includes detailed information that will be presented during the speech.

prewriting: the first stage of the writing process in which the writer will conduct an audience analysis, consider the purpose, decide upon a topic, research and gather information, brainstorm, and organize the document.

project: the process by which a speaker will cast forward his voice so that it is heard throughout the audience.

pronunciation: a process by which a speaker forms words and sounds accurately.

proxemics: a person's perception of space.

publication: the final stage of the writing process which produces a final draft to be submitted to the instructor.

purpose: a goal set up as an end to be attained.

rate: a measurement of the degree to determine how fast or how slowly the speaker is speaking.

rehearsal: to perform or practice a speech prior to the actual presentation.

research: the process of finding material to support a speech.

revising: the third stage of the writing process which focuses on content.

signal verb: a verb that is used to signal the audience that the speaker is planning to interject research to support a point.

spatial cues: non-verbal cues or signals given, whether knowingly or inadvertently, to indicate a person's conception of space.

speech group: a group of people formed within a fundamental speech class that lends support to the speaker by offering peer evaluations, editing, and advice, tips, or support.

standard outline form: an acceptable outline format which uses numbers, letters, headings, and subheadings to indicate the relationships among the sections of a speech.

startling statistics: numerical data provided within a speech. They can be used as the introduction, attention step, conclusion, or simply to support main ideas within the body of the speech.

strategies: a careful plan or method involving action toward reaching one's goal.

tech team: a group of people formed within a fundamental speech class that lends technical support to the speaker by handling visual aids, handouts, lights, sound, setting up, and breaking down.

transitions: connectors or a passage from one subject to another within a speech.

values: a person's perception of right or wrong.

verbal communication: the use of written or spoken language used to communicate with a listener.

visual aids: aids used within a speech to visually augment the main points being made by the speaker. They come in the form of PowerPoint Presentations, video/DVD, posters, objects, pictures, graphs or charts, and sometimes may include the speaker's body.

vocal variance: indicates a speaker's ability to vary volume, rate, pitch, and pauses to emphasize a point within a speech.

volume: indicates the loudness or softness of a speaker's voice.

working outline: a handwritten outline that lists three main points and may also include sub-points.

Photo Credits

p. 1 courtesy of Ryan McVay.

p. 16 courtesy of MBI / Alamy.

p. 17 courtesy of Corbis Super RF/ Alamy.

p. 25 courtesy of MBI / Alamy.

p. 39 courtesy of Corbis Super RF / Alamy.

p. 44 courtesy of Radius Images / Alamy.

p. 83 courtesy of arek_malang / Shutterstock.

p. 89 courtesy of Blend Images / Alamy.

p. 101 courtesy of PhotoAlto / Alamy.

p. 153 courtesy of Cultura Creative / Alamy.

p. 160 courtesy of Corbis Super RF / Alamy.

p. 166 clip art courtesy of Nova Development Corporation.

p. 177 courtesy of amana images inc. / Alamy.

p. 335 courtesy of Radius Images/Corbis.

Quotation Credits and Acknowledgements

p. vii Quote: Anonymous.

p. 4 Quote: James Calvin Joyner.

p. 4 Quote: Mark Twain.

p. 7–8 Acknowledgement: George L. Grice and John F. Skinner.

p. 25 Quote: William H. (Bill) Waddell.

p. 39 Acknowledgement: Peanuts.

p. 44 Quote: Anonymous.

p. 83 Quote: Vince Lombardi.

p. 98 Quote: Ralph Waldo Emerson.

p. 153 Quote: Albert Schweitzer.

p. 159 Quote: Unknown.

p. 159 Acknowledgement: Albert Mehrabian.

p. 161 Quote: Martin Luther King.

p. 172 Quote: Abraham Lincoln.

p. 177 Quote: Abraham Lincoln.

p. 255 Quote: Elbert Hubbard.

p. 256 Acknowledgement: Monroe's Motivated Sequence.

p. 335 Quote: Ruth Rowell Joyner.

"Success? You can do anything that you make up your mind to do, and that is success."

RUTH ROWELL JOYNER

PEARSON ALWAYS LEARNING

Going from Stress to Success

A Student Workbook for the Fundamentals of Speech Class

Seventh Edition

by Penny Joyner Waddell, Ed.D.

Excerpts taken from

Simon & Schuster Handbook for Writers, Ninth Edition
by Lynn Quitman Troyka and Douglas Hesse

DK Guide to Public Speaking
by Lisa A. Ford-Brown

Cover Art: Courtesy of Photodisc/Getty Images.

Excerpts taken from:

Simon & Schuster Handbook for Writers, Ninth Edition
by Lynn Quitman Troyka and Douglas Hesse
Copyright © 2009 by Pearson Education, Inc.
Published by Prentice Hall
Upper Saddle River, New Jersey 07458

DK Guide to Public Speaking
by Lisa A. Ford-Brown
Copyright © 2011 by Pearson Education, Inc.
Published by Allyn & Bacon
Boston, Massachusetts 02116

Copyright © 2013, 2012, 2011, 2010, 2009, 2007, 2006 by Pearson Learning Solutions
All rights reserved.

This copyright covers material written expressly for this volume by the editor/s as well as the compilation itself. It does not cover the individual selections herein that first appeared elsewhere. Permission to reprint these has been obtained by Pearson Learning Solutions for this edition only. Further reproduction by any means, electronic or mechanical, including photocopying and recording, or by any information storage or retrieval system, must be arranged with the individual copyright holders noted.

All trademarks, service marks, registered trademarks, and registered service marks are the property of their respective owners and are used herein for identification purposes only.

Pearson Learning Solutions, 501 Boylston Street, Suite 900, Boston, MA 02116
A Pearson Education Company
www.pearsoned.com

Printed in the United States of America

5 6 7 8 9 10 V0UD 19 1817 16 15

000200010271780898

EEB/VP

ISBN 10: 1-269-44796-3
ISBN 13: 978-1-269-44796-6

New to This Edition

The Revised 5th Edition of *Going from Stress to Success* has been designed to include important changes in structure, appearance, and content that make this text more user friendly for students and instructors.

Structure and Content:

- The structure of the textbook has changed to a coil bound text with perforated tear-out worksheet pages.
- The textbook contains instructional material, worksheet pages, and is bundled with **Tools for Success**, a course online access card.
  - **Instructional Material**
    - The Fundamentals of Speech
    - Organizing a Speech
    - Conducting Research
    - Delivering a Speech
    - Types of Speeches
  - **Worksheets**
    - Speech Evaluation Worksheets
    - Peer Evaluation Worksheets
    - Self-Evaluation Worksheets
    - Outline Evaluation Worksheets
    - Assignment Worksheets
  - **Tools for Success**
    - MyCommunicationLab
    - E-Book—*Going from Stress to Success*
    - Resources
      - Alternative Media Index
      - Video Quizzes
      - American Rhetoric Quizzes
      - 100+ Classic and Contemporary Speeches
      - National Communication Association
      - ABC News Top Videos
      - ABC News Top Stories
    - Composition Assistance
      - MyOutlineBuilder
      - Topic Selector
      - New York Times Topics Index
      - Pearson Online Writing Tutor
    - PowerPoint presentations
      - First Day of Class
      - Overcoming the Fear of Public Speaking

- Audience and Speaker Responsibilities
- Organizing a Speech
- Selecting a Topic
- Writing an Outline
- Conducting Research
- Creating Effective Visual Aids and Handouts
- Presentation Skills
- Dressing for a Speech
- Non-verbal and Verbal Communication Skills
- Public Speaking Confidence Center
  - Quick and Dirty Tips
- Research
  - MySearchLab
  - Avoiding Plagiarism
  - Plagiarism Check
  - MLA, APA, CMS Guidelines
  - Autociting Tool
  - Understanding a Research Assignment
  - Examples of Written and Verbal Citations
- MySpeechFeed
  - Recent Speeches in the News
  - Applicable Questions
- MediaShare
  - Upload Video for Instructor
  - Upload Video for Peer Review
- Multimedia Library
  - Audio and Video
  - Classic and Contemporary Speeches
  - Introduction Speeches
  - Informative Speeches
  - Persuasion Speeches
  - Special Occasion Speeches
  - Speech Preparation Tools
- Quizzes and Exams
  - American Rhetoric Video Quizzes
  - Chapter Quizzes
  - Comprehensive Exams
- Pearson 24/7 Tech Support

MyCommunicationLab

Contents